The

# Spells
# Bible

# The
# Spells
# Bible

## The definitive guide to charms and enchantments

Ann-Marie Gallagher

 A GODSFIELD BOOK

An Hachette UK Company
www.hachette.co.uk

First published in the U.K. in 2003 by Godsfield Press, a division of
Octopus Publishing Group Ltd
Endeavour House, 189 Shaftesbury Avenue, London WC2H 8JY
www.octopusbooks.co.uk

This edition published in 2009

Designed and produced for Godsfield Press by The Bridgewater Book Company

ISBN: 978-1-84181-371-4

A CIP catalogue record for this book is available from the British Library

Printed and bound in China

10 9 8 7 6 5 4 3

Photography: Mike Hemsley at Walter Gardiner Photography
Senior designer: John Grain
Project editor: Sarah Doughty
Designer: Jane Lanaway
Prop-buyer: Claire Shanahan
Model: Genevieve Appleby

# CONTENTS

# PART 1

# BEFORE YOU BEGIN

# INTRODUCTION TO THE SPELLS BIBLE

The craft of magic is making something of a comeback—not that it ever went entirely away—and the resurgent public interest in myth and magic shows no signs of abating. It may seem odd that in the age of technology people are still intrigued by ancient traditions and beliefs and interested in casting spells. There are many theories for this renewed interest, all with their particular attractions, but it is likely that growing concern for the environment, our diets, and our lifestyles have generated a similar concern about a spiritual vacuum that is not answered by established religions. This has led to a search for meaning that has taken many people beyond the church or temple door to ask themselves new questions about our place in the cosmos.

Exploring spirituality outside of the strictures of organized religion can be extremely liberating, but it can be quite scary, too. For this reason, many people look for inspiration to the old ways and ask what our ancestors believed and did.

To the delighted surprise of many of us, there is a whole history of spirituality and magic just waiting to be discovered. Embedded in folklore, superstition, and tales of gods and goddesses are clues to the importance of magic in the life of our forebears. We know, from spells inscribed on cave walls or sheets of lead found in sacred wells, that our ancestors practiced and believed in the efficacy of magic. We know that they lived closer to nature and respected and utilized the natural energies and forces they found within and around them. You will find within this spell book many references to the traditions behind some of the ingredients, tools, and techniques of spell work, and hopefully you will yourself contribute to its many customs as you become confident enough to design spells of your own!

What can you expect to find in the *Spells Bible*? Well, with spells for love, passion, work, career, health, beauty, and protection, all key life concerns are catered to. Moreover, as you will see, there are generally a number of spells to choose from, each approaching similar circumstances from a different angle. This enables the reader to select the spell that most nearly addresses the specific need in question. All of the spells

spells designed to coincide with the ancient festivals that mark the wheel of the year.

Reading through the *Spells Bible* should also be something of an education in itself. It is designed as a directory, with easily identifiable sections with background information and guidance, making it easy to dip into it at need, but it also contains kernels of ancient wisdom and magical knowledge. If you read through the introductory texts for each spell, you will find discussed within them elements of folk and magical lore as well as the origins and meanings of certain magical customs and traditions. In addition, within the spells themselves, you will find descriptions of magical techniques from all around the world and practical lessons in the principles of magic.

This book is a veritable Aladdin's Cave of magical information covering history, customs, symbolism, and magical correspondences within the texts accompanying the spells. Between its covers you will discover a range of charms and enchantments using chants, talismans, amulets, poppets, fith-faths, herbs, incenses, candles, cords, and many other unexpected ingredients. If any of these are unfamiliar to you, both the

carry brief explanations and advice, making it simpler to match the spell to the occasion. In addition, there are magical workings for banishing or binding—designed to prevent harm—as well as divination spells through which you will be able to discern and act on life patterns revealed within spell work. The importance of the natural rhythms and energies of nature are also recognized here, and there is a section of seasonal introductory section of this book and the texts of the spells themselves offer clear explanations and guidance to their uses. The accounts of magical practices offered within this *Spells Bible* should also go some way toward discounting some of the more ignorant assumptions about wax figures and large pins that have found their way into popular culture through the distorting lens of Hollywood and the uninformed scribblings in sensationalist novels!

Welcome, then, to the *Spells Bible*, your comprehensive guide to spells for all areas of your life. Whatever your need, you are sure to find a choice of charms and enchantments within

these pages to answer it. Here you will find a blend of the ancient and modern, all flavored with the customs and traditions of magical crafts from around the world, set in a directory that lists the purposes, timing, and background to each spell. Within the pages that follow, you will discover a world of knowledge and ideas that can, ultimately, guide you toward developing your own very individual magical strengths.

*Materials for charms and enchantments*

# WORKING WITH MAGIC
## ETHICS, ATTITUDE, AND PRACTICALITIES

Before attempting any spell work, it is important that you first grasp certain principles regarding the use of magic and your attitude toward it. The attitude with which you approach magical work is the key to its success and has a bearing on your development as a magician. In case you are tempted to pass over this section, let me add that failure to do the basic work described here will result in wasted effort as far as spell casting goes. Further, you may find yourself in a pickle if you ignore the advice offered.

Don't worry, you are not going to be given a heavy lecture on the abuse of magical power; as you will come to realize while you progress in your work,

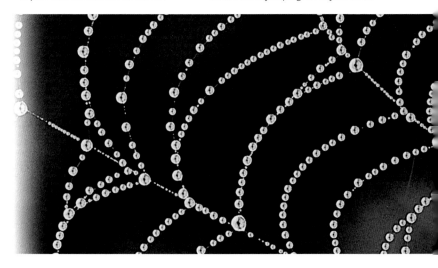

it is not in the nature of magic to accommodate misuse in the way often depicted in films and literature. However, magic operates in such a way that you do need to be sure that the changes you are seeking to make are truly for the good of all concerned.

One way of describing magic is as connection. Imagine, if you can, that all things in the world are connected by invisible threads, all of which join up as a series of webs. All of these webs in turn are connected with each other, making a multi-dimensional pattern that describes all life. As large as this web is, it is so delicate that an event on one part of the web affects the whole. This is because the matter from which it is made is spirit, which in the magical tradition behind most of the spells in this book is known as the *fifth element*. When we work rituals or do spells, we are weaving new patterns into this great spirit web, and these interventions need to be considered in the context of the whole. In short, the questions we need to ask ourselves prior to spell work are those that ensure that we respect the well-being of the whole web—not just the part of it that we inhabit. On the whole, this isn't such a bad way of approaching everyday life!

There are certain questions you need to ask before "casting off." First of all, be practical; consider whether you really need to be casting a spell at all. Magic should never be used as an alternative to material action—this just wastes everybody's time, enables people to avoid facing reality, and feeds whatever delusions they may be harboring that their problems can be solved with no effort on their part.

Secondly, ask yourself what is really needed. Nine times out of ten, someone asking for a love spell actually needs help in another area of their life. Some people, for example, believe that finding a partner will resolve their lack of confidence; others assume that meeting someone will make them happy with their lives. What they are asking for may not actually be what they need; commonly, what is needed is counseling or healing and thereby some work and effort on their part to build their inner resources and self-esteem. A spell for their self-esteem can be very empowering and complement the practical steps that are actually being taken, but what will be utterly wasted on them at this point in their lives is a love spell—"Do I really need to cast a spell?" and "What is really needed?"—if you ask

yourself these two questions before proceeding with spell work, you won't go far wrong. There are, however, a number of other issues that you need to take into consideration in your magical work, and these are related to the difference between what people think magic is and how magic actually does work.

There are laws of magic in the same way there are laws of physics, and while some of these are pretty obvious, others are less so and will be discovered as you progress in the craft. One of the most

common pieces of magical lore quoted at beginners is something called the Law of Threefold Return. Although some magicians take this very literally as an absolute, cast-in-stone natural law, it is more accurate to say that it refers to a belief that whatever we send out into the universe comes back to us, multiplied by three. Acceptance of this law has been important to some witches and magicians in their attempts to dispel fears about the "dangers" of what they do. There is absolutely no point, it is

reasoned, for witches or magicians to send out a "curse" when they know that such an action would simply rebound on them multiplied by three. It makes much more sense, or so the theory goes, to send out blessings and cast spells to do good, as magic will ensure that these are likewise multiplied and sent back to us. It is a nice theory, and it has performed some good public relations work for us magical folk, but it is not a law. It is actually a spiritual principle that has been taken rather too literally.

When we claim that what we send out we get back, we are probably right. If we all did good deeds, then they would be repaid in kind at some point. Similarly, it is observable that destructive behavior engenders an increase in negative conduct, rather than otherwise—hence sayings such as "Violence begets violence" or, more biblically, "He who lives by the sword shall die by the sword." The trouble is that this is not a hard-and-fast magical law. When somebody is behaving in a damaging way, they are doing themselves damage in that they are failing to grow psychologically and spiritually, and ultimately this will rebound on them. However, this is not the same as having what you send out revisited upon you three times. The knowledge that someone is restricting their spiritual development, furthermore, is no consolation for those suffering as a result of their appalling behavior. The fact is that though we may feel that wrongdoers harm themselves in the end, this does not add up to a specific law whereby all damage is visited upon them in kind three times over.

Reference to cause and effect, however, is highly relevant to magical ethics. Just as we need to be careful about what we deal out in terms of our everyday behavior, we need also to take note of our magical actions. This means that the changes we seek need to be weighed carefully, both in the context of our own lives and the lives of others.

It is not possible, for example, to change another person's free will by magic; neither should it be an aspiration to do so. A person who attempts to subject the will of another to their own,

eventually finds themselves rendered indecisive, confused, and easily misguided—for the reason that the lack in them that drove them to demand obedience from another will simply be magnified. This reflects a general law that bending magic toward selfish purposes will not have the effect the magician intends; rather, it will focus on and emphasize their own shortcomings.

This raises another general law observed in magic—that of the magnifying properties of the magical circle. Most spell work takes place within a magical circle—a space where the energy raised from spell casting is contained until it is ripe to be released into the cosmos to go about its business. Whatever you bring with you is magnified and brought to your attention until you deal with it. If you cast a spell that is about greed, lust, or obsession, this will simply amplify the flaw in yourself that initiated such a need, until you deal with it.

All in all, the ethics of magic are practical and based largely on common sense. If you enter the circle of magic with an attitude of respect for yourself and respect for others, you will find success and enrichment.

# SPELL WORK
## RANGE AND TYPES OF SPELL, MAGICAL TECHNIQUES, TOOLS, AND INGREDIENTS

Each of the spells in the directory section offers a brief explanation of its purpose, the ingredients required, the symbolism deployed, and the appropriate timing to work with. They also supply brief descriptions of the techniques employed, and as you read through the different sections, you will inevitably accumulate a working knowledge of magical tools and techniques.

Magic has survived through the ages because a good magician can improvise and find resources all around them. This is reflected in the large number of spells in this book that use everyday objects. Others use more arcane materials— specific herbs and incenses—for their established properties, in keeping with traditional correspondences. The majority of spells in this volume arise from a tradition of sympathetic magic, a system that uses symbols to represent the people, objects, and intents of the spell. Many of the ingredients, tools, and techniques used are adaptable to a

variety of uses and purposes. When you develop more confidence as a seasoned magician, you will no doubt test their flexibility yourself.

Sympathetic magic is very straightforward. In addition to its system of transference, which symbolizes "like with like," it also draws on a range of other symbolic systems. One such example is the use made of the phases of the moon. Although there are physical energies at work at different times—

evident from tides and animal and plant responses—there is an element of symbolism attached to lunar phases. The waxing, or growing moon, for example, is seen to favor spells for growth, increase, and attraction. The waning, or shrinking moon, on the other hand, symbolizes decay, banishment, and repulsion. The dark moon, known more conventionally as the new moon, favors new projects, building protection, and disposal. The full moon is symbolically linked with reflection, illusion, revelation, and wholeness.

Other symbolic correspondences include the days of the week, linked to planetary influences which themselves represent different aspects of human existence. Monday is linked with the mysterious powers of the moon, and favors dreams, psychic activity, and money. Tuesday is the day of Mars, the fierce planet of courage, will, and defense. Wednesday is ruled by Mercury, the planet of communications, while Thursday is the day of Jupiter, the generous and expansive luck planet. Friday is dedicated to Venus, planet of love and harmony. Saturday is dedicated to ringed Saturn, the disciplinarian, and Sunday to the sun, bringer of joy and success.

An important system used here in magic is that of the five sacred elements: earth, air, fire, water, and spirit. Their symbolic correspondences cover all matters of human existence. Earth represents the material world and our need for shelter, food, and physical health. Air is the element of communication, memory, ideas, and learning. Water is associated with love, healing, and dreams, while fire symbolizes courage, willpower, and inspiration. Spirit, the fifth sacred element, is the element of connection and transformation. It oversees birth, communion, and death, as well as the realm of magic.

In addition to these symbolic systems, the spells occasionally refer to gods and goddesses. Where they are invoked in this book, there is generally an explanation of why their influence is considered significant, except in cases where a figure is generally well known.

The spells in this book are divided into sections that reflect key life concerns, but across these dividing lines, many of the spells share common techniques. One of the most common techniques used is that of making a declaration of intent. This is usually announced at the opening of the ritual—when the first candle is lit, for example. Speaking the declaration aloud has a dual purpose: to knock on the doors of your subconscious in order to awaken your latent magical abilities; and to focus your attentions on the energies you are invoking.

Raising energy to empower the spells in this book is generally achieved through chanting, concentration, or visualization. In some of the spells, the means of energizing are obvious from the directions, for example, where the words to a chant are provided or where guidance is given on how to visualize outcomes. In other spells, you are being asked to focus all your concentration on the spell. When your confidence grows, you may consider exercising other techniques, such as dance, drumming, or trance.

Whereas chanting is pretty straightforward, visualization needs a little practice, and it is a good idea to "rehearse" beforehand using relaxation techniques such as breathing slowly, stilling your thoughts, and sitting quietly for a short length of time. If you are considered a bit of a daydreamer, it is likely that you are already a natural!

The tool kit of magic is pretty simple. Although some magical systems insist on a complex specification of swords, wands, and cords, the tools used in this book are very basic. Traditionally, magicians have a wand or a knife to direct their energies, but it is not expected that you have a dedicated tool

of this type. Most of the tools required for the spells in this book can also be described as ingredients—candles, cords, herbs, oil burners, charcoal disks, incense, and so on.

*Juniper berries*

The best guideline to follow in any spell work is to keep it simple. The rules for the spells found here are uncomplicated. Allow the candles to burn down in safety unless otherwise directed. You do not need new element candles for each spell. When you are asked to keep something "safe," this means that you do not dispose of it or return it to its usual use until what you have asked for has been achieved.

*Rosemary*

*Mugwort*

# SEASONS AND FESTIVALS
## CELEBRATING AND TUNING INTO THE NATURAL RHYTHMS OF MAGIC

Many of us who work frequently with magic consider it a natural part of life that comes from within us and from our surrounding environment. Our understanding of our place in the world and in the cosmos is our spirituality, so working magic, for us, is a spiritual practice. The way we attune to the energies we find around us is also part of that practice, and the more closely we work with and try to understand the rhythms of nature, the more we develop magically and spiritually.

In order to become acquainted with the natural energies we draw on for spells and rituals, we need first to become acquainted with the tides and seasons of the earth. The correlation between the phases of the moon and spell work is generally well known. However, the most intuitive and gifted magicians know that, in order to work with earth energies, we need to assimilate the planetary rhythms of continuity and change. This involves learning about the

seasons of the earth, attuning ourselves to our passage through the solar system, and experiencing the changes around us independently of the calendar that hangs in the kitchen or the office. Approaching the changing seasons experientially and learning about the old traditions associated with them is the best way of beginning to understand the nature of magic, which comes from the world around us.

The wheel of the year, as seen from the magical traditions in the West, is divided into eight festivals, all linked to the natural flow of the seasons and astronomical events. These festivals are sometimes depicted as eight spokes in the wheel of the year, and this is a quite useful image to hold on to, if this is new to you. Strictly speaking, there is no beginning and no end to the year, even though different cultural traditions have at some point nominated one or two of them as candidates for the title of "New Year." Because they observe the natural

YULE/WINTER SOLSTICE
DECEMBER 21–22

IMBOLC
FEBRUARY 1–2

SAMHAIN
OCTOBER 31–NOVEMBER 1

EOSTRE/VERNAL EQUINOX
MARCH 21–22

MABON/AUTUMN EQUINOX
SEPTEMBER 21–22

BELTAINE
APRIL 30–MAY 1

LAMMAS/LUGHNASADH
JULY 31–AUGUST 1

LITHA/SUMMER SOLSTICE
JUNE 21–22

rhythms of nature rather than the dates on the Gregorian calendar, beginnings and endings are seen as integral parts of the festivals, which are themselves seen as interlinked with each other. The festivals are a mixture of solar events—solstices and equinoxes—and fire festivals from Celtic and Nordic cultures. The four solar festivals occur on the day of the astronomical event in question: Yule, the shortest day, or winter solstice, usually on December 21 or 22; Litha, the longest day, or summer solstice, on June 21 or 22; Eostre, the vernal equinox, on or around March 21; and Mabon, the autumnal equinox, on or around September 21. These are interspersed with the fire festivals—so called because of the custom of setting bonfires at these dates: Imbolc, "ewe's milk," falls at the beginning of February when the first snowdrops appear; Beltaine, or May Day, occurs around May 1, or when the May blossom appears; Lammas, or Lughnasadh, comes at the beginning of August with the grain harvest; and Samhain, "first frosts," the feast of the ancestors, on or around the end of October.

There are a number of customs connected with the eight seasonal festivals, and you will find on pages 206–255 a number of spells that are particularly relevant to their celebration. Each spell is accompanied by an explanation, but it is useful to know something of the framework that guides them.

Yule is an ancient festival, taking its name from an Old Norse word thought to mean "wheel." From the alignment of several prehistoric stone monuments in England, Scotland, Wales, and Ireland, it is clear that our ancestors considered the winter solstice an important part of the ritual year. We know that it was being celebrated in the fourth century C.E., as records from that era state that the Christian church expressly declared December 25 as Christ's birthday in order to persuade Christians participating in the pagan midwinter festival to commemorate the Nativity instead! On the shortest day, darkness triumphs over light. At the same time, however, we know that thereafter the hours of daylight will increase, and so the sun is "reborn." In some quarters, the winter solstice is called "sun return" to emphasize the promise of lighter days to come. Although at this time solar

energies are at an ebb, Yule is still seen as a festival of light, hope, and promise. At this time many of us feel the lack of light and warmth, and we gather together to brighten up the long, dreary winter nights. Some of us even feel the need to hibernate—thus the common occurrence in the Northern Hemisphere of the winter blues, or "seasonal affective disorder." This is a time to go into the dark and seek the potential that lies within us. For magicians seeking to tune into the cycle of the seasons, this is the time to meditate, work on our creative potential, and take note of our dreams, which at this time of year are deeper, richer, and more vivid. It is also a time to take note of what is around us, and to note the passage of the moon and the bright points of the winter stars and planets. Yule is a season of contemplation and the search for power within.

Imbolc, when the snowdrops emerge in Europe at the end of January, comes at the time when lambs are born. This festival marks the thawing of the earth in preparation for planting and crop sowing. A Celtic fire festival, Imbolc is sometimes known as the festival of Brigid, a much beloved Celtic fire and healing goddess. Brigid has the reputation of being fiercely protective of women, children, and newborn animals, so this is seen as a time of justice. It is also a time of renewal, when the winter loosens its grip on the earth and sets the rivers and streams awash with the melted snows. Daylight is of noticeably greater length now, and just as Brigid is invoked as a midwife to the newborn lambs, Imbolc is seen as the midwife to the spring.

This is the time to witness the earth awakening and feel the energies around us gearing up toward the surge of life that characterizes spring and early summer. Imbolc is the season for beginning to look outward again after the long nights of winter, which means that it is a good time to consider "spring cleaning" our own lives in anticipation of the season to come.

Eostre marks another astronomical event—the spring equinox, when day and night are of equal length and in perfect balance. Thereafter, the hours of daylight will outstrip those of darkness until the summer solstice, when the sun will triumph altogether on the longest day. Eostre is sacred to a fertility goddess of that same name. Her totem is the

hare, and we see in depictions of Easter bunnies and the giving of chocolate eggs remnants of old fertility rites. Now the sap is rising, the earth is green again, and the hours of light are set to increase. Themes of balance, fertility, and growth run through the festival of Eostre, and this is a good time to think about balance in our lives and our potential for growth, and to tap into the rush of natural energy around us. This is a good time of year to meditate with your back to a tree and to try to feel the life rising through its roots, trunk, and branches. Eostre is also known as the Festival of Trees—this is a good time to acquaint yourself with traditions, customs, and magical knowledge associated with trees.

Beltaine, celebrated when blossoms deck the May tree or from sundown on the eve of May I, is another fertility festival. It marks the beginning of summer and is the time of the Green Man and Woman, Jack in the Green, Robin Hood, and Marian. Now the spirits of the greenwood are abroad, and the veil between the world of humans and the Celtic otherworld, the land of the sidhe or "fairy people," is at its thinnest. Beltaine is a time of rampant sensuality. For this reason, over the centuries its celebration has been discouraged by the more puritanical Christian churches. Celebrated with the use of phallic and yonic symbols such as the Maypole and the wreaths of flowers that crown it, May Day festivities are accompanied by the images of sexuality that are a testimony to its origins as a fertility festival. The people's defiance of prohibitions against celebrating Beltaine mark this festival with a tradition of disobeying authority. May Day is also used to celebrate workers' rights and is increasingly a signal for the people to protest on the streets of Western cities.

Beltaine is a time to communicate with the spirits of the greenwood, to make promises and pledges, and to honor your sensuality.

*Corn dolly*

Litha, the summer solstice, celebrates the triumph of the hours of daylight over the hours of darkness. The longest day is greeted in parts of the British Isles at stone circles, on hillsides, or at other significant sacred prehistoric sites, by crowds of people who camp out overnight to keep vigil together for the rising sun. This is a time when you can draw strength and energy from the triumphant sun—Sol Invicta—and concentrate on your outgoing energies. This is a time of year to get out into the open air, meet new people, and learn new things about the world. It is a perfect time to go camping away from city lights, where you can sit out and appreciate the beauty of the night sky. With the better weather, it may also be possible for you to travel to the sea or other large expanses of water and there attune to the energies of the waters— the origin of all life.

Lammas or Lughnasadh marks the bringing in of the grain harvest. It has many traditions associated with it, particularly relating to corn dollies and casting out evil. At this time, when the wheat is separated from the chaff, we can focus on things in our own lives that need casting aside and also celebrate our personal harvest. It is a good time to ensure that the blessings we have are shared and to ensure that the bounty of the harvest returns to us at this time next year. This festival has ancient precedents and customs, and it is good to know that many of our ancestors' concerns are reflected in our own. For the magician, this is the time to tap into the fruitfulness of the season and listen to the spirits of the land.

Mabon, the equinox in the fall, marks the time of perfect balance between light and darkness. At this festival, however, the balance turns thereafter in favor of the darkness, and so there is a certain sadness attached to it as we say goodbye to the best of the summer. In the wheel of the year, Mabon is in the west—the place of the sunset and, for our ancestors, the direction the soul traveled after death. It is the time when we go into the dark, and we remember the many myths around the world that account for the time of darkness and barrenness of winter on the earth. It is a time to travel into the darkness with some of these characters in order to find wisdom and truth and to obtain arcane knowledge. It is also a good time to cast aside sorrow and place the past where it belongs—behind us.

Samhain, sometimes described as the Celtic New Year, marks the time of the first frosts and the descent into the dark days of winter. We commemorate the dead at this point of the year's turning and honor the ancestors. Now the veil between the world of the living and the world of the dead is thin, and the spirits of the dead are invited to visit with us. Samhain is considered an auspicious time for divination, and at this time of year our dreams become more vivid and telling. This season provides an opportunity to explore our developing psychic abilities and a space in which to consider our own mortality. The mysterious forces around at this time of the year remind us of the mysteries of life and death and our connection thereby with every other living thing. It is a time to consider the nature of death and to question our beliefs.

Becoming attuned to the rhythms and tides of the earth as we travel the solar system is a brilliant way of developing our own magical abilities. If you work through the solar cycle, noting the phases of the moon and the planets, you are already on your way to becoming one of "the wise" and adept at using the power you find within and around you.

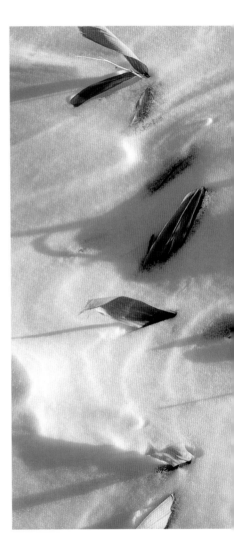

# SACRED SPACES
## CREATING AND RECOGNIZING SPIRITUAL SPACE

Space that we create for the purpose of spiritual activity is sacred. Within this space, we may come to recognize our place in the universe and acknowledge certain truths about the human condition. We may even develop an understanding about what some people refer to as "divinity." Or we may practice the sacred art of magic—sacred because it draws on spiritual knowledge in order to effect change.

Creating sacred space is simple, but it requires concentration, clarity of purpose, and an ability to withstand the mental and physical distractions of your particular circumstances. You can create a space for meditation or spell work within your own home without having a room set aside for that specific purpose. This involves claiming a physical space in your home for the duration of the spell and later returning that room to its original purpose. For many of us, clearing the physical space is the easy part. But psychological debris is sometimes a little

harder to shift, and this will take practice. In time, and when you have undertaken the tasks described in this section several times over, switching to ritual mode inside your head will seem as easy as preparing the physical space in your home.

The most natural shape of a sacred space is a circle, and this has been used for centuries as a boundary—and for protection—for the casting of spells by magicians. Casting a circle is very straightforward. If you are working at home, choose a room in which you will

not be disturbed for the duration of your task; usually this will mean at least one hour. Clear a space in the center of your room, so that you can sit comfortably on the floor in the center of it. Place four candles—one yellow, one red, one blue, and one green, all in secure holders safely away from fire hazards around the room—in directions that roughly equate with east for yellow, south for red, west for blue, and north for green. These candles represent four of the five sacred elements: air, fire, water, and earth. In the center, you should place a purple candle in a secure holder, representing spirit, the fifth magical element.

Most magicians like to psychically "cleanse" the space before a circle is properly cast, and this means purifying water and blessing salt, then mixing the two, and sprinkling this around the room. All you have to do is to place your hand over half a wineglass or vessel of water, then visualize any energy that the water may have absorbed as dark smoke coming out of the glass, and declare: "I exorcise thee, o creature of water." Now place your hand on the salt and bless it, saying: "Blessings be upon this creature of salt." Place the salt into the water and stir, then sprinkle it around the room clockwise.

*Wand*

Using a wand, a knife, or your forefinger, and beginning at the east, move clockwise, or deosil ("sunwise"), around the room; "describe" a circle of light in the air all around it. This should move outward to encompass the whole room. Draw energy from the earth up through your feet, through your trunk, and down your arms into your wand, knife, or forefinger. When you have completed this circle, you should declare it cast. For example: "I conjure thee, o circle of power, that thou be a boundary and a protection for this space between the worlds."

When the circle is cast, the elements should be invoked. Some people like to visualize these as humanoid and see them in angelic or god or goddess form. Others prefer to visualize the raw energy of the elements. Whatever your inclination, it is important to acknowledge the elements when you are building the circle. When we invoke the elements, this does not mean that we summon the mighty forces represented by them to that particular spot for an

hour or so—rather it means that we call up their meaning within ourselves. Externally, we acknowledge their presence in all things and symbolize and unify that presence for the duration of the circle in the appropriate direction. It is best to keep the wording of any declaration very simple. Beginning in the east, welcome the element of air; then move around the circle deosil, hailing the elements appropriate to the direction and adjusting the following wording for each as appropriate: "In the east, the element of air, you are honored in this sacred circle." When you have welcomed the outer elements, move to the center and welcome the element of spirit. You should light the candle for each element when you have welcomed it in, saying: "Hail and welcome."

When your spell or ritual is completed, move around the circle counterclockwise, or *widdershins*, to close it, blowing out the candles in reverse order, beginning with earth and ending with spirit.

It is customary to move deosil within the circle at all times. There are occasional exceptions—for example, when casting some banishing spells— but generally this tradition should be observed. You should not walk through the boundaries of the circle or leave this sacred space for the duration of your ritual, unless an emergency occurs which necessitates disruption. This helps to keep the focus and concentration necessary for magical undertakings and contains the power raised within the circle until you are ready to release it.

Circles of standing stones, ditches, and earthworks have been found in many Neolithic sacred sites and are thought to symbolize the mysterious cycle of life, death, and rebirth, as celebrated by the ancients. In magic, when we talk about work in the circle, we actually mean very much the same thing as our ancestors did when they chose to build their monuments—that all circles are one great circle, and that the nature of all existence is cyclical.

*Describing a circle*

# MAKING AN ALTAR
## A FOCAL POINT FOR MAGICAL WORK AND SPIRITUAL GROWTH

It is possible to build altars—focal points of spiritual contemplation—almost anywhere. An altar can be as simple as a space set apart, in your home or place of work or study, in which you can place objects that are special or sacred to you. Alternatively, it can be more elaborate, with candles, pictures, figures, or symbols representing a deity, natural element, or moon phase with which you have a particular affinity. The loveliest altars can be built in gardens, using rocks, wood, and natural materials. If you need to be relatively discreet about your magical and spiritual interests, altars that are out in the open can be passed off as garden décor, while the indoor variety can be officially listed as a place where you keep things that you don't want moved. If you are lucky enough to have a whole room set aside for meditation and magical work, you can afford to dedicate some of this space to constructing an altar, to provide a focus for your circle work and your spiritual development.

Many magicians like to have this focal point while they are doing circle work. Some prefer to have a table in the center of the circle, while others choose to place one in the north of the circle, a direction particularly sacred to pagans and witches.

This type of altar is generally set up for the duration of the circle, then dismantled, and the objects are packed away carefully until the next one. It is very much an individual taste as to what is included on an altar of this kind, but there are general guidelines as to what you might include.

*Athame*

It is usual to represent the five sacred elements present on the altar during circle work. Traditionally, incense represents air; an athame (a witch's knife), a candle, or an oil lamp represents fire; a chalice or cup represents water; and a pentacle (a five-pointed star) set in stone or wood represents earth. The magician's cords or measure (cords measuring the exact height and the measurement around the heart and head) represent spirit. The first four of these are considered to be traditional tools of witchcraft, even though in practice it is more common for magicians to use a wand, an athame, or their own hands to direct energy during spell casting. Other element symbols can serve just as well, and some people like to have a feather for air, a flame of any kind for fire, a shell for water, a potted plant for earth, and a crystal for spirit.

What really matters is that the symbols you choose are meaningful to you and bring to mind the nature of the five sacred elements, all of which are drawn on in magic. Symbols of the sun and moon are quite common, too, and can be found in candlesticks or small statues. Planetary and zodiac symbols are also quite popular, though these tend to appear on hangings or altar cloths. Gods and goddesses, if included at all, are depicted in framed pictures, small statues, or in totem form. For example, my favorite representation of Athena, the goddess of wisdom, is a carved wooden owl that I own.

One or two candles are usually in place, in addition to any other candles used in the circle. Their color is generally representative of the ritual being undertaken during any particular circle.

*Symbols of the
sun and moon*

This may be influenced by the season (if celebrating one of the eight festivals), the type of spell that is being cast, or the phase of the moon that is being marked. Many magicians use the altar as a power point and as a center for spell work. It is not necessary to carry out spells on an altar in order to make them successful, but if this aids concentration, which many magicians feel it does, then it is a good idea to build this into your working practices. If at all possible, it is useful to have an altar that you can leave set up following circle work, as this can provide a place where you can leave magical items undisturbed.

Altars can play a part in our spiritual development outside of the context of spell casting, too. A small, personal space specifically dedicated to contemplation and spiritual expression can invoke

*Representing
the elements*

powerful responses and its importance should never be underrated. The simple act of lighting a candle in memory of someone at your own altar can engender more spiritual meaning than an entire requiem performed in a cathedral. Remember—a personal altar is pertinent to your own spiritual path and to the meanings you attribute to whatever you may wish to include.

Creating an altar of your own can be immensely empowering and indeed this should be regarded as integral to your spiritual, as well as your magical, growth. Consider setting aside some space in your home or your garden in order to build your own personal sacred site.

You will be joining a long ancestral line of magicians who have, through the ages, built altars for both sacred and magical purposes! Your altar is a space dedicated to what *you* hold sacred.

# PART 2
# THE SPELL DIRECTORY

# HOW TO USE THE SPELL DIRECTORY

The following section of the book, from pages 46–383, contains 150 spells. They have all been placed in sections according to their key themes. The titles of each section are generally self-explanatory, but you are nonetheless advised to read the introduction to the section very carefully to ensure that you are looking in the right place for the right spell.

Once you have identified the spell that seems most suited to your purpose, read through the opening text of the spell carefully, and check the advice under the section titled "Purpose." The "Background" section will offer useful counsel and sometimes include a little of the history or meaning of the symbols or ingredients used. It is important that you read this guidance thoroughly, as your understanding of their purpose contributes toward the energy raised within your spell work. The intent with which you cast a spell is crucial to its working and so is your understanding of its key components.

The ideal "Timing" for each spell is given just below the section that offers some background. This will refer to the moon phase, considered important in magic, and sometimes the most auspicious day, with some reference made to the planetary influence at work. You are advised to take the advice regarding timing seriously—particularly when it comes to the difference between waxing and waning phases of the moon, which are used for very different purposes. Where a spell refers to the dark moon, this means the phase that astronomers term the new moon.

The full moon and half-moon phases are often logged in diaries or on calendars. Many daily national newspapers list the dates of the new, full, and quarter phases of the moon, so until you tune into the rhythms of the moon more instinctively, you should be guided by charts and lists of this type.

As a rough guide, in the Northern Hemisphere a waxing moon is one that is growing from the right side and filling up toward the left. A waning moon shrinks from the right toward the left. You can identify the waxing or waning phase by observing on which side the circular outline of the moon appears. If the regular curve is on the right, this is a waxing (growing) moon; if on the left, this is a waning (shrinking) moon. A waxing half-moon, therefore, is lit on the right-hand side, while a waning half-moon is lit on the left-hand side.

All spells, apart from those that specifically indicate otherwise, should be cast within a circle in accordance with instructions set out on pages 32–35. If you are lacking the correct number or color of candles to cast a full circle, you should be prepared to improvise. This may mean, at a pinch, gathering together a few tea-lights in jars and situating them at the appropriate point of the circle in place of the standard yellow, red, blue, green, and purple candles.

If there are other reasons why you cannot prepare a circle in the way described—for example, if your mobility is impaired either permanently or temporarily then directions to walk around the circle can be safely ignored, and you can visualize the casting of the circle instead. This is not difficult—it simply involves directing the energy you raise with the power of your mind rather than with the power of your feet and arms. The circle will be just as cast as one that has been walked around and directed through an athame or a finger!

You will notice that some of the spells incorporate the use of essential oils. These are very powerful and should be used with a carrier oil when being applied directly to the body, because they could cause irritation. They should not be used during pregnancy or by anybody with hypertension. If you have any serious medical condition, consult a medical advisor before exposing yourself to any of these oils. They are therapeutic, used in the appropriate context, but may be dangerous if used in the presence of people with certain medical conditions.

All candles used as part of a spell should be placed in secure holders and, unless the spell specifically advises otherwise, allowed to burn down in safety, meaning under supervision. This does not apply to the element candles; these can be extinguished at the end of the circle and used again and again. Ensure that all candles are placed away from drafts and drapes or flammable materials. It is advisable to keep a home fire extinguisher in the room in case of any accidents.

Incense sticks and cones should be placed in safe holders that have a "catchment area" in which secreted hot ash can burn out safely. Charcoal disks can be placed in fireproof dishes or censers, but orb censers, which can be swung to distribute the perfume, should be avoided because they often cause accidents. Be aware that whereas sticks and cones cool off quickly, disks take a little longer and should be treated with caution when clearing up.

Many of the ingredients required for the spells are easily obtainable. Remember that some of the herbs used in the spells are toxic and care should be taken in the home to keep them away from children and pets. If you have trouble tracking down some herbs and incense gums, you can order these by mail from suppliers advertised in specialist magazines or order them over the Internet.

With only one exception—and that is made clear in the directions—the spells in the following sections are specifically designed for those who do not have a good deal of magical experience. Cast them with respect and love, and magic will be kind to you.

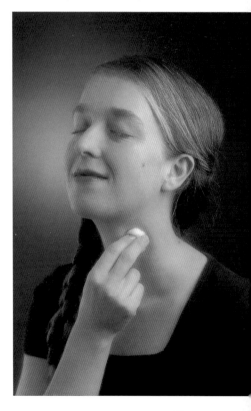

# LOVE AND
# PASSION SPELLS

# INTRODUCTION TO LOVE AND PASSION SPELLS

Spells for love are probably the most frequently requested in a magician's repertoire. The extent and regularity of demands for love spells are testimony to the emphasis that many of us place on partnerships and the need to feel attractive. There are a wide range and variety of spells in existence, both traditional and modern, which focus on romance and passion. The fact that some of these spells have quite ancient antecedents confirms that love is a perennial concern of humans. It is poignant, and perhaps comforting, to think that this obsession with love gives us common cause with our ancestors who lived thousands of years ago.

In the following pages you will find spells that cover a range of situations. There are spells to enhance and increase your powers of attraction, to signal that you are ready for a new lover to come into your life, or to gain the notice of one to whom you are attracted. Magical recipes for love are not just about new romances, either. This section contains

spells to revive passion, aid communication, and secure harmony within existing relationships. If your current relationship is stuck in a rut, there are plenty of magical recipes here to pep up your love life!

If you feel unsure whether you need a love spell or something else, you could always consult the Health, Beauty, and Well-being section (pages 134–177) for a spell to help build self-esteem or attain inner harmony. Sometimes working on yourself in this way can help you to make important decisions about what you want from a relationship in the future. Remember—loving and accepting ourselves bestows the kind of confidence that makes us attractive as partners.

Before you delve into this section, however, a word of advice is in order. The stereotypical view of love magic is that it will cause the object of your desire to fall hopelessly and inextricably in love with you. This view could not be more mistaken. You cannot change the free will of another by magic. Should you attempt to, it would simply misfire. If you try to use magic to enforce your will, you are failing to advance yourself spiritually, and magic works on the level of spiritual development. In love magic, it is positive action that attains positive outcomes!

# ROSE PETAL SPELL
## TO SUMMON TRUE LOVE

**PURPOSE**  To help those who are single and ready for true love. It will send out the magical message that you are now ready to settle down with the right person.

**BACKGROUND**  Roses have long been symbols of love and physical attraction, their beautiful scent often captured in perfume formulas to create a romantic and erotic ambience. Red roses, in particular, carry the symbolism of true love and passion—essential ingredients in a lasting, loving relationship. In the lexicon of magic and pagan spirituality, roses are sacred to Venus, the ancient Roman goddess of love and sexual passion, and her powerful influence is an essential element of this enchantment.

   This spell draws on the ancient symbolism of the rose in order to signal your willingness to welcome a worthy and true lover into your life. In order to ensure that everything does "come up roses" for you, be sure to choose roses with lots of petals, as this spell uses them to create a path of love to lead your true love to your door—and beyond.

## HOW TO CAST THE SPELL

**TIMING** Cast this spell on a waxing moon to draw true love toward you. The best day for this spell is Friday, day of Venus. Work after sunset.

### CASTING THE SPELL

1 Cast a circle in accordance with the guidelines on pages 32–35, visualizing a circle that surrounds your entire home.

2 Light the red candle, saying:
*Bright Venus, bless this circle well.*
*Honor and empower my spell.*

3 Taking the wineglass in your left hand, hold your right hand palm down over the water, saying:
*This water, blessed in purity is blessed by*
*the goddess.*
*Blessed by me and charged to draw true*
*love to me.*
Sprinkle the water over the rose petals, saying:
*May the love I receive be as pure as my*
*intent.*

4 Take out three petals, and take the remainder in the bowl to your front door. Trail the petals to lead from the doorstep to your bed.

### YOU WILL NEED

One red candle, 6–8"/15–20 cm in length

Matches or a lighter

One quarter wineglass of pure spring water

Petals from six red roses, placed in a bowl

One fine sewing needle

One 48"/120 cm length of fine red cotton sewing thread

5 Double-threading the needle, pierce the remaining three petals at their base to form a rose-petal pendant and necklace. Wear it overnight, then keep it under your pillow for one lunar month.

6 Thereafter, place your rose petal charm into a natural water source, and await the appearance of your true love.

# CHERRY STONE SPELL
## TO ATTRACT A NEW LOVER

PURPOSE  To help those looking for a new lover. It sends the signal that you are ready, willing, and able to embark on a new romance.

BACKGROUND  The association of cherries with magic and divination goes back a long way. The custom among single people of counting out cherry stones to find out when and if they will marry is still widespread today. In addition, the old children's rhyme "Tinker, Tailor, Soldier, Sailor, Rich Man, Poor Man, Beggar Man, Thief" originally accompanied the counting out of cherry stones as a way of predicting the future. Both practices echo the ancient custom of casting stones or bones for divination purposes.

## HOW TO CAST THE SPELL

### YOU WILL NEED

One white candle, 6–8"/15–20 cm in length

One red candle, 6–8"/15–20 cm in length

Matches or a lighter

Nine ripe red cherries

One glass of white wine

One teaspoon of clear honey

One 4"/10 cm square piece of red cloth

One 24"/60 cm length of thin cord or twine

**TIMING** Best cast on a waxing moon, to draw your object toward you. Avoid Saturday, when restrictive Saturn rules. Work after sunset.

### CASTING THE SPELL

1 Cast a circle in accordance with the guidelines on pages 32–35.

2 Light the white candle, saying:
*Firm of purpose, pure intent.*
*The same be said of [he/she] who's sent.*
Light the red candle, saying:
*Passion's fire, heart that's true.*
*This guiding light I send to you.*

In the days before mass-produced cosmetics, staining the lips with cherries was a way to accentuate your attractiveness. This spell carries a little of that association with it.

In magical terms, the cherry also symbolizes partnership, fruitfulness, and a glowing future. This symbolism is so well established that in some cultures another way of saying that life is good is to claim that "life is a bowl of cherries." In this spell the cherry stones represent the qualities your future lover will bring with them, so you will need to keep the stones safe to ensure a romance in your future!

3 Now eat the cherries, and spit the stones into the wine, reciting one of the following words for each stone you spit:

*Beauty, Sweetness, Vigor, Youth, Faith, Loyalty, Passion, Truth, Love.*

4 Stir the honey into the wine, saying:
*Sweetness draw you to me*
*Love intoxicate thee.*

Sip the mixture until only the cherry stones remain.

5 Place the stones in the center of the red cloth, and tie it into a pouch with the cord.

6 Hang the pouch over your bed until your new lover joins you there; then bury the cherry stones in your garden to ensure that love will grow.

# APHRODITE'S TALISMAN SPELL
## TO INCREASE YOUR POWERS OF ATTRACTION

PURPOSE   To help those who wish to attract the notice of potential lovers.

BACKGROUND   In magic, a talisman is a charm that is charged with the magical potential to perform a particular task. Here, the aim is to magnify the attraction of the wearer in order to gain the attention of potential lovers. In order to charge the talisman successfully in this way, you are asked to concentrate on your most engaging attributes. These qualities may be physical: appealing eyes or lovely hair, for example. They may be

personality traits such as a good sense of humor or a cheerful nature. Anything that you can identify in yourself as an attractive quality is a valid attribute to focus on when working this spell.

One of the symbols used in this spell is sacred to Aphrodite, the Greek goddess of love, counterpart of the Roman Venus. The symbol (a circle with a conjoined cross at the bottom) is still used in astronomy and astrology to symbolize the planet Venus, the celestial body associated with love deities for thousands of years.

## HOW TO CAST THE SPELL

**TIMING** Work on a waxing moon, preferably close to the full moon, and if possible on a Friday, which is sacred to Venus. Avoid Saturday—Saturn's day.

### CASTING THE SPELL

1 Cast a circle in accordance with the guidelines on pages 32–35.

2 Light the incense first; then light the candle, saying:

*I invoke thee, star of the evening*
*Rising in beauty from the sea*
*Shine on the beauty within me.*

3 Using the point of the nail, inscribe the sign for Aphrodite on one side of the copper disk. On the other side inscribe your first initial.

4 Hold the disk between your palms, envisaging your most attractive attributes, and charge the talisman by chanting the following at least nine times:

*As the serpent sheds her skin*
*Shines the beauty that's within.*

5 Show the talisman to the four elements—air, earth, fire, and water. Pass it through the incense smoke; pass it through the candle flame; sprinkle it with water; and breathe hard on it.

### YOU WILL NEED

One stick of ylang-ylang incense

One green candle, 6–8"/15–20 cm in length

Matches or a lighter

One sharp nail

One small copper disk, perforated for wearing

One teaspoon of spring water

One 24"/60 cm length of fine cord for wearing

6 By the time the "serpent" of the rhyme—the green candle—has shed its skin by burning down, the talisman will be ready to wear by attaching the cord.

# MAGIC MIRROR SPELL
## TO VISIT A LOVER IN DREAMS

PURPOSE   To draw your lover's thoughts to you or, to send comfort when apart.

BACKGROUND   Mirrors have a special place in magical lore, and they are used in many traditions the world over. Their ability to reflect three dimensions on a flat surface, and to magnify and distort, has earned them the reputation of being powerful amplifiers of magical energy.

There is an old superstition that the mirror has the mystical ability to hold our "soul" in the reflection it provides. In this spell you will send your own reflection— to enter the dreams of the person whose thoughts you wish to turn toward you.

### HOW TO CAST THE SPELL

#### YOU WILL NEED

One jasmine incense stick or cone

One white or silver candle, 6–8"/15–20 cm in length

Matches or a lighter

One mirror, full or half-length, covered with a black cloth

One large bowl of spring water

**TIMING** Best carried out at full moon, after dark. Any day will suffice, with Monday (moon day) being the most auspicious.

#### CASTING THE SPELL

1 Cast a circle in accordance with the guidelines on pages 32–35.

2 Light the incense.

3 Light the candle, saying:
*I call upon the powers of the full moon
Sun's light reflected in the night sky
To empower my spell and carry my likeness
To light my lover's dreams in the darkness.*

This "thought form" has a limited life span and purpose, so don't worry that you will be sending out a likeness of yourself to take on a life of its own or that you are abandoning a piece of your soul!

To cast this spell is to set out on something of a psychic adventure; you can use it to comfort an absent lover or to ascertain, by their reaction to their dreams, how serious they are about your relationship. Mirror magic can bring you closer to your beloved but should not be used once a relationship is broken.

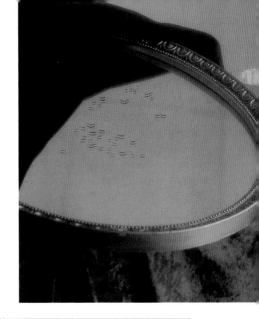

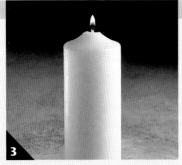

4 Uncover the mirror, and concentrate on fixing your reflected image in your mind's eye.

5 Sprinkle a little water from the bowl onto your mirror image, saying:
*I name thee [insert name of choice—not your own].*
Then, speaking to your reflection, raise your arms and intone the following:
*[Name], I give you life for one moon only*
*To go to [lover's name] in [his/her] dreams*
*To put them in mind of me*
*So mote it be.*

6 Cover the mirror immediately and snuff out the candle.

# WATER WISH
## A POWERFUL REQUEST FOR LOVE TO COME INTO YOUR LIFE

PURPOSE   To help those who are serious
about a new love match.

BACKGROUND   Of the five sacred
elements, water is the one most associated
with love. In the material sense, water is one of
the most powerful forces on the planet. It has
the ability to sustain life or engulf it. Little wonder,
then, that its magical reputation is built on its twin
properties of subtlety and power. Deep, loving
relationships draw on both qualities, and love, it can
be argued, shares water's claim to being among the
most powerful energies in the world.

   The element of water symbolizes our emotional self
and the subconscious and is often invoked for psychic work
and dreaming. In magic, to wish on water is to invoke all of
the delicate nuances and powerful attributes of its material
and its symbolic meaning. Those who go to water to look for love
should brace themselves for a surprisingly powerful response—one
that may creep in quietly like lapping lakeside water but carry the
emotional force of a tsunami!

   This spell work is performed outdoors by a body of natural water,
be it ocean, sea, river, or lake.

## HOW TO CAST THE SPELL

### YOU WILL NEED

One ripe apple

One penknife

One thick embroidery needle

One teaspoon of sugar

One blue candle of any type

**TIMING** Test this spell on a waxing moon, on Monday, in honor of the moon, queen of tides. If the water is tidal, cast when the tide is incoming and near turning.

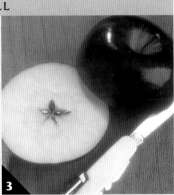

### CASTING THE SPELL

1 Find a safe, private place by the waterside.

2 Breathe deeply, relax, and center yourself.

3 Cut the apple in half horizontally to reveal the five-pointed star at its core. Cupping one half in each hand, look out on the water, and intone the following nine times:

*By the water in my blood*
*By the rivers of the earth*
*By the tides of the moon*
*Bring me one who knows my worth.*

4 Put aside the half-apple in your right hand, and on the other inscribe an equilateral downward pointing triangle (the symbol for water), the letters of your first name, and the shape of a waxing crescent moon, using the needle.

5 Pour on half a teaspoon of sugar, and cast it as far into the water as you can. Place the remaining sugar on the other half-apple, and eat it.

6 Once home, light the blue candle to honor your wish. Allow the candle to burn down safely.

# LOVE OIL
## A BLEND TO ATTRACT POTENTIAL LOVERS

PURPOSE  To help those who are looking for loving fun as well as those who are looking for romance with a touch of spice.

BACKGROUND  Most seasoned magicians become aware, at some point in their careers, of legends concerning oil blends that attract the most reluctant of suitors and turn the shyest wallflower wanton. Such oils remain myth rather than reality. However, certain fragrance blends have observably positive effects on the mood and state of mind of those who are exposed to them.

## HOW TO CAST THE SPELL

### YOU WILL NEED

One red candle, 6–8"/15–20 cm in length

One blue candle, 6–8"/15–20 cm in length

Matches or a lighter

Thirty drops of almond carrier oil

Four drops each of cinnamon, geranium, and orange essential oils

One teaspoon of water

One oil burner with tea-light

One sterile oil bottle with a lid

Four sterile droppers

**TIMING** Cast on a waxing moon to attract attention, on any day of the week. Friday, day of the love planet Venus, is the most powerful.

### CASTING THE SPELL

1 Cast a circle in accordance with the guidelines on pages 32–35.

2 Light the red candle, then the blue candle, saying:

*I invoke the spirit of water*
*I invoke the spirit of fire*
*To turn interest to attraction*
*And attraction to desire*
*An' it harm none.*

This is useful to note in the case of wishing to attract romantic attention, as some essential oils are noted for helping fancy turn into love. Blending oils that promote emotional engagement with those that invoke sensuality can have some interesting results. The blend employed in this case carries some powerfully evocative qualities. In this spell, cinnamon, associated with the sun, is used to fire up the passions, while geranium, which emits powerful love-vibes, is deployed to attract affection. Essential oil of orange is used to attract love—and to make the wearer delectable.

3 Using a different dropper for each oil, place five drops of almond and three drops each of cinnamon, geranium, and orange, along with the water, into the oil burner dish.

4 Place thirty drops of almond oil into the empty bottle. Add to this one drop each of cinnamon, geranium, and orange; stir and seal.

5 Light the burner. Breathing in the fragrance, sit in the center of the circle, then envisage an attractive figure walking toward you and see yourself opening your arms in welcome.

6 When you are ready, dab some oil from the bottle on your pulse points, and extinguish the burner flame. Wear the blend daily until it is all used.

# SNAKESKIN SPELL
## TO ENHANCE THE LIBIDO
## AND PEP UP YOUR LOVE LIFE

**PURPOSE** To revive a decreased libido and to send out sexual vibes to appropriate interested parties. It is suitable for those already in a relationship and for those who are actively seeking passionate liaisons.

**BACKGROUND** Snakeskin is among the more arcane of magical ingredients recommended in this book. Traditionally, it has been used in spells and charms to promote sexual potency. Apart from the obvious phallic symbolism of the snake, there is also an ancient symbolic connection between serpents and female sexuality, so this magical charm is suitable for both sexes.

The skin shedded by a serpent carries powerful spiritual connotations. In particular, the ability of the snake to renew its appearance and to slough off the old, spent skin

represents transformation and vigor. This is directly relevant to the aims of the spell: to reenergize, and thus transform, your libido so that your sexually charged attractions encourage the amorous attentions of a present or prospective lover.

Sometimes sloughed snakeskin is found in the wild, but if you are a city-dweller, you may be able to strike a deal with a local pet store in order to obtain one.

## HOW TO CAST THE SPELL

**TIMING** Test this spell on an early waxing crescent moon for maximum effect. Any day of the week is suitable, but Tuesday, day of energetic Mars, is favored.

### CASTING THE SPELL

1 Cast a circle in accordance with the guidelines on pages 32–35.

2 Light the incense, then the candle, saying:

*I light this fire*
*To honor the snake*
*That gifted its skin*
*For passion's sake.*

3 Open the snakeskin out, and spoon the nutmeg, pepper, chili, and soil into the middle.

4 Roll the snakeskin into a packet to contain the ingredients, and fasten it crosswise with the ribbon.

5 Hold the snakeskin packet out toward the candle flame, and sprinkle the ash onto it, saying:

*Out of the ashes*
*Comes a fire*
*Out of the serpent*
*Comes desire.*

### YOU WILL NEED

One vanilla incense cone or stick

One red candle, 6–8"/15–20 cm in length

Matches or a lighter

One shed snakeskin

One 24"/60 cm length of thin red ribbon

One teaspoon of nutmeg

One teaspoon of diced red pepper

One teaspoon of chili powder

One teaspoon of fresh soil

One pinch of ashes from an open fire

6 Place the snakeskin charm under your pillow, where it should stay for one moon cycle; then bury it in earth.

# CATNIP SPELL
## TO ATTRACT AND PROMOTE PLAYFULNESS AND PASSION

**PURPOSE** To encourage a partner to exercise their imagination in bed. Ideal for those in established relationships wishing to spice up their love life.

**BACKGROUND** The plant *Nepeta cataria*, better known as catmint or catnip, is noted for the amazing effect it has on domestic cats. Magical correspondences for catnip include the element of water and the planet Venus—both associated in magic with love. This association, along with the wild effect it has on the most sedate of pets, makes it ideal for turning your lover from an absolute pussycat into a tiger. A few teaspoons of the chopped, dried herb sewn into a cloth sachet soon has puss frolicking and rolling about the floor in ecstasy. The aim in this spell is to get your lover to do the same by loosening up some inhibitions and letting their amorous imagination run riot!

Catnip is sacred to Bast, the Egyptian cat goddess, hence the invocation to her at the beginning of this spell.

## HOW TO CAST THE SPELL

### YOU WILL NEED

One oil burner with a tea-light

Nine drops of ylang-ylang essential oil

One teaspoon of water

One green candle, 6–8"/15–20 cm
in length

One red candle, 6–8"/15–20 cm in length

Matches or a lighter

Two tablespoons of dried catnip

Two 3"/7.5 cm square pieces of
cheesecloth

One 30"/75 cm length of red thread

One sewing needle

**TIMING** Spell casting should coincide with a waxing or full moon and take place on Friday, day of Venus and of Freya, a Norse goddess who rides in a chariot pulled by cats.

### CASTING THE SPELL

1 Cast a circle in accordance with the guidelines on pages 32–35.

2 Put the essential oil and water in the oil burner. Light the tea-light, then the candles, saying:

> *I call upon Bast, lady of cats*
> *To witness, bless, and empower*
>   *my charm.*

3 Place the catnip in your right palm, and cover it with your left. Visualize yourself and your lover making love in a way that you would like them to initiate. Hold onto the feeling that this evokes, and direct that energy into the catnip.

4 Place the catnip in the center of one of the cheesecloth pieces, and place the other on top. Sew all of the edges together firmly with the thread doubled, and fasten off.

5 Pass the catnip sachet through the oil burner's steam nine times and then over the candles dedicated to Bast.

6 Keep the sachet in the bed you share with your lover for at least one moon cycle.

# PURPLE CANDLE SPELL
## FOR RED-HOT PASSION

**PURPOSE** To help those who desire a passionate encounter without the need for a long-lasting relationship. It is most suitable for confident singles who are not looking for commitment.

**BACKGROUND** Traditionally, the color purple is said to raise energy vibrations and magnify the power raised during the casting of a spell. In magical terms, it is seen as the color of spirit, the fifth sacred element, which represents connection. This spell seeks to obtain connection of the more physical kind and so draws on the earthier aspects represented by this hue as well as the powerful vibes it sends out.

## HOW TO CAST THE SPELL

### YOU WILL NEED

Sixty drops of grapeseed oil

Three drops each of patchouli and ylang-ylang essential oils

Three sterile droppers

One sterile oil bottle

One purple candle, 6–8"/15–20 cm in length

Matches or a lighter

One open lily or orchid flower head

One acorn, the cup intact

One small drawstring pouch

**TIMING** Cast on any day of the week, after dark and after moonrise on the night before the full moon.

### CASTING THE SPELL

1 Perform this spell naked.

2 Cast a circle in accordance with the guidelines on pages 32–35.

3 Using separate droppers for each oil, place the amounts in the empty bottle, and stir. Anoint with a little oil, in the following order, your thighs, lower abdomen, breasts, and throat.

The Purple Candle Spell has achieved a certain notoriety among magicians, due to its erotic effects. The version included here is the most straightforward and should be treated with respect. Some magicians disapprove of spells to attain sexual gratification, but then the same people also disapprove of sexual gratification outside of a committed relationship. This magician takes the view that sexual desire is a need as natural as hunger or thirst, so the only warning here is to be sure that this is what you want, and to act responsibly; and needless to say, with safety in mind.

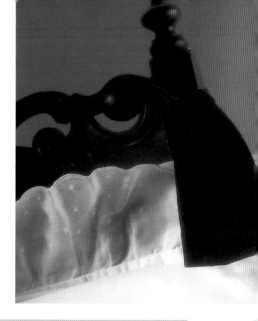

4 Smear the candle with oil, avoiding the wick, beginning at the bottom with upward strokes, then from top to bottom, stopping halfway. Repeat three times.

5 Kneeling, anoint the flower and acorn, saying:

> *As I anoint thee now with oil*
> *Thou shalt anoint me with thy pleasure*
> *Draw unto me with sweet desire*
> *And taste a passion without measure.*

6 Light the candle, and leave it to burn down completely. Seal the flower and acorn in the pouch. Hang it on your bedpost until your wish has come to pass; then bury it in the earth.

# FAITH BRACELET
## TO SEAL A LOVE PLEDGE

PURPOSE   To help lovers who wish to endorse a declaration of fidelity magically.

BACKGROUND   Berries are traditional ingredients of love pledges, perhaps because they bear both the nourishment of fruit and the seed of future fruition. In this spell, the berries cover and effectively "house" a blood pledge, while bringing their own magical properties into play to make it fully effective. If you are squeamish about obtaining blood, then you and your partner can use saliva—although this is not as romantic as the version outlined below! Use sterile needles and take care not to let any wounds or abrasions (including the pinprick you make for this spell) come into contact with a partner's blood, for health and safety reasons.

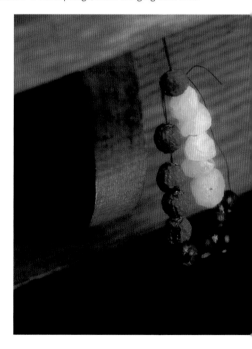

Here, holly berries are used to represent fidelity; juniper berries protect your pledge; and mistletoe's fertility connection enables your relationship to grow. Placed together in this way, these berries signify a serious commitment to be faithful and loyal to to each other, and accepting of positive change.

## HOW TO CAST THE SPELL

### YOU WILL NEED

Three sterile fine sewing needles

Ten each of dried holly, juniper, and mistletoe berries

One 30"/75 cm length of black thread

One white candle, 6–8"/15–20 cm in length

One red candle, 6–8"/15–20 cm in length

One green candle, 6–8"/15–20 cm in length

Matches or a lighter

One pot with a lid, for needle disposal

Two adhesive dressings

**TIMING** Cast on a waxing or full moon, on Saturday, day of serious-minded Saturn.

### CASTING THE SPELL

1 Cast a circle in accordance with the guidelines on pages 32–35.

2 Say together:
> We are present in this circle
> To seal our love and commitment
> To each other
> May vows made here
> Hold for one year.

3 Thread a needle, doubling the thread and fastening it with a large knot. Using another needle, prick your thumb, then

squeeze out a drop of blood and smear it onto the thread. Dress the "wound," and dispose of the needle used to extract blood immediately.

4 Get your partner to do the same, using the other sterile needle onto another part of the thread, avoiding the blood placed there by you.

5 Sew five holly berries each onto the thread, and light the white candle, saying:
> That we keep faith.

Do the same with the juniper berries, and light the red candle, saying:
> That faith holds true.

Repeat the process with the mistletoe berries, and light the green candle, saying:
> That love flourishes under this pledge.

6 Tie the berries into a circle and fasten it off, then hang it over your hearth for a year and a day.

# CHILI PEPPER SPELL
## TO REVIVE PASSION IN A RELATIONSHIP

PURPOSE   To help when passion has faded in an otherwise loving and committed relationship.

BACKGROUND   Occasionally, magical symbolism is very literal, and this spell is one where the theory matches the reality in a very immediate and palpable way! Chili peppers are noted for their hot taste as well as their ability to heat up physically those who dine on them. This makes them ideal ingredients for a spell that seeks to put the heat back into a relationship where passion has cooled of late.

## HOW TO CAST THE SPELL

### YOU WILL NEED

One cinnamon incense cone or stick in a holder

One red candle, 6–8"/15–20 cm in length

Matches or a lighter

Six red and two green fresh chili peppers

One strand of your partner's hair

One 12"/30 cm length of fine red ribbon

One 36"/90 cm length of florist wire

One sharp kitchen knife

Scissors, to cut wire

**TIMING** Cast on a waxing moon, on Friday to bring Venus's love of pleasure into play, or alternatively, on Tuesday to invoke the impulsive energy of Mars.

### CASTING THE SPELL

1 Cast a circle in accordance with the guidelines on pages 32–35.

2 Light the incense, then the candle, saying:
*Element of fire*
*Raise [his/her] desire*
*Flame grow longer*
*Heat grow stronger.*

Here, green and red chili peppers represent different aspects of passion—respectively, sexual desire within the individual and passion for the other partner. The chilies that remain once the charm is completed should be used to prepare a spicy dish for your lover—for example a lively chili or hot curry—as an overture, perhaps, to a romantic evening! At any rate, this spell should certainly pep up your love life.

Take care not to get any chili juice near your eyes or any other delicate membranes, as the burning can be very painful.

3 With the knife, make a slit on the side of a green chili. Place your partner's hair inside, and reseal the chili, binding it with the ribbon—this is the "torso."

4 Thread five red chilies with florist wire, leaving 1 inch/2.5 cm of wire protruding at one end of each. Thread the beribboned chili using two lengths of wire, which should join at the thin end and emerge separately at the thicker end—this is for the "legs."

5 Join the four red chili "limbs" to the torso, and select the fattest red chili to secure as a "head." Hold your doll before the candle flame to energize it.

6 Keep the doll under your bed until passion is restored. Cook the remainder of the chili peppers in a spicy dish for your lover.

# CLADDAGH SPELL
## TO SECURE PEACE AND CONCORD IN A RELATIONSHIP

PURPOSE  To bring peace and harmony to a loving relationship that occasionally strays into stormy and volatile territory.

BACKGROUND  The tradition of the claddagh is quite well known. It is the symbol of two hands clasped around a heart, and with a crown, denoting friendship and loving understanding. This symbol, which originated in Ireland, is often seen in items of jewelry, especially rings, and both lovers and friends buy them for each other. In many cultures, clasping hands represents the end of enmity, or assurance that friendly approaches are being made, as in the custom of the handshake. In this spell, the clasped hands signal the desire to bring peace to a relationship undergoing a difficult period.

Before casting this spell, it is important that you give some thought to why a relationship is becoming unsettled. If your partner is displaying signs of a dangerous and violent temper, magic is not going to resolve this problem for you. Seek help and advice, and get out before it is too late. If this is not the case, and you find that you are simply touchy with each other, perhaps some relationship counseling will help—as will this spell.

## HOW TO CAST THE SPELL

**TIMING** Put this spell to the test at the full moon, on any day of the week.

### CASTING THE SPELL

1 Cast a circle in accordance with the guidelines on pages 32–35.

2 Light the candle, saying:
*Blessed be the full moon*
*And the high tide*
*Enmity washed away*
*Harmony washed in.*

3 Place your right palm down on one sheet of paper, and use the pen to outline it on the page. Now draw an outline, freehand, of what you think the outline of your partner's left hand looks like, and write their initial on the palm.

4 Placing your right palm on your imprint and your left on your partner's, chant the following nine times:
*Let there be peace and harmony*
*As I will it, so mote it be.*

5 Clasp your own hands together, palm to palm, saying:
*May what I have in my hands take root.*
Place the two outlines palm to palm, and fold them five times.

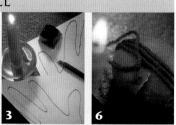

### YOU WILL NEED

One pale blue candle, 6–8"/15–20 cm in length

Matches or a lighter

One ink pen with black ink

Two 8"/20 cm square pieces of plain white paper

One large potato

One sharp kitchen knife

One 24"/60 cm length of fine red cord

6 Cut the potato in half and scoop it out, then replace the insides with the folded paper. Bind the halves together with the cord, and bury them in earth immediately.

# CHAIN SPELL
## TO AID COMMUNICATION IN A RELATIONSHIP

PURPOSE  To encourage partners in a relationship to be more open and communicative with each other.

BACKGROUND  An easy flow of communication is important in any relationship. Difficulties in this direction can lead to misunderstandings, which in turn may cause arguments or bad feeling. Having a partner who is clearly troubled, but unable to communicate their worries, can also be upsetting. This spell calls on the element of air to encourage the openness and clarity that is found in good, strong relationships.

### HOW TO CAST THE SPELL

#### YOU WILL NEED

One cone or stick of lavender incense

One yellow candle, 6–8"/15–20 cm in length

Matches or a lighter

One feather quill pen

One bottle of green ink

One package of paper chain decorations

**TIMING** Work on a waxing moon to bring ease of communication, on a Wednesday, sacred to Mercury the messenger.

#### CASTING THE SPELL

1 Cast a circle in accordance with the guidelines on pages 32–35.

2 Light the incense, then the candle, saying:
*Element of air, carry my prayer.*

3 With the quill pen, write your name on one side of a paper chain strip and your partner's name on one side of another paper chain strip.

In this spell a symbol of air doubles as a practical magical tool: a feather made into a writing quill, with the use of a sharp knife and a little experimentation. Practice first on a few feathers, and rehearse your quill-writing skills before casting the spell.

The "paper chains" used here are thin paper strips, with adhesive at one end, that you thread through each preceding link to form a chain. If you cannot obtain ready-made "paper chains," you should use plain paper strips approximately 4" x 1"/10 cm x 2.5 cm, and glue in place of adhesive.

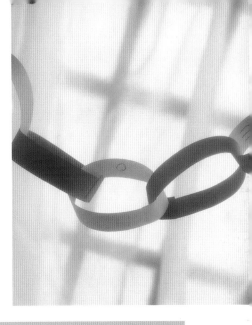

4 Using one side of the paper only, one word to a strip, write the following seven separate strips: *Speak, Listen, Look, Touch, Give, Receive, Trust*. Allow them to dry. Fasten the strip with your name into a loop with the writing side inward.

5 Thread through the seven strips in the order outlined above, fastening them into links to make a chain. To the final strip, link the strip bearing your partner's name.

6 Hang the paper chain over the window of the room in which you spend the most waking time together, so that the light coming in shines on your paper chain.

# SHOE CHARM SPELL
## TO GAIN THE NOTICE OF SOMEONE TO WHOM YOU ARE ATTRACTED

PURPOSE  To obtain the attention of someone who has taken your fancy.

BACKGROUND  This is one of the rare love-related spells in this book that is designed to work on a specific person. As already stated, you cannot make someone fall in love with you, and as a rule spells for attraction should not be aimed at a particular person. However, the ethical rules of magic are not being disregarded here, as this charm is designed, not to attract someone to you, but to grab their attention and so offer them the chance of regarding you as a potential partner.

The Shoe Charm is a very old magical device, based on herbal and floral lore and sympathetic magic. You are expected to gather the ingredients by hand for this spell, and it helps if you, or an understanding friend, have a garden. Otherwise a quick visit to a garden center will enable you to buy the various potted varieties of the stipulated flowers and herbs.

## HOW TO CAST THE SPELL

### YOU WILL NEED

One white candle, 6–8"/15–20 cm
in length

Matches or a lighter

Two mint leaves

Petals from two pansy flowers

Two borage leaves

Two sprigs of marjoram

One small earthenware bowl

**TIMING** Work on an early waxing moon to
draw attention to you, on any day but a
Saturday.

### CASTING THE SPELL

1 Cast a circle in accordance with the
guidelines on pages 32–35.

2 Light the white candle, saying:
*I invoke the lady of the moon*
*To make me shine in [name of*
*    person]'s eyes*
*I invoke the evening star*
*To form me in beauty before [her/him]*
*I invoke the morning sun*
*To warm [name]'s heart toward me*
*I invoke this holy flame*
*To light [her/his] way to me*
*So mote it be.*

3 Place the mint into the earthenware
bowl, saying:
*Draw [her/his] eyes to my presence.*
Add the pansy petals, saying:
*Ease [her/his] heart when I am near.*
Put in the borage, saying:
*An [he/she] like me, give [her/him]*
*    courage.*
Add the marjoram, saying:
*Joy to [her/him] that holds me dear.*

4 Place the bowl and ingredients in open
moonlight for one hour.

5 Secrete the ingredients inside your
shoes the next time you are with the
object of your affection. Wear them until
the day after the full moon.

6 If they have not expressed interest
within one moon cycle, cease to consider
them as a potential love interest.

# CRYSTAL SPELL
## TO HELP YOU CHOOSE BETWEEN LOVERS

PURPOSE  To help you come to a decision when there is more than one suitor, and it is time to make your choice.

BACKGROUND  If there are two people contending to share your life, deciding which is the better prospective partner can be tough going. We often take a liking to different people for different reasons, all of which can be equally valid as far as our emotions are concerned. This can make it hard to decide which relationship to keep and which to let go.

In truth, you already know the solution to the problem, and this lies deep within your subconscious. After casting the spell, the answer will reveal itself to you in your dreams, which often hold clues to the inner wisdom that is there to guide us whenever we are prepared to listen.

The tumbled stones you are asked to use are available in many rock and crystal stores and New Age outlets. You are asked to select a stone for each of your two suitors, matching their properties or appearance to the qualities of the person they are chosen to represent.

## HOW TO CAST THE SPELL

**TIMING** Cast this spell as near to the first crescent of the waxing moon as possible, on any day of the week.

### CASTING THE SPELL

1 Cast a circle in accordance with the guidelines on pages 32–35.

2 Light the incense and the candle.

3 Close your eyes, and taking your time, imagine walking downstream in a small, shallow river which gradually gets deeper and flows more strongly. When the river is above your head, swim underwater toward its source. When the waters are completely dark, open your eyes.

4 Take the rose quartz, and place it in the goblet, saying:
   *May my heart know my heart.*
Place one of the other stones into the goblet, saying:
   *My heart knows [name of suitor].*
Repeat this with the other stone.

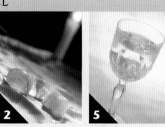

### YOU WILL NEED

One jasmine cone or incense stick

One blue candle, 6–8"/15–20 cm in length

Matches or a lighter

One small tumbled rose quartz

One goblet, chalice, or wine glass

Two tumbled stones to represent your suitors

One bottle of fresh spring water

5 Fill the goblet with springwater. Before bedtime, drink half the water. Keep it at your bedside until the day after the full moon, after which pour away the water and secrete the stones under your pillow. The answer will come in your dreams within a month.

# PILLOW CHARM
## TO DREAM OF YOUR TRUE LOVE

**PURPOSE** To catch a glimpse of your true love in your dreams.

**BACKGROUND** There are many old spells and charms whose object is to reveal the identity of your true love. Additionally, there are a number of interesting folk beliefs concerning actions to be taken at propitious times of year, superstitions that are distortions of earlier magical wisdom. Among some of these are kernels of magical knowledge gifted to us by our ancestors. This spell, which will reveal your true love to you, draws on this ancestral knowledge.

### HOW TO CAST THE SPELL

**YOU WILL NEED**

One pale blue or silver candle, 6–8"/15–20 cm in length

Matches or a lighter

One half-length mirror

One ripe and flawless apple

One sharp black-handled knife

One black cloth to cover the mirror

Mortar and pestle

Two 3"/7.5 cm square pieces of cheesecloth stitched together on three sides

One 8"/20 cm length of fine blue ribbon

**TIMING** The spell is cast in two parts, the first to take place on the day of the dark moon at true midnight (exactly between sunset and sunrise), the second to take place at true midnight on the night of the full moon.

**CASTING THE SPELL**
**PART ONE**

1 Cast a circle in accordance with the guidelines on pages 32–35.

2 Light the candle; then address your reflection in the mirror thus:
> *Placed out of moonlight but in the mirror's seeming*
> *Reflect my true love's secrets into my dreaming.*

The means by which you will "see" your true love is in dreams. Our dreams frequently offer hints about our life's journey, clues which, when pieced together, provide vital information as to the correct path to take. This magical working will prompt dreams in which symbols, puns, and maybe even literal images will serve to reveal the identity of your true love. If these do not point to someone you presently know, then they will help you to recognize your true love when that person does appear. Keep watching the horizon!

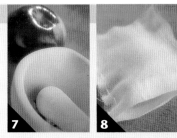

3 Peel the apple in one continuous piece; then, looking into the mirror, toss it over your shoulder.

4 Cover the mirror and extinguish the candle, then place the apple to dry near a source of heat.

**PART TWO**

5 Cast a circle in accordance with the guidelines on pages 32–35.

6 Light the candle.

7 Using the mortar and pestle, grind down the dried apple peel.

8 Place it in the cheesecloth bag. Tie the bag with the ribbon, and place it under your pillow. Make careful note of unusual dreams over the following two weeks.

# LOVE SACHET
## TO DRAW LOVE AND AFFECTION TOWARD YOU

PURPOSE To help those who feel the need of love and support around them, whether from a lover, family, or friends.

BACKGROUND Just as there are many forms of love, there are many different types of love spell. This one is geared toward drawing love and affection toward you from a variety of sources, including relatives, friends, or colleagues. We all need to feel loved, especially at times when we are not feeling as strong or confident as we would wish to. This touch of magic encourages people around you to let you know you are

## HOW TO CAST THE SPELL

### YOU WILL NEED

Two teaspoons of water

Six drops of geranium essential oil

One oil burner with a tea-light

Matches or a lighter

One pink candle, 6–8"/15–20 cm in length

Three drops of rose water and violet water

Cheesecloth bag 2"/5 cm square

One small piece of absorbent cotton

Six pink rose petals

Six hyacinth flower heads

One teaspoon of dried orris root

One 30"/75 cm length of fine black cord

TIMING Perform this spell on a waxing moon to draw affection, and on a Friday, sacred to love deities.

### CASTING THE SPELL

1 Cast a circle in accordance with the guidelines on pages 32–35.

2 Place the water and geranium oil in the burner dish and light it.

3 Light the candle, saying:
*Loving spirits, heed me*
*When the need is near me*
*Smother all affliction*
*With heartfelt affection.*

held in affection. It also works by encouraging you to love yourself, something you may have forgotten to do if you have been too busy or too blue to remember. The Love Sachet is stocked with ingredients traditionally associated with love and affection, including violet and rose. Whilst roses are more popularly associated with love, violets draw forth amity. Rose water is an acceptable substitute for the prohibitively expensive rose absolut and is available from many herbalists and general stores. Similarly, violet water is often more easily available than violet essential oil.

4 Drop the rose water and violet water onto the absorbent cotton, and place it in the cheesecloth bag. Add to it the rose petals, the hyacinth, and the orris powder.

5 Holding the sachet between your palms, intone the following chant to charge it with power and energy:

*All will be well*
*All will be well*
*All is completed*
*Under love's spell.*

Experienced magicians will feel the energies peak, but if you are new to circle work, ensure that the chant is repeated at least twenty-one times.

6 Fasten the bag with the cord, and make it into a pendant. Wear your love sachet about your person at all times.

# LOVE PHILTER
## A LOVE POTION TO ENHANCE YOUR POWERS OF ATTRACTION

PURPOSE   To help those who are single and wish to make themselves attractive to others.

BACKGROUND   The stereotypical—and inaccurate—concept of a love philter is of a mysterious and potent liquid that is slipped into another person's drink in order to bedazzle them. This love potion is drunk by the person who wishes to become more attractive. Drinking it activates your most attractive qualities, and when these are emphasized, you are naturally more attractive to others. It is also chock-full of healthy, wholesome ingredients, which variously offer a vitamin boost or aid the digestion, so even if it doesn't exactly turn you into a smoldering Morgan le Fay type, it has the added bonus of lending youa healthy glow!

The word *philter* simply denotes "a magical liquid," and this spell creates a tea brewed from magical ingredients. Prior to casting the circle, you may need to grind the whole dried mint leaves and the dried apple pieces yourself. The base for the philter is blended in the circle and empowered by the spell work you do within it, but should be drunk once a day until the mixture is all gone.

## HOW TO CAST THE SPELL

### YOU WILL NEED

One green candle, 6–8"/15–20 cm in length

One white candle, 6–8"/15–20 cm in length

Matches or a lighter

Mortar and pestle

Three heaping tablespoons of ground dried mint

Three heaping tablespoons of ground dried apple

One tablespoon of dried marjoram

One tablespoon of rose petals

One large box or chest for holding tea

**TIMING** Cast this spell between a waxing half-moon and full moon, on any day except Saturday.

### CASTING THE SPELL

1 Cast a circle in accordance with the guidelines on pages 32–35.

2 Light the green candle, saying:
*For that which is without.*
Light the white candle, saying:
*For that which is within.*

3 Grind all the listed ingredients together, chanting as you do:
*Everything that I am I will be*
*Everything changes from within me.*

4

4 Place the blend in the caddy and seal it. Then, holding it in both hands, close your eyes and visualize yourself entering a room directly opposite a full-length mirror. See yourself as others might see you: bright, attractive, with a kind smile, nice eyes, and so on.

5 When the vision is fixed in your mind, open the caddy, and on your next out-breath, breathe the power of that vision into the mixture. Seal it immediately.

6 When you wish to have a cup of tea, pour 8 fl oz/225 ml of boiling water onto two teaspoons of the mixture, and leave it to brew; then pour it through a strainer, and add honey to taste.

# HERBAL RING CHARM
## TO DISCOVER IF A LOVER IS DECEITFUL

PURPOSE  To uncover a lover's deceit.

BACKGROUND  When we have cause to doubt someone in whom we have placed our trust, it is easy to fantasize about a foolproof method of discovering the truth. But in spite of the invention of lie detector machines and "truth serums," there is no guarantee that what a person tells us is genuine. In love, this uncertainty can be torment, as we risk a great deal emotionally when we make ourselves vulnerable and

## HOW TO CAST THE SPELL

### YOU WILL NEED

One censer with a charcoal disk

Matches or a lighter

Frankincense grains

One black candle, 6–8"/15–20 cm in length

Three sewing needles

One white candle, 6–8"/15–20 cm in length

One white tea-light

One large bundle of lady's mantle

One large bundle of yarrow

A long length of blue woolen yarn

**TIMING** Cast this spell on the day of the dark moon, after sunset. This spell takes some time, so you will need to ensure privacy for at least 2–3 hours.

### CASTING THE SPELL

1 Cast a circle in accordance with the guidelines on pages 32–35.

2 Light the charcoal disk, and sprinkle on frankincense. Light the black candle.

3 Heat the point of a needle in the flame, and stick the point into the side of the white candle, ½ in/1 cm from the wick, saying:
   *Truth.*

**86**

trust someone. This spell is designed to help the truth to come to light and is based on a very old charm traditionally applied to uncover a wrongdoer.

It is a powerful spell, and all the consequences of magical misuse apply. Cast it inappropriately and it will bring out truths about yourself that you may not be happy to have uncovered. So use this spell only in need and where you have genuine reason to seek its aid. On a practical note, if you are having doubts early in a relationship, this may be a signal to end it.

Repeat with a second needle, spacing it away from the first, saying:
*Proof.*
Repeat with the third needle, saying:
*Right.*
Light the white candle, saying:
*Light.*

Using the first needle that falls, inscribe on the tea-light the rune daeg—two even triangles with one point touching.

4 Place the herbs in a ring approximately 12"/30 cm in diameter around the tea-light, and light the candle, saying:
*Fire lies under stone*
*Truth lies under bone.*

5 When the rune is no longer visible, using the wool, gather the herbs into a ringed garland 4"/10 cm in diameter.

6 Hang the ring in a window so that it casts a shadow in the room. The truth will come to light within a moon cycle.

# GARLAND SPELL
## TO KEEP LOVE EVERGREEN

PURPOSE  To bless a strong relationship
and to keep it fresh.

BACKGROUND  The symbolism of plants
is frequently drawn on in magic, and no wonder,
as some of the first magical—and medical—
ingredients known to humans were found growing
in the ground around us. In nineteenth-century
England, there was a concerted effort to collect and
compile a comprehensive list of the symbolic language
of flowers, and this included some genuinely ancient
meanings. However, the magical associations and properties
of some plants have been known for a great deal longer, and this
is true of the plants used in this spell.

In the vocabulary of plants, holly represents fidelity, ivy constancy, and
yew endurance. Holly, or *tinne* as it is known in Gaelic, is also a protective herb and
is said to guard against bad temper—a bonus for the well-being of any relationship!
Ivy, or gort, encourages cooperation and mutual aid, while yew, or ioho, promotes the
resilience and growth a relationship needs to endure through life's many changes.

This magical blessing garland is ideal to offer as an anniversary gift to a couple
who have been together for some time.

## HOW TO CAST THE SPELL

**TIMING** This spell should be cast on a waxing moon, and on a Friday, the day sacred to Venus, friend of lovers.

### CASTING THE SPELL

1 Cast a circle in accordance with the guidelines on pages 32–35.

2 Light the candle, saying:
*I light a candle to shine upon*
*This deed*
*That the light of the evening star*
*Shine upon [names of couple].*

3 Divide the holly, ivy, and yew into smaller sprigs, and insert them stem first into the oasis, intertwining all three in a regular pattern.

4 When the oasis is completely invisible and the garland is covered in greenery, place it before the candle.

5 Hold the glass of water in your left hand, and cover it with your right hand, with the palm downward, saying:
*I bless and consecrate this water*
*To bestow life and love*
*Wherever it flows.*

6 Sprinkle a few drops of water over the greenery; then pour the rest onto the oasis to be absorbed by it and by the plants.

### YOU WILL NEED

One green candle, 6–8"/15–20 cm in length

Matches or a lighter

One large bunch of holly (preferably with red berries)

One large bunch of ivy sprigs

Several large sprays of yew

One green oasis florist ring, 7–9"/17.5–22.5 cm in diameter

One wineglass of spring water

# CAREER AND
# WORK SPELLS

# INTRODUCTION TO CAREER AND WORK SPELLS

The enormous range and scope of spells concerning career and work can be seen in the variety found in the following pages. If you browse through the twenty spells in this section, you will notice that "career and work" are interpreted to include issues having to do with enterprises and initiatives as well as employment. Education and preparation for advancement in the workplace are also covered, as is communication—one of the most important aspects of education, qualification, work, career, promotion, and enterprise. Although paid work is a fairly recent idea in human history, having the means to ensure shelter and sustenance is not, and so many older spells and traditions lend themselves well to employment matters.

Among the spells in this section you will find magical workings to find gainful employment, to obtain promotion, and to remove obstacles in your career path. Others found here are designed to enhance your workplace or educative abilities, and so you will find spells with an emphasis on confidence and courage,

the ability to concentrate, and verbal and written communication skills. For those seeking help and guidance, there are charms to attract a mentor and to draw attention to your work and ideas.

The atmosphere in the workplace and at school or college is important to work and study. A little magic can aid in achieving harmony in your working environment. Communication—so important in work and education situations—can be improved by deploying any one of several spells in this section. There is also help at hand in the form of protective magic, if you find you are being blocked in your progress, or if an atmosphere of negativity pervades your workplace or classroom.

If you do experience difficulties in your workplace, school, or college, and it is due to bullying or discrimination, you should seek advice and take the appropriate action. Magic can help in various workplace situations, as you can see from the extensive list in this section, but plain common sense travels along the same lines and you can achieve much in a practical way, too.

Spells in this section are powerful and potent workings based on ancient traditions and magical knowledge. They are, however, also flexible and can be applied in a variety of contemporary work, career, or study contexts. Because of this, they can justifiably claim to be ancient and modern both in concept and application!

# TYR AMULET
## TO GAIN EMPLOYMENT

**PURPOSE**  For those wishing to find paid employment of all kinds.

### BACKGROUND

In the language of the sacred runes, *tyr* represents "success and victory in a quest." It is the rune of the Norse god known as Tiw, a mighty warrior and a good entity to have on your side in times of adversity. In the 24-rune alphabet, tyr is the first of the eight runes over which Tiw is said to preside, and so brings with it all the blessings of energy, determination, and steadfastness associated with him. Invoking the magical properties of this rune will strengthen the resolve and resourcefulness you need to ensure that your search for gainful employment is successful.

You will notice from the illustration that tyr resembles an arrow; this emphasizes the importance of having a clear target in mind when seeking a job. It also denotes shelter, indicating that this spell is invoked for need rather than greed and is thus more likely to bring material success if it is used in this spirit.

## HOW TO CAST THE SPELL

**TIMING** Test this spell on a waxing moon to draw your target closer. Wednesday, day of communications and planet Mercury, is best, with Tuesday, named for the god Tiw, as a close second choice.

### CASTING THE SPELL

1 Cast a circle in accordance with the guidelines on pages 32–35.

2 Light the candle, saying:
*Spirit of sure victory*
*Look well and kindly upon me.*

3 Hold the pebble firmly between your palms, and visualize yourself looking happy, setting off to work, and having money in your wallet or pocket.

4 When you are ready, take a deep breath, and breathe onto the stone, envisaging all that you have just wished for yourself going into the stone, and say:
*By my breath*
*I charge thee.*

5 Paint onto its flat surface the rune tyr. Leave this to dry next to the candle.

6 The next day, pop the pebble into your coat or pants pocket, and carry it with you wherever you go. When your object is achieved, cast the pebble into the nearest natural water source.

### YOU WILL NEED

One yellow candle, about 6–8"/15–20 cm in length, if casting on a Wednesday
*or*
One red candle, about 6–8"/15–20 cm in length, if casting on a Tuesday

Matches or a lighter

One small pebble with a flat surface— light enough and small enough to carry in a coat or pants pocket

One small pot tube of oil-paint

One fine model paint-brush

# SOLAR CROSS CHARM
## TO FIND THE CORRECT CAREER PATH

PURPOSE  To aid decision-making in planning for your career.

BACKGROUND  Deciding on your future occupation, or mapping your progression in your chosen career, can be difficult. After you have spoken to your friends, family, colleagues, and career advisor, the next step is yours alone. But which direction should you take?

When you are drowning in information, help, and advice and can progress no farther, it is time for inner knowledge to take over! This spell activates that wisdom by applying tradition to a thoroughly modern context.

The mark inscribed on this charm is an ancient symbol that has nothing to do with the more recent influence of Christianity. The solar cross, as it is known, is characterized by arms of equal length. As well as its solar associations, this sign represents the meeting of the spiritual and earthly planes of existence. The equality of length and intersection of the lines are a visual example of the magical maxim "as above, so below". This spell draws on both meanings and adds a third—the tradition of reaching a crossroads—in order to promote your inner awareness of the direction you should take.

# HOW TO CAST THE SPELL

## YOU WILL NEED

One censer with a charcoal disk

A mix of myrrh, benzoin, and cinnamon incense

One gold, yellow, or orange candle, 6–8"/15–20 cm in length

Matches or a lighter

One thumbnail-size ball of self-hardening hobby clay

One dull knife

One 30"/75 cm length of fine black cord

**TIMING** Cast this spell on a dark moon—also known as the new moon—which favors new projects and beginnings. Any day will suffice, but Sunday, with its solar associations, is most favorable.

## CASTING THE SPELL

1 Cast a circle in accordance with the guidelines on pages 32–35.

2 Light the charcoal, and sprinkle on incense.

3 Light the candle, saying:
*Eternal sun*
*Lamp of the universe*
*Shine upon and bless my pathway*
*Light my way forward.*

4 Roll the clay between your palms, and flatten it into a round disk. Take the knife, and make an imprint of a solar cross on one side. Use the knifepoint to drill a hole at the top, on the vertical cross shaft.

5 Holding this disk in the incense smoke, visualize yourself at a crossroads at midnight. Hold this image for as long as you can; then set the disk aside to dry.

6 When the disk is hardened, thread it with the cord, and wear it until you have made your decision. The answer will come to you within one lunar month.

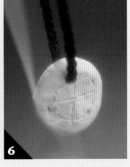

# BLACK PEPPER SPELL
## TO AID CONCENTRATION IN INTERVIEWS OR EXAMS

PURPOSE   To enhance concentration levels when studying or preparing for exams or interviews—and to help to retain focus for the event itself.

BACKGROUND   A lot can hang on a test, exam, or interview, but the associated pressure can make it hard to concentrate. This ritual bestows the ability to focus during periods of preparation and study and can even help you stay calm and centered on the great day itself.

Aromatherapy is a well-established alternative treatment which uses olfactory or fragrance signatures to stimulate nerve endings that carry messages to the brain. The volatile oils used by practitioners are also absorbed into the bloodstream via inhalation. This spell harnesses the powerful properties of black pepper essential oil to give your concentration levels a wake-up call.

Black pepper, or *Piper nigrum*, is a renowned stimulant. It is also a muscle relaxant, which makes it ideal as an aid to study and to keeping some of the physical symptoms of anxiety at bay when under pressure in an examination or interview situation. Think carefully before using it near bedtime, especially if you have trouble sleeping. Its aphrodisiac qualities may be of benefit, but not if you are looking for rest!

## HOW TO CAST THE SPELL

### YOU WILL NEED

One yellow candle, 6–8"/15–20 cm
in length

Matches or a lighter

Two teaspoons of water

One oil burner with a tea-light

One bottle of black pepper (*Piper nigrum*)
essential oil

One ounce of dried juniper berries

One 7"/17.5 cm square piece of cheesecloth

**TIMING** Use on a waxing moon. Saturday,
day of disciplinarian Saturn, is best.

### CASTING THE SPELL

1 Cast a circle in accordance with the
guidelines on pages 32–35.

2 Light the candle, saying:
> *I summon the element of air*
> *To bring me clarity of purpose*
> *To aid me in my firm intent*
> *And help to keep my mind in focus.*

3 Place the water in the oil burner dish,
and light the tea-light.

4 Hold the bottle of black pepper oil
between your palms, and focus on your
goal. Place six drops of oil into the oil
burner dish.

5 Place the berries in the center of the
cheesecloth, and add six drops of oil; then
tie the opposite corners together to
secure it.

6 Hang this pouch in your study area.
Use oil in the burner whenever you are
studying and immediately prior to the
exam or interview.

# SIGIL SPELL
## TO AID WITH INTERVIEW SUCCESS

PURPOSE  To obtain a successful outcome to an interview.

BACKGROUND  A sigil is "a compound symbol containing all the separate symbols, or letters, that form the name of the thing it represents." The traditional way of forming a sigil is to leave out all vowels, write the consonants in cubic letters, and superimpose them on each other. The resulting symbol embodies what is named in a powerfully concentrated form.

In this spell, you construct a sigil to signify victory in order to obtain a successful outcome to an interview. A successful outcome is one that is right for you and that

### HOW TO CAST THE SPELL

**YOU WILL NEED**

One yellow or white candle, 6–8"/15–20 cm in length

Matches or a lighter

One ink pen

One bottle of green ink

One 4"/10 cm square piece of thick drawing paper

**TIMING** Cast this spell on a waxing moon to bring success, and on a Sunday, sacred to the wholesome rays and blessings of Sol.

benefits all concerned. This interpretation builds in a safeguard to ensure that your interests are protected in ways that are not always immediately obvious. It may, for example, prevent you from getting a job that is wrong for you.

Spells to help you in interview situations are not going to be of the least use if you are unprepared or unqualified for the job or promotion to which you aspire. Remember, then, that the Sigil Spell is designed to give you the edge *in addition to* your preparedness and appropriateness for the situation you seek.

**CASTING THE SPELL**

1 Cast a circle in accordance with the guidelines on pages 32–35.

2 Light the candle.

3 Dip the nib of the pen into the ink, and in the center of the paper inscribe the letters *V*, *C*, *T*, and *R* in squared script, one on top of the other.

4 Write the following three phrases, one to a line, to form an equilateral triangle around the sigil you have formed:

*Auxilio ab alta*
*Sol victorioso*
*Sol omnipotens.*
Light the candle, and dry the ink by the heat of the flame.

5 Fold the paper in half, then in quarter, saying:
*Victory be mine*
*Fortune be kind.*

6 Carry your sigil with you to your interview.

# IRON SPELL
## TO PROMOTE CONFIDENCE AND COURAGE FOR INTERVIEWS AND EXAMS

PURPOSE  To help those who suffer from debilitating nervousness in interview or exam situations.

BACKGROUND  Examinations and interviews can reduce the most sensible and well-prepared person to jelly. The Iron Spell is designed to bestow the confidence and courage to help the most nervous candidate acquit themselves with calm assurance.

Iron is a proverbial symbol for bravery and endurance in the face of adversity; we even use phrases such as "iron-willed" or "nerves of steel" to describe someone with

---

### HOW TO CAST THE SPELL

#### YOU WILL NEED

Two teaspoons of water

Two drops of basil essential oil

Two drops of borage essential oil

One oil burner with a tea-light

Matches or a lighter

One red candle, 6–8"/15–20 cm in length

Approximately two tablespoons of fine sand

One saucer

One 6"/15 cm iron nail

**TIMING** Cast this spell on a waxing moon to draw courage. Tuesday, sacred to Mars, is the best day on which to cast this powerfully affirmative spell.

#### CASTING THE SPELL

1 Cast a circle in accordance with the guidelines on pages 32–35.

2 Place the water and oil in the oil burner dish, and light the tea-light.

3 Light the candle, saying:
*Spear of Mars*
*Pierce timidity*
*Iron sword*
*Check humility.*

---

admirable resources of steadfastness. In the tradition of alchemy, iron is the metal of Mars and a symbol of willpower and determination. Here, it is used to support magically the steadfastness and poise required to perform to the best of your abilities in a high-pressure situation. The form of the iron used will also help you to "nail" the problem of those pesky, undermining nerves.

This spell can be repeated as often as you please. Because it doubles as a form of self-affirmation, it has a powerful cumulative affect that is very beneficial to those who suffer from nervousness.

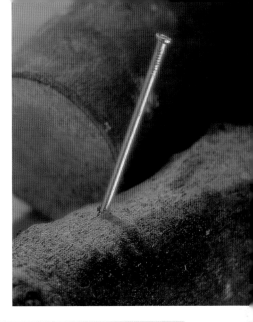

4 Place the sand in the saucer, and level the surface. Using the nail point, write the word "FEAR" in the sand. Shake the sand to obliterate the letters. Next, draw an X encircled.

5 When the candle has burned completely down, take the sand outdoors, and cast it into the wind.

6 Carry the nail with you in your pocket in the days leading to the interview. On the day of the interview, drive the nail partway into a piece of wood near your hearth.

# ARROW SPELL
## TO OBTAIN PROMOTION

PURPOSE To help those seeking to get ahead in their careers—including those who are planning to move from one job or line of work to another.

BACKGROUND Many of us experience a feeling of stagnation in our working lives from time to time, particularly if we feel that our career has ground to a halt. This spell is designed to light the fuse of your career so that it can take off in a satisfactory direction. Primarily a ritual to obtain promotion, it is also useful for those who wish to leave their present position and progress into work that is more rewarding financially, psychologically, or spiritually.

## HOW TO CAST THE SPELL

### YOU WILL NEED

Two teaspoons of water

Three drops of basil essential oil

Three drops of mint essential oil

One oil burner with a tea-light

Matches or a lighter

One red candle, 6–8"/15–20 cm in length

One yellow candle, 6–8"/15–20 cm in length

One sheet of paper approximately 10" x 3"/25 cm x 7.5 cm

One pen with red ink

Two paper clips

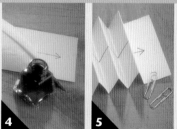

TIMING This spell should be cast on a waxing moon to attract your target ever nearer, with Tuesday, ruled by go-getting Mars, as the most auspicious day.

It may interest you to know that arrows have been used in magic from ancient times. Arrowheads were sometimes carried in pouches as amulets of protection, and there is even a branch of divination—belomancy—that uses the direction in which arrows fall as a means of prediction. Here, the arrow is used to signify the forward direction in which your future lies. Folding the paper on which it is drawn—to bring the end of the arrow close to its point—symbolizes the speed with which you wish to attain your target. May your journey take you somewhere wonderful.

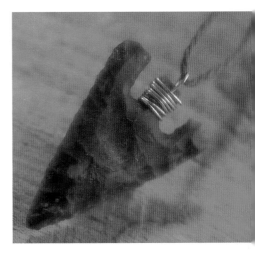

### CASTING THE SPELL

1 Cast a circle in accordance with the guidelines on pages 32–35.

2 Place the water and oil in the oil burner dish, and light the tea-light.

3 Light the red candle, saying:
*Great Mars, launch this arrow well.*
Light the yellow candle, saying:
*Swift Mercury, direct this spell.*

4 With the longest side horizontal, draw on the paper an arrow pointing right.

5 Fold the paper into a concertina, so that the arrow is foreshortened, its point close to its end. Fasten it with paper clips.

6 Hold this between both palms and concentrate on your target, then chant the following six times:
*Wind of change*
*Carry me forward*
*Flight of arrows*
*Carry me onward.*
Keep the folded paper in a safe place.

# DANDELION CHARM
## TO GET YOURSELF NOTICED AT WORK OR AT SCHOOL OR COLLEGE

PURPOSE  To help those who get overlooked at work. It is designed to help them attract notice, make friends, and gain popularity.

BACKGROUND  Dandelions, or *Taraxacum officinale*, have a wonderful history of herbal and magical traditions associated with them. Sometimes called "wet-the-beds," they have diuretic properties that are well known to herbalists, as are the highly nutritious and detoxifying properties of their leaves. Among the magical traditions is the belief that the yellow flowers, if rubbed all over the naked body, have the power to ensure that a person thus anointed will make friends wherever they go. This conviction probably arose from the dandelion's reputation as a flower of the fairies, who have the ability to bestow the "gift of the gab."

This charm is for those who feel overlooked in the workplace or classroom. It helps them to attract the notice of colleagues and employers so that they can really shine for others to see. If this applies to you, getting into the habit of drinking dandelion tea following this spell will aid your confidence. This is because dandelion dispels emotional blockages and can release the resentment and hurts that boil away under the surface. In this respect, dandelions are truly food for thought.

## HOW TO CAST THE SPELL

**TIMING** Perform this spell on a waxing moon to attract notice, and on a Sunday, day of the blessings of the sun.

### CASTING THE SPELL

1 Perform this circle naked.

2 Cast a circle in accordance with the guidelines on pages 32–35. Light the tea-light.

3 Cupping the dandelions in your hand, visualize a recent incident in which you were overlooked but wished to be noticed. Mentally re-create the scene, this time with a more positive outcome.

4 Place the dandelions in the cheesecloth. Add the lemon balm and six drops of oil. Fasten the cloth into a pouch, using the ribbon.

5 Light both candles, saying:
*Power of the sun*
*Caress me*
*Flower of the sun*
*Now bless me.*
Rub the cheesecloth sachet over your body, avoiding your eyes and other delicate parts.

6 Carry the sachet in the workplace. At home use six drops of oil in your bath, for each subsequent bath, until it is all gone.

### YOU WILL NEED

One tea-light

Matches or a lighter

Six fresh yellow dandelion heads

One handful of dried lemon balm leaves

Six drops of melissa oil diluted in sixty drops of almond carrier oil

One 6"/15 cm square piece of cheesecloth

One 12"/30 cm length of yellow ribbon

Two yellow candles, 6–8"/15–20 cm in length

# SESAME SPELL
## TO REMOVE OBSTACLES TO YOUR CAREER

PURPOSE  To help those who feel blocked in their efforts to progress in their career.

BACKGROUND  If you have been trying to get ahead in your career, but have been frustrated by obstacles that spring up in your way, this spell is just the one for you. It works by releasing the potential that is being blocked, and it does this in a rather dramatic fashion that emphasizes the spell's aim—which is to blast through opposition! Using sesame seeds, which symbolize discovery and openings, will aid you in your cause.

## HOW TO CAST THE SPELL

### YOU WILL NEED

Twelve sesame seeds

Water

One ice tray with twelve compartments

One bunch of dried white sage

Matches or a lighter

One fireproof dish

One black candle, 6–8"/15–20 cm in length

Two teaspoons of sesame oil

One bunch of dried garden weeds

Dry wood and kindling

**TIMING** This working should be performed on a waning moon to destroy obstacles, and on a Saturday, day of Saturn the banisher.

### CASTING THE SPELL

Prior to the spell, freeze one sesame seed per cube in an ice tray.

1 Cast a circle in accordance with the guidelines on pages 32–35.

2 Light the sage leaves, and allow them to smolder. Use the smoke to cense the circle clockwise. Place the leaves in the fireproof dish.

This element of the spell will involve using a balefire, which is a "fire made for magical purposes," so you will need to work outdoors for the second part of the spell. The fire should be composed of the usual fuel—dry wood and kindling—but do not be tempted to add anything artificial to it, such as gasoline or charcoal lighter. The magical ingredients to be cast into the fire as part of this spell will require a well-established blaze in order to ignite or disperse appropriately. You should therefore ensure that the fire is at its peak temperature before throwing these in.

3 Anoint the candle with sesame oil, using upward strokes, avoiding the wick. Place the candle in the holder, and light it, saying:

*Destroyer of barriers*
*Purify this flame*
*Turn it to thy work*
*No hindrance remain.*

4 Close the circle, and carry the ice tray, weeds, sage, and lit candle outside. Use the black candle to light the fire. Once the fire is at peak temperature, cast on the weeds, saying:

*Away, all that chokes*
*Disappear in smoke.*

Cast the ice cubes into the fire separately; these should evaporate instantly.

5 Circle the fire counterclockwise with sage smoke three times. Cast the sage into the fire.

6 Allow the candle to burn down completely in safety.

# FIRESTONE SPELL
## TO BRING INSPIRATION TO YOUR WORK

PURPOSE  To seek inspiration in a work or study situation.

BACKGROUND  You may have heard the saying that inspiration often "strikes like lightning." This spell takes that very literally and calls on the powers of Oya, a great African goddess, who is associated with lightning storms. She is certainly deemed a fierce goddess, so any boon that she brings, when invoked, is difficult to ignore!

In order to find the ingredients for this spell, you may need to go out into your garden or to a local park or green space. This is so that you can find a stone that has been out in the heat of the sun. The stone should be small enough to slip into a pocket or purse and smooth enough to close into your palm. It should also have at least one flattened side so that you can paint on a small symbol during the casting of the spell. Use your instincts— if a stone feels good when you hold it, it is obviously the one for you.

The paint for this spell should be available from most hobby or model craft stores.

## HOW TO CAST THE SPELL

**TIMING** Cast on a waxing moon to invite inspiration, on any day of the week apart from Saturday, day of restrictive Saturn.

### CASTING THE SPELL

1 Light the charcoal disk, and blend the frankincense with the oils.

2 Cast a circle in accordance with the guidelines on pages 32–35.

3 Sprinkle the incense blend onto the hot charcoal disk.

4 Light the candle, saying:
*Oya, I invoke you*
*Lady of the lightning stroke*
*Lady of the sudden fire*
*May it strike as I desire.*

5 Paint onto the stone a vertical zigzag of lightning surrounded by the outline of a flame. Pass the stone through the incense smoke, then through the heat of the candle flame. Hold it in your cupped hands, saying:
*I seek inspiration*
*In the name of Oya*
*And by all of her names*
*Known and unknown.*

### YOU WILL NEED

One charcoal disk in a censer or in a fireproof dish

Matches or a lighter

One teaspoon of frankincense

Three drops of ginger essential oil

Six drops of cinnamon essential oil

One red candle, 6–8"/15–20 cm in length

One stone

One fine artist's paintbrush

One tube of copper oil paint

One can of clear varnish

6 Visualize lightning striking the stone, and imagine that energy passing into it. Close the circle. When the paint is dry, seal the symbol with clear varnish. Whenever you seek inspiration, summon it by clasping the stone.

# SILVER CANDLE SPELL
## TO AID QUICK-WITTEDNESS IN STUDY AND IN THE WORKPLACE

PURPOSE  To help you gather your wits together more quickly in study and in the workplace.

BACKGROUND  In a world of information overload, it is crucial to be able to function by making prompt decisions and by selecting and absorbing essential information quickly. Busy lifestyles call for speed in such matters, so keeping our wits about us is just as important now as it was when our ancestors took risks to gather the right herbs and fruits while avoiding large predatory animals! This spell will aid your wits in study or work situations.

## HOW TO CAST THE SPELL

### YOU WILL NEED

One silver candle, 6–8"/15–20 cm in length

Matches or a lighter

One 6" x 6"/15 cm x 15 cm square piece of yellow paper

One pen with black ink

One tube of hobby glue, with a fine-holed applicator

One tube of loose silver glitter

**TIMING** Perform this spell on a waxing moon to attract quick-wittedness, and on a Wednesday in honor of Mercury, patron of this spell.

### CASTING THE SPELL

1 Cast a circle in accordance with the guidelines on pages 32–35.

2 Light the candle, saying:
*Silver-heeled Mercury*
*Lend me your swift aid*
*Let my head judge quickly*
*Gift my wits with speed.*

This spell calls on Mercury, the swift messenger of the gods. The metal mercury, named for the divine messenger, is also known as quicksilver, "quick" meaning "live." It is noted for its mutable qualities, such as expanding and shrinking at different temperatures and flowing to fit the shape of the space it is poured into. This quality of mutability is just as relevant to this spell, as is the reputation of Mercury as the patron of swift communication. We need to remain adaptable and flexible in the fast-changing world of work and study in order to soak up, select, and assess the information we are expected to act on.

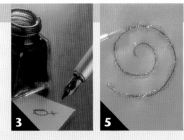

3 In each corner of the paper, draw the sign for Mercury (similar to the symbol for Venus, with "horns" on the top of the circle).

4 Beginning from the center of the page, draw with a line of glue an outwardly increasing spiral. Keeping the flow of glue constant, turn the line back on itself to trace an inward-moving spiral.

5 Pour the silver glitter onto the paper. Wait a few seconds; then pour the excess glitter away. Allow the glue to dry completely in the light of the candle.

6 Hang this silver spiral, representing Mercury and swift thought, in the place where you do most of your thinking.

# AIR INCENSE SPELL
## TO COMMUNICATE YOUR IDEAS AT WORK OR IN CLASS

PURPOSE   To ensure that your ideas are carried at work or in class.

BACKGROUND   In magic, the element of air is closely associated with communication. In this spell, designed to help your ideas take wing in the workplace or classroom, the magical association between incense and the air element is put into action. Incense not only produces smoke, making the physical element of air momentarily visible, it also distributes perfumes, which are perceived via the sense of scent—a sense very much associated with air.

## HOW TO CAST THE SPELL

### YOU WILL NEED

One charcoal disk in a fireproof dish

One yellow candle, 6–8"/15–20 cm in length

Matches or a lighter

Two teaspoons of benzoin granules

One teaspoon of pine needles

One teaspoon of dried lavender

Mortar and pestle

Three drops of pine essential oil

Three drops of lavender essential oil

**TIMING** Be sure to cast your spell on a waxing moon to encourage a flow of communication, and on a Wednesday, day of Mercury.

### CASTING THE SPELL

1 Cast a circle in accordance with the guidelines on pages 32–35.

2 Visualize a bright silver circle surrounding the ritual area.

3 Light the charcoal disk, then the candle, saying:

*I invoke the element of air*
*To witness and empower my spell.*

The ingredients used in this air incense recipe carry symbolic properties, as well as the physiological benefits. Lavender, sacred to the communication planet Mercury, is an excellent relaxant when inhaled, rendering those who breathe it both eloquent and receptive to ideas. Benzoin, symbolically associated with air in herbal or incense tables, carries a resonance that works positively in work or class. Pine is an air-related tree in terms of symbolism, and its scent initiates levels of awareness that make bystanders alert to conventional *and* subliminal messages.

4 Place all dry ingredients in the mortar bowl, and grind to a fine consistency, chanting:

*Flower of Hermes*
*Leaf of pine*
*Carry my words*
*Let them be heard.*

Blend in the oils.

5 Sprinkle a little incense onto the glowing disk. Closing your eyes, imagine your words darting through the air, powered by feathers. Visualize positive reactions from those with influence and those whose respect you wish to win.

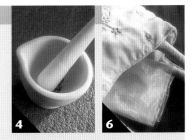

6 Place the remaining incense in an airtight bag for future use in communication spells. When you wish for an all-round boost of power, wear the incense in a pouch around your neck.

# OWL CHARM
## TO ENHANCE YOUR WRITING ABILITIES

**PURPOSE**  To boost your writing skills and help your written communications flow more smoothly and impact more effectively.

**BACKGROUND**  These days, in addition to "paper" qualifications, we are often required to have a number of additional skills. Employers and educators agree that abilities such as interpersonal skills and the capacity to take responsibility or to be self-managing are crucial qualities for successful students and workers. Foremost among the many skills we are now required to attain are communication skills—and this means confidence and competence in written, as well as spoken, communication.

This spell invokes the blessing of Athene, the Greek goddess of wisdom, learning, and communication—and the patron of writing. Her totem is the owl—an archetypal symbol of wisdom—and the gift of writing well is sometimes dubbed the "owl gift." You will need to obtain an owl feather for the charm. This should be naturally shed, so you may need to visit a bird center or sanctuary and ask the staff to help.

If you are genuinely worried about poor writing skills, you can register for a basic writing skills class at your local college. This spell will aid your learning process and help you to concentrate on written tasks generally.

## HOW TO CAST THE SPELL

**TIMING** Cast this spell on a waxing moon to increase your writing powers, and on a Wednesday, day of Mercury.

### CASTING THE SPELL

1 Cast a circle in accordance with the guidelines on pages 32–35.

2 Light each candle in turn, saying:
*This flame I light in honor of wisdom*
*This flame I light in honor of learning*
*This flame I light in honor of the owl gift*
*May each be mine*
*In time.*

3 Holding the feather in your writing hand and the stone in the other, envisage your written work gaining the approval of your teachers or employers.

4 Hold the feather out in front of the candles, and say:
*Athene, you know my thoughts*
*Help me bring them to paper.*
Do the same with the stone, saying:
*Athene, you know my wishes*
*Help me to bring them to pass.*

5 Place the stone in the pouch, and fasten it. Wind the thread around the base of the feather, and fasten it securely to the outside of the pouch.

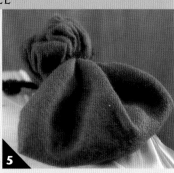

**5**

### YOU WILL NEED

Three yellow candles, 6–8"/15–20 cm in length

Matches or a lighter

One owl feather

One smooth thumbnail-size white stone

One small brown drawstring pouch

One 30"/75 cm length of thick brown embroidery thread

One 30"/75 cm length of fine cord or thong

6 Attach the cord, and hang the charm in the room where you do most of your writing.

# CLARY SAGE SPELL
## TO AID VERBAL COMMUNICATION

PURPOSE   To bestow the gift of clear and persuasive speech.

BACKGROUND   This is the magical equivalent of the Blarney stone—a magical stone in Ireland which, if kissed, is said to impart the "gift of the gab," or the ability to charm with words. Clary sage, or *Salvia sclarea*, the main ingredient of the spell, is said to confer wisdom as well as the gift of clarity, both important ingredients in the power of clear and persuasive speech. Used as an herbal remedy, it enhances confidence and aids perception.

The power of good speakers was recognized by many ancient cultures, particularly in those traditions whose survival depended on the skills of storytellers, bards, priests, and priestesses. The Celts particularly prized the skills of speech, and the power attributed to skilled speakers is evident from legends that claim St. Patrick magically struck dumb the pagan priests and counselors of the people he was sent to convert to Christianity. The ability to always speak fair words and to charm any company is also said to be the gift of the fairies, or the "good folk." The endurance of such beliefs signifies the importance in which eloquence is still held in some traditions.

*Blarney Castle*

## HOW TO CAST THE SPELL

**TIMING** This charm is best performed on a waxing moon for increase, and on a Monday, day of the Moon.

### CASTING THE SPELL

1 Cast a circle in accordance with the guidelines on pages 32–35.

2 Light the charcoal disk and candle, saying:

*Power of the old ones*
*The high ones*
*The low ones*
*Power of the moon*
*Bestow fair speech*
*An it harm none.*

3 Sprinkle sandalwood onto the charcoal disk, and add three clary sage leaves saying:

*This I offer to the old ones.*

4 Bind three leaves together with thread, and place them beneath the candle, saying:

*This I offer to the moon.*

5 Place three leaves in a cup and pour on a teaspoon of honey. Then fill it with boiling water, saying:

*This I offer to myself.*

When the drink is cool enough, drink it straight down, and bury the leaves in soil outside your home.

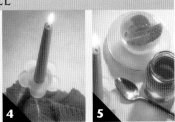

### YOU WILL NEED

One charcoal disk in a fireproof dish

One silver or white candle, 6–8"/15–20 cm in length

Matches or a lighter

White sandalwood incense

Nine clary sage leaves

One 18"/45 cm length of black sewing thread

One teaspoon of honey

One cup/250 ml of boiling water

6 At the next full moon, take the bound leaves outside. Offer them up to the moon, kiss them, then cast them into a natural water source as soon after as possible.

# HARMONY OIL SPELL
## FOR HARMONY IN THE WORKPLACE

PURPOSE  To aid in creating a harmonious atmosphere in the workplace, particularly if colleagues are involved in conflict.

BACKGROUND  When our surrounding work environment is out of balance, we tend to get out of balance, too, and our home life as well as our work can suffer. This is particularly the case when the quarrels of colleagues get out of hand and others are dragged in, often involuntarily. Even if you are wise enough to keep out of such disputes, you are still likely to be affected by the ensuing hostile atmosphere and therefore justified in taking magical measures to restore harmony.

### HOW TO CAST THE SPELL

**YOU WILL NEED**

One green candle, 6–8"/15–20 cm in length

Matches or a lighter

Five elder leaves

Five drops of sandalwood essential oil

Five drops of camomile essential oil

Five drops of ylang-ylang essential oil

Four sterile droppers

One sterile oil bottle

One 4" x 8"/10 cm x 20 cm piece of cheesecloth, sewn into a sachet

One 12"/30 cm length of white thread

One needle

**TIMING** Blend on a waxing moon for maximum impact, and on a Friday, day of harmony planet Venus.

**CASTING THE SPELL**

1 Cast a circle in accordance with the guidelines on pages 32–35.

2 Light the candle. Hold the elder leaves before the flame, saying:
   *Elder for protection*
   *Love to lend direction.*

The magical potion brewed in this spell is intended to smooth things over and restore some equilibrium on the work front. You and your co-workers will benefit from its beneficial aromatherapeutic effects—so everybody wins! However, if there is real bullying involved in the quarrel, advise the party concerned to seek help from personnel or from their union. This spell will still help calm things down, but magic helps those who are grounded and resourceful, so ensure practical measures are sought where appropriate. Remember to tend your pot plant once the spell is cast.

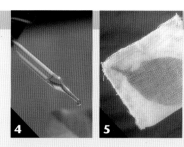

3 Place five drops of sandalwood oil into the sterile bottle, saying:
   *Away negativity.*
Add five drops of camomile oil, saying:
   *Forward with harmony.*
Add five drops of ylang-ylang oil, saying:
   *Quarrel mend peacefully.*

4 Place three drops of the blended oil onto each of the five elder leaves. Sew one leaf into the cheesecloth sachet.

5 Hide one leaf at each of the four corners of your workplace, and carry the sachet with you at all times to spread the harmony around.

6 Once the atmosphere calms, bury all five leaves beneath a potted plant, which should remain in the workplace.

**WARNING** A medical condition or pregnancy can be adversely affected by the oils in this recipe.

# ASH CIRCLE SPELL
## TO GUARD YOU FROM THE ENVY OR SPITE OF A CO-WORKER

**PURPOSE**  To provide protection against a troublemaker in the workplace.

**BACKGROUND**  The unpleasant behavior of a colleague, particularly when it is difficult to prove or pin down, can make work hell. This spell is designed both to defend you from spite and to cause their plans to misfire.

The protective nature of an ash circle is well known to seasoned magicians. Cinders and ash from a hearth fire symbolize, in concentrated form, the protection of fire and the shelter of hearth. In this spell, there are two ash circles—one representing the present situation, and one representing an improved future situation. These draw, respectively, on the inherently protective qualities of ash and on ash as a condenser. This latter aspect comes from the notion that a burned item condenses, and thus concentrates, the power of whatever the item symbolizes. For example, if you burn an effigy of a spiteful person, the resultant ash contains and represents their spite in concentrated form. The way that the ash is then acted on will be what happens to the behavior it represents— in this case, you literally blow it away!

A final word: magic works on the basis of common sense and resourcefulness. If you are being victimized, get advice and support prior to casting this spell.

**122**

## HOW TO CAST THE SPELL

**TIMING** Cast on a waning moon to banish bad behavior. Saturday, dedicated to Saturn the disciplinarian, is best.

### CASTING THE SPELL

1 Cast a circle in accordance with the guidelines on pages 32–35. Light both candles.

2 Hold up the quartz, and say:
*I name thee [your name].*
Place the quartz on the upturned mirror.

3 Draw a likeness of the troublemaker on one sheet of paper. Set the paper alight using the black candle, and place it in the pot. Sprinkle the ashes in a circle around the stone, saying:
*Evil to fail*
*Good to prevail*
*Go thee hence and*
*Get thee gone!*
Blow the ashes away.

4 Draw an eye on the second sheet of paper. Set it aflame using the white candle. Place it in the pot.

5 Sprinkle the ashes from the pot in a circle on the floor. Step into it, and say:
*As I stand in this circle now*
*May I ever be protected so.*

6 Place the stone in the pouch, then fasten it and keep it safe.

### YOU WILL NEED

One white candle, 6–8"/15–20 cm in length

One black candle, 6–8"/15–20 cm in length

Matches or a lighter

One small tumbled quartz

One small mirror

One pencil

Two sheets of paper

One fireproof pot

One small drawstring pouch

# TAROT SPELL
## TO ATTRACT A HELPFUL ADVISOR AND PATRON IN YOUR WORK

PURPOSE   To help you obtain a mentor and patron in your work.

BACKGROUND   The voice of experience is always worth listening to, and gaining the counsel and interest of an experienced or influential person in your place of work can be extremely useful. This spell helps you to draw the notice of an appropriately helpful mentor and patron toward you by using the age-old wisdom of the tarot.

In all tarot decks, the cards most associated with advisors are the court cards depicting the Kings and Queens of Cups, Wands, Swords, and Pentacles. Prior to spell

## HOW TO CAST THE SPELL

### YOU WILL NEED

One oil burner with a tea-light

Two teaspoons of water

Six drops of heliotrope essential oil

One deep blue candle, 6–8"/15–20 cm in length

Matches or a lighter

One tarot card

One sprig of chickweed, or *Stellaria media*

One small free-standing mirror

TIMING Test this spell on a waxing moon to draw your advisor, and on a Thursday, ruled by generous Jupiter.

### CASTING THE SPELL

1 Cast a circle in accordance with the guidelines on pages 32–35.

2 Light the oil burner, placing the water and oil in the dish.

3 Light the candle, saying:
   *Good Jupiter, I invoke thee*
   *Bring fair advice to me.*

4 Choose a card. Stand your card against the mirror, with both facing toward you.

casting, select an appropriate advisor from the list below, choosing a queen for a female advisor or a king for a male:

King or Queen of Pentacles—both offer good advice on financial matters.

King or Queen of Cups—both offer creative ideas and advice, particularly in the areas of art, the sciences, and travel.

King or Queen of Wands—both aid communication, particularly in teaching, journalism, or in commercial situations.

King or Queen of Swords—both are incisive and perceptive and offer excellent advice in the areas of law and insurance, and in career advancement generally.

**4**

5 Pass the chickweed through the rising aroma from the oil burner, saying:
*Bring fair words.*

Now pass it through the heat of the candle flame, saying:
*Bring fair counsel.*
Lay the chickweed in front of the card, saying:
*Generous counselor and wise*
*Look to me with friendly eyes*
*Before another moon is past*
*Seek me out to give advice.*

6 Keep the card in front of the mirror for one moon cycle, or until the right advisor appears.

# IVY SPELL
## TO PROCURE SUCCESS IN A NEW BUSINESS OR ENTERPRISE

PURPOSE  To protect a new business or enterprise and thereby procure its future success.

BACKGROUND  This spell offers a blessing and protection for a new business and a boost to improve its chances of future success. It uses ivy, known to the Celts as *gort*, which is associated with protection and endurance, both of which will benefit a brand-new enterprise. Ivy is fast growing, as well as tenacious, and has the ability to find its way over and around obstacles. Any project blessed by the power of ivy is sure to find such qualities useful.

Although setting up your own enterprise can be exciting, it can also feel pretty scary—particularly when you are set to stand or fall by your own actions. Trading in employee status for self-employment offers the chance to make your own way in the world, but it brings with it responsibilities and risks that you may not have encountered head-on in your previous working life. At the same time as this spell works to protect and advance your new project, it also works to erase worries and steady the nerves of the proud new owner/manager! In order to maximize this particular benefit, burn juniper berries every night for seven nights prior to the full moon, and secure a twist of ivy to place around your bedpost.

## HOW TO CAST THE SPELL

**TIMING** Work on a waxing moon to attract success and build protection and endurance, and on a Thursday, day of fortuitous Jupiter.

### CASTING THE SPELL

1 Cast a circle in accordance with the guidelines on pages 32–55.

2 Light the charcoal disk, then the blue candle, saying:
   *Fortuna, mother of fortune*
   *Smile upon your child.*
Light the green candle, saying:
   *Erce, mother of evergreens*
   *Smile upon my venture.*

3 Burn the juniper berries on the disk.

4 Pass the twig of mountain ash (rowan) through the scented smoke, saying:
   *Steadfast and pure*
   *Hold fast and endure.*

5 Twist the ivy around the stick, bottom to top and back again, and pass it through the incense smoke again, saying:
   *Semper, semper, semper.*

6 Place the entwined twig in front of the candles, and using both hands, direct the incense toward your heart, saying:
   *Guard and protect me; I harm none.*

### YOU WILL NEED

One charcoal disk in a fireproof dish

One deep blue candle, 6–8"/15–20 cm in length

One green candle, 6–8"/15–20 cm in length

Matches or a lighter

Two teaspoons of dried juniper berries

One 8"/20 cm forked twig of mountain ash (rowan)

One long twist of wild ivy, approximately 24"/60 cm in length

# MAGNET SPELL
## TO DRAW CUSTOMERS
## TO A BUSINESS OR ENTERPRISE

PURPOSE  To draw customers toward a new business. To be used in need, not greed.

BACKGROUND  It can be immensely disappointing, indeed, damaging, when the goods or services you offer remain unused through lack of customer interest. This spell works to drum up interest to gain the notice of potential paying customers in order to get them through the door—literally or metaphorically. The rest, of course, is up to you and your goods and services, but as many failed businessmen and women will testify, half the battle is getting people to the point of seeing what is being offered.

### HOW TO CAST THE SPELL

#### YOU WILL NEED

Two teaspoons of water

Three drops of lavender essential oil

One oil burner with a tea-light

Matches or a lighter

One needle

Five white tea-lights

One 6" x 6"/15 cm x 15 cm square piece of yellow paper

One small magnet

One teaspoon of honey

One spider's web

**TIMING** Perform this spell early in the waxing moon cycle, and on a Wednesday, ruled by commercial patron Mercury.

#### CASTING THE SPELL

1 Cast a circle in accordance with the guidelines on pages 32–35.

2 Place the water and oil in the oil burner dish, and light it.

3 Inscribe with a needle on the surface of each tea-light a matchstick humanoid figure.

4 Place the tea-lights in a circle on a heatproof surface, around the paper.

This spell works on the basis of age-old metaphors and symbols. Everybody recognizes the symbolism of drawing bees to a honey pot, and this is the effect that you wish to have on potential customers. Similarly, the proverbial properties of a spider's web in catching prey and the attraction of magnets are well known. Here, all three are used to catch the curiosity of the public, although presumably you will not be "preying" on customers but offering goods and services from which they will benefit—and from which you will make a living.

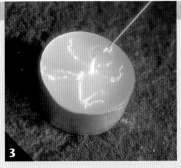

Place the magnet on the paper, saying:
*I draw you forth*
*By the power of the north.*
Place a teaspoon of honey on the magnet, saying:

*I draw your money*
*As bees fly to honey.*
Place the web on the honey, saying:
*Stick close by*
*As the web to the fly.*

5 Light all five tea-lights, saying:
*By this bright light*
*And Mercury's might*
*By iron, web, and sting*
*I draw you to this ring.*

6 When all have burned down, fold the ingredients into the paper, and hide it in your place of business.

# BROOMSTICK SPELL
## FOR ENSURING COMMERCE AND PROSPERITY FOR YOUR BUSINESS

PURPOSE   To bring prosperity blessings for an established business.

BACKGROUND   The broomstick is the archetypal symbol of witchcraft and abounds in Hollywood B-movies as well as in historical depictions of witchery. Its association with witches is interesting, as traditionally the symbol of the broom has functioned more to define boundaries than to depict flight. In the days before sidewalks and asphalt roads, the broom tracks and sweep patterns left on the ground around your home marked out your territory. The broomstick was often left by the front door to indicate when the inhabitant was at home, or away.

In this spell, the broomstick is used as a blessing on the boundaries of your business, in the hope that it will continue to take flight unimpeded. The elements of air and earth are called to empower your enterprise with the commercial viability and stability it needs to continue.

You will need to purchase a broomstick for this spell. These are generally easy to obtain from reputable garden centers. Once the spell is cast, the broomstick should be placed inside the room above the lintel of the door through which customers access your premises.

## HOW TO CAST THE SPELL

### YOU WILL NEED

One charcoal disk in a fireproof dish

Matches or a lighter

One teaspoon of benzoin granules

One teaspoon of chopped basil

One green candle, 6–8"/15–20 cm in length

One yellow candle, 6–8"/15–20 cm in length

One broomstick

One large bunch of fresh rosemary

Two yards of natural twine

One 12"/30 cm length of freshly strung dried juniper berries

Six drops of mint essential oil

**TIMING** Work this charm on a waxing moon for growth, and on a Wednesday, ruled by the king of commerce, Mercury.

### CASTING THE SPELL

1 Cast a circle in accordance with the guidelines on pages 32–35.

2 Light the charcoal disk, and sprinkle on the benzoin and basil.

3 Light the green candle, saying:
*Earth, witness this spell.*
Light the yellow candle, saying:
*Air, carry it well.*

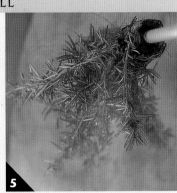

4 Tie the rosemary around the band fastening the handle to the brush, wrapping the twine around until it is completely used, chanting as you do:
*Born of earth*
*Carried in air*
*Increase worth*
*Away with care.*
Fasten it off; then tie the strung juniper berries around the twine.

5 Anoint the handle and brush with the mint oil; then pass the broomstick over the incense smoke three times, saying:
*Once I invest thee*
*Twice I impress thee*
*Thrice I then bless thee.*

6 Keep this broomstick charm over the doorway of your business premises.

# SUNBURST TALISMAN SPELL
## TO REVIVE THE FORTUNES OF AN AILING ENTERPRISE

PURPOSE   To aid a failing enterprise.

BACKGROUND   It can be distressing to see that a business you have built from nothing, with a lot of hard work, is failing. Sometimes projects fail because they were not well thought through, publicized, or supported financially. Other times, an enterprise can take a dive because of circumstances entirely beyond your control. If the latter applies to you, and you have taken all possible practical steps to ensure the continuation of your business, then this spell can give it just the edge it needs to survive.

In magic, as in many divinatory systems such as the tarot, the sun represents joy, happiness, and success. The symbol of the sunburst, a central disk with a zigzag penumbra surrounding it, was used by many ancient peoples to denote divine blessing. We recognize the significance of the sun's blessing in sayings such as "fortune shines upon them" when describing somebody's luck or success in their endeavors.

The Sunburst Talisman is designed to attract the blessing of the sun and all its associated powers to save your business. If successful, you should ensure that a small portion of all earnings from that business in the future is dedicated to those less fortunate than yourself.

## HOW TO CAST THE SPELL

**TIMING** The talisman should be made on a waxing moon to favor increase, and on a Sunday, ruled by the sun.

### CASTING THE SPELL

1 Cast a circle in accordance with the guidelines on pages 32–35.

2 Light the charcoal, and sprinkle on the frankincense. Light the candle, saying:

*I call upon the infinite sun*
*To shine upon this*
*enterprise/shop/business.*

3 Cover the clay disk with the foil; then inscribe on it with the dull pencil the shape of a sunburst.

4 In the center of the sunburst, draw a dot, and around this write the words:

*Bel, Sol, Salve.*

5 Blend the benzoin, cinnamon, and saltpeter in the mortar, and throw them onto the charcoal disk, repeating the words you have written on the disk. Pass the talisman through the incense smoke.

6 Hang the talisman from the highest central point inside your business premises.

### YOU WILL NEED

One charcoal disk in a fireproof dish

Matches or a lighter

One teaspoon of frankincense

One orange or gold candle, 6–8"/15–20 cm in length

One circular clay disk prepared with a hole through it

Gold-colored foil to cover the disk

One dull pencil

One pinch of benzoin

One pinch of cinnamon

One pinch of saltpeter

Mortar and pestle

One 30"/75 cm length of fine cord

# HEALTH, BEAUTY, AND WELL-BEING SPELLS

# INTRODUCTION TO HEALTH, BEAUTY, AND WELL-BEING SPELLS

Each of the categories covered in this section is interpreted broadly in order to encompass the many senses in which health, beauty, and well-being are perceived. Health is seen here as a positive and whole state of physical and mental existence—not simply the absence of pain. Similarly, the concept of well-being incorporates our own sense of inner peace and balance. Beauty, the most subjective of ideals, is interpreted here as going beyond a social or cultural sense of perfection to embrace alternative notions of physical and spiritual beauty.

Taken together, the interpretations of health, beauty, and well-being offered in this section have, arguably, more validity than the sometimes arbitrary and limited senses in which they are so commonly defined. Perhaps this is because magic does not have a spending budget that curtails cures, a vested interest in making women anxious about their bodies, or a tendency to overload participants with anxiety, beyond that of getting enough space and privacy to practice!

Some of the spells for physical healing in this section have a very worthy lineage; our ancient ancestors used magic to heal or disperse sickness or disease. For millennia prior to the professionalization of medicine and surgery, healers had extensive anatomical and herbal knowledge, which was often blended with folk magic and religion. Many healing spells have been preserved in the annals of folk beliefs, having been passed from the hands of the old village or country practitioners known as cunning men and wisewomen into the hands of collectors of folk customs and other curiosities. Other spells have passed from generation to generation—often from mother to daughter—surviving as "superstitions" or "old wives' tales"—tellingly, an epithet that links such knowledge with the aforesaid wisewomen. As well as spells

to ease physical symptoms, you will find magical recipes to overcome emotional pain, ease grief, and work against a sorrowful disposition. This is because health and well-being are so much more than simply being able to function. Ridding yourself of unhealthy habits and attaining physical and mental balance are important elements of both. The quality of beauty, both physical and spiritual, is intimately connected with self-esteem, health, and inner peace—which in turn are key elements of well-being. Thus, in this section, you will find that the spells and their objectives all flow into each another with the ease that you would expect in a tradition that encourages holism and wholesomeness.

# HEALING STONE SPELL
## FOR HEALING PHYSICAL AILMENTS

PURPOSE  To heal a variety of physical problems.

BACKGROUND  This spell is taken from a very old tradition in sympathetic magic, based on the idea that sickness or blight can be transferred to another, or to an inanimate object. In less enlightened times, an ailment might be symbolically transferred to a living animal; one old charm to cure warts, for example, included instructions to rub them on a toad, which was then weighted down and drowned in a pond.

You will be happy to learn that although this spell acts in line with the ancient principles of symbolic transference, it does not resort to such cruelty. Rather, it employs an ingredient that is not harmed during the making of the spell—a stone. Using an inanimate object is not a second-rate option; the power of stones and crystals and other earth-based objects was well known to our ancestors, and many old transference spells mention the use of specific types of stones or pebbles.

Prior to working this charm, you will need to find a smooth, white, oval-shaped pebble that fits snugly in the palm of your hand. It should be shaped naturally by water or weather, so you are likely to need an expedition to the sea, or to a river or lakeside.

## HOW TO CAST THE SPELL

**TIMING** This spell should be cast on a waning moon to take ailments away, and on a Monday, day of the mysterious moon.

### CASTING THE SPELL

1 Cast a circle in accordance with the guidelines on pages 32–35.

2 Visualize a white circle encompassing the entire room.

3 Using the nail, score an X-shaped cross onto the surface of the tea-light, with the wick at the intersection of the X, saying:

*Ill things are scored out*
*And sickness brought to rout.*

4 Light the candle, then fold the cheese-cloth in half and sew up the sides with double thread to form an open pouch.

5 Rub the pebble on the part of the body that is troubling you, visualizing what you wish to expel as black smoke drawing from your body into the stone, while repeating the following:

*The waning moon*
*Shall shrink to bone*
*And take with her*
*What's in this stone.*

### YOU WILL NEED

One sharp iron nail

One white tea-light

Matches or a lighter

One 4" x 8"/10 cm x 20 cm strip of cheesecloth

One sewing needle

One 24"/60 cm length of white sewing thread

One white, naturally oval-shaped pebble

One 9"/22.5 cm length of fine black cord

6 When you are done, place the pebble in the pouch and tie it firmly with the cord, then cast it into the deepest local natural water source.

# HEART CHALICE SPELL
## TO INCREASE SELF-ESTEEM

PURPOSE   To build self-esteem.

BACKGROUND   The pressures of modern fashions and ever-changing ideas of physical perfection can make it difficult for us to appreciate what we have and who we are. This spell is the perfect antidote to the type of thinking that sees beauty and worth in the looks of the exceptional few; it will help you to focus on the beauty and value of your looks, your personality, your spirit.

The symbolism of the chalice is ultimately bound up with many of the legends of northern and western Europe, the quest for the Holy Grail being a more recent, Christianized version of a cup representing healing and spiritual quest. In the *Mabinogion*—the book of ancient Welsh spiritual traditions and stories—a magical cauldron is associated with the gift of renewal. In Western magical traditions the chalice represents the magical healing qualities of water and the accompanying correspondence of that element—love.

The chalice of this spell is a cup of healing *and* love, as building self-esteem is really about coming to love yourself and healing the damage caused by distorted social values.

## HOW TO CAST THE SPELL

### YOU WILL NEED

One stick of frankincense in a secure holder

One green candle, 6–8"/15–20 cm in length

One pale blue candle, 6–8"/15–20 cm in length

Matches or a lighter

One sharp tack

One clean copper disk

One wineglass or goblet

One red rosebud

One sprig of rosemary

Apple juice, 3 fl oz/85 ml

Natural spring water, 3 fl oz/85 ml

**TIMING** Work on a waxing moon to enhance feelings of self-worth, and on Friday, day of loving and harmonious Venus, after moonrise.

### CASTING THE SPELL

1 Cast a circle in accordance with the guidelines on p. 32–35.

2 Light the incense and the green and blue candles.

3 Using the tack, inscribe the initial of your first name and a heart symbol on the copper disk.

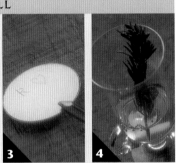

4 Place it in your chalice, saying:
*By that which I hold dear.*
Add the rosebud, saying:
*By that which I love best.*
Add the rosemary, saying:
*By that which I value.*
Pour on the apple juice and water, saying:
*By what is sweet*
*By what is pure.*
Hold the chalice in both hands before the candles, and say:
*May I hold myself dear*
*May I love myself well*
*May I be that which I value.*

5 Leave the chalice undisturbed in the open in moonlight for an hour; then drink the potion.

6 Bury the disk, rosebud, and rosemary beneath a beloved plant in your garden or in a nearby green space.

# FOUR WINDS SPELL
## TO PROMOTE HARMONIOUS LIVING

PURPOSE  To bring harmony and balance into all areas of your life.

BACKGROUND  This charm calls on the power of the four winds to bring balance into all areas of your life. It does not guarantee protection against all of life's crises but works toward a balance in your life that enables you to deal with them as they arrive.

There are many traditions concerning control of the winds, many of them associated with witches, who were accused at the height of the witchcraft persecutions in Europe of conjuring up storms in order to cause shipwrecks and ruin crops. One of the methods by which witches were said to summon high winds was by "knotting" them into a cloth or cord.

Of these superstitious tales, only the account of knotting in magical work comes anywhere near the truth; witches have used knotting as a means of sealing a spell for time out of memory—though not to unleash bad weather. In the making of this charm, you will be using a technique that is truly ancient.

## HOW TO CAST THE SPELL

**TIMING** Cast on a waxing half-moon—the day of the week is immaterial, as the moon phase must take precedence.

### CASTING THE SPELL

1 Cast a circle in accordance with the guidelines on pages 32–35.

2 Place the water, salt, incense, and tea-light at equidistant points around the circle. Light the charcoal disk and the tea-light; then light the candles, saying:

*I stand between the darkness and the light.*

3 Tie four knots at equidistant points along the cord, one after each of the following lines:

*I invoke the east wind, by my breath*
*I invoke the south wind, by my body's heat*
*I invoke the west wind, by the water in*
    *my blood*
*I invoke the north wind, by my flesh*
    *and bones.*

4 Bury it in salt, saying:
*I show you to earth.*
Soak it in water, saying:
*I show you to water.*
Pass it through the incense smoke, saying:
*I show you to air.*

5 Pass it through heat from the tea-light, saying:
*I show you to fire.*

### YOU WILL NEED

One bowl of water

One bowl of salt

One pinch of frankincense

One tea-light in a holder

One charcoal disk in a fireproof dish

One black candle, 6–8"/15–20 cm in length

One white candle, 6–8"/15–20 cm in length

Matches or a lighter

One 24"/60 cm length of pale blue silken cord

6 Hold the cord up, and declare:
*May all around me balanced be*
*Whenever the four winds blow on me*
*May I retain true harmony*
*Blessed and so mote it be!*
Keep the cord safe.

# PEACE INCANTATION SPELL
## TO ATTAIN TRANQUILLITY AND INNER PEACE

PURPOSE   To help those wishing to achieve a sense of inner peace.

BACKGROUND   All of us experience troubles from time to time, and we are better equipped for dealing with them when we have inner resources of calm and tranquillity. Sometimes this is easier said than done, as attaining peace within requires patience, persistence, and determination. This spell goes a long way toward touching a place of inner calm—and can be repeated as often as needed. Your sense of peace will increase each time you use it.

### HOW TO CAST THE SPELL

#### YOU WILL NEED

Thirteen white candles of varying heights

Matches or a lighter

One charcoal disk in a fireproof dish

Two tablespoons of incense blended from equal parts sandalwood, camomile, and myrrh and six drops of apple essential oil

One small handbell

**TIMING** The night of the full moon, on any day of the week, is ideal for casting this spell.

#### CASTING THE SPELL

1 Place the candles in a circle around the area in which you are working. Cast a circle in accordance with the guidelines on pages 32–35.

2 Light the charcoal disk and sprinkle on the incense.

3 Beginning in the east of the circle and moving clockwise, light all the candles. Sit in the center of the circle, and slow your breathing until you feel calm. Say aloud:
> *Iris, goddess of peace*
> *Aid me in my quest.*

The practice of chanting is a very ancient technique, one found in many world religions. One theory holds that chanting occupies the logical left-hand brain, enabling the right-hand brain, allegedly the more spiritual center, to come to the fore. Certainly the rhythm and act of chanting can alter our levels of consciousness and promote different states of being. Repetition can be very soothing, and although you can go back into the circle as often as you wish to cast the whole spell, you will find that using the Peace Incantation outside of the circle is also very strengthening.

**4** Ring the bell to signal that you are ready to begin.

**5** Chant the following, finding as you chant a pattern of notes to match the rhythm of the words:

*Air flows within me and around me*
*Air flows around me and within*
*Life flows within me and around me*
*Life flows around me and within.*
Continue to work your way through the five elements—air, fire, water, earth, spirit—and end with the following lines:
*Peace flows within me and around me*
*Peace flows around me and within.*

**6** Repeat this entire incantation nine times; then ring the bell to signal the end of your chant.

# CANDLE THORN SPELL
## TO PROMOTE MENTAL HEALTH AND HYGIENE

**PURPOSE**  To help drive away nagging worries and mental "clutter."

**BACKGROUND**  At a time when stress is a major health problem in industrialized countries, finding a way to drive worries away is somewhat of a health priority! Part of maintaining a healthy mental state is the ability to wash away the worries that hang on long after we are able to do anything about them. This is particularly the case at the

end of a working day or on the weekend when work-connected worries continue to nag, even when we are not in a position to tackle them head-on. If this happens to you, then this spell could help you take the sting out of the most irritating of anxiety states.

It is not difficult to see where the symbolism for this spell comes from— if a person is a constant nuisance or worry to us, we say they are a "thorn in the side." Here, more abstract worries are represented by the thorns that are pressed into the side of a candle. As the candle burns down, the worries are released, leaving you with a clearer head and the ability to shuck such burdens from your shoulders more effectively in the future.

## HOW TO CAST THE SPELL

### YOU WILL NEED

One charcoal disk in a fireproof dish

Matches or a lighter

One tablespoon of dried juniper berries

One pale blue candle, 6–8"/15–20 cm in length

One black candle, 6–8"/15–20 cm in length

Sufficient rose thorns to represent each of your worries

**TIMING** Work on a waning moon to take worries away, on any day of the week.

### CASTING THE SPELL

1 Cast a circle in accordance with the guidelines on pages 32–35.

2 Light the charcoal; sprinkle on some juniper berries.

3 Light the blue candle.

4 Hold the black candle between your palms, and closing your eyes, concentrate on the anxiety that besets you; envisage it as a dark cloud drawing out of you and going into the candle.

5 Hold the black candle over the heat of the blue candle flame to soften the sides. Pick up the thorns, ready to press them into the softened wax, naming them as you do, for example:

> *I baptize thee [anxiety over money/worries belonging to the office, etc.]*

6 When you are satisfied that you have covered all the anxieties, light the black candle, saying:

> *As you burn,*
> *You will release*
> *Anxiety*
> *Which hence shall cease*
> *As you burn*
> *The thorns shall slough*
> *All worries*
> *Then shall be cast off.*

# BOTTLE SPELL
## TO ENCOURAGE FEELINGS OF WELL-BEING

**PURPOSE** To promote a sense
of well-being.

**BACKGROUND** A sense
of well-being comes both from
enjoying general good health
and from a sense of wholeness
that comes from within.
Sometimes it is possible, with
a little magic, to begin the task
of bringing your life, health, and
work into balance by starting off
with a sense of well-being.

   This spell is designed to kick start your
plans to balance your life more effectively
by drawing on the powers of the sun—the
traditional patron of good health and fortune.
It centers on achieving a sense of well-being, through which
you can explore those parts of your life and health that need to be
brought into balance or that simply need tending to. If you are intent on neglecting
some aspects of your health or lifestyle, be warned that casting a spell alone will not
compensate. The sense of well-being achieved via this charm is but a taste of what can
be accomplished with patience, thought, and effort.

## HOW TO CAST THE SPELL

### YOU WILL NEED

Two teaspoons of water

Six drops of cinnamon essential oil

One oil burner with a tea-light

Matches or a lighter

One orange or gold candle, 6–8"/15–20 cm in length

One marigold flower head

One wineglass

Pure water, 2 fl oz/50 ml

One sterile bottle with a lid and dropper

**TIMING** Cast this spell during the daytime, on a waxing moon and on a Sunday, day of the munificent sun.

### CASTING THE SPELL

1 Cast a circle in accordance with the guidelines on pages 32–35.

2 Place the water and oil into the oil burner dish, and light it.

3 Light the orange candle, saying:
*May the sun's Eternal power*
*Found within this gentle flower*
*Grant me good health from this hour.*
The flower, or candle-flame, should be held up to greet the four cardinal directions, then brought back to the center.

4 Place the marigold in the wineglass, and pour on the water. Take it outside to allow the sun to shine on its contents. Return with it to the circle, and pour it into the bottle.

5 Place three drops of the water on your tongue, saying:
*That which I seek*
*So might it speak.*
Now anoint your eyelids with the water, saying:
*That I would know*
*I will understand so.*
Anoint your ears with the water, saying:
*That I would receive*
*So might I achieve.*
Anoint your forehead, saying:
*That wisdom come near*
*Let it begin here.*

6 Keep the bottle in a safe place, and use the water any time you wish to feel the power of the sun.

**149**

# DAWNTIDE SPELL
## TO ACHIEVE BEAUTY

**PURPOSE**   To bring out the beauty in you.

**BACKGROUND**   Perceptions of what is beautiful are notoriously subjective, differ from culture to culture, and change over time. What is thought beautiful in one era is often thought unattractive in another, and what is deemed the epitome of beauty in one culture may be disregarded in another, or even considered ugly! There is no such thing, in short, as a universal measure of physical beauty.

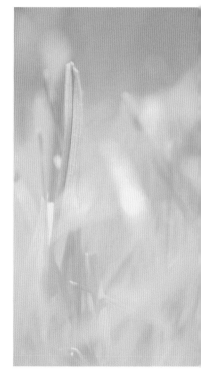

If you wish to bring out your most attractive features and draw out your inner beauty, this is just the spell for you. Based on a very old custom, it requires access to grass uncontaminated by crop spraying or chemicals, in order to gather pure morning dew. It is best performed in the summer, from May onward, at sunrise, so you will need to get up and out early for this one!

This spell is, unusually, performed in the open air, so you will need to ensure privacy. Given the time of day when you will be out and about, this shouldn't be too difficult. Please give some thought to your safety, too, and take a friend along if at all possible.

## HOW TO CAST THE SPELL

### YOU WILL NEED

One shortened green candle, in a jar

Matches or a lighter

A grass meadow, full of dew in the morning!

**TIMING** Work at dawn on a waxing moon, between May 1 and August 31, and on any day but Saturday.

### CASTING THE SPELL

1 In place of casting a circle in the usual way, work out your position by the sun; as you bow, respectively, to the east, south, west, and north, speak the line appropriate to the direction, as follows:

*In the east, I honor the element of air*
*In the south, I honor the element of fire*
*In the west, I honor the element of water*
*In the north, I honor the element of earth.*

2 Then, facing the rising sun, say:
*At the center of all, I honor the element*
*of spirit.*

3 Light the green candle, saying:
*I call upon the spirit of this green field*
*And the essence of nature*
*To reflect in me your glory and*
*natural beauty.*

4 Gathering dew from the grass with both hands, bathe your face with it.

5 Repeat this action nine times, each time reciting the words above.

6 Blow out the candle, and take it home to re-light at sundown; allow it to burn out completely.

# HEALING CAULDRON SPELL
## TO HELP HEAL GRIEF AND EMOTIONAL PAIN

**PURPOSE** To bring closure to grief and emotional pain.

**BACKGROUND** Without wishing to sound morbid or pessimistic, it seems reasonable to say that grief and emotional pain are part of human experience. Indeed, some may argue that if we do not give ourselves the time and space for these emotions, we cannot grow and mature. When the time for grief and pain is past, it is healthy to let these feelings go. This is not always easy, and some cultures acknowledge this by providing rituals to mark the end of mourning.

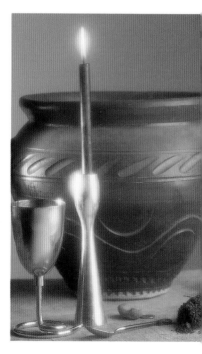

Death is not the only situation that causes us to grieve—the end of a happy time or the breakup of a relationship can also cause deep distress. The healthy way to deal with grief is to take time to express it, remember the person or time we have lost, then move on and grow from that experience. If moving away from grief is difficult, and you are finding it hard to let go of painful feelings because they have become a habit rather than a healthy way of dealing with loss, this ritual will help you to move on.

## HOW TO CAST THE SPELL

### YOU WILL NEED

One black candle, 6–8"/15–20 cm in length

Matches or a lighter

One copper or bronze-colored coin

One large metal cauldron or rounded ceramic pot

One small, dark, rounded pebble

One teaspoon of water

Two trowelfuls of soil or potting soil

Red wine or grape juice, 4 fl oz/125 ml

**TIMING** Cast this spell on a waning moon to carry grief out with the tide, on any day of the week, with Saturday, day of Saturn the banisher, the most favorable.

### CASTING THE SPELL

1 Cast a circle in accordance with the guidelines on pages 32–35.

2 Light the candle, saying:
*Light upon grief*
*Cast out all pain*
*Tears to be lost*
*Happiness gained.*

3 Place the coin in the cauldron, saying:
*Ties are now rent*
*Anger is spent.*
Now place in the pebble, saying:
*Banished the frown*

*Weighing me down.*
Pour in the water, saying:
*Hence the last*
*Teardrop passed.*

4 Cover these with the soil or potting soil; then raise the glass of wine, saying:
*A toast to sorrows gone*
*That will not come again.*

5 Drink half, and pour the remainder onto the soil, saying:
*The earth to soak up*
*The last of this cup.*

6 Stand the cauldron by the candle until it is completely burned down. Then remove it and keep it in a hidden place for one moon cycle. Then bury the soil and its contents after dark, away from your home.

# BALEFIRE SPELL
## TO DESTROY WORRIES

PURPOSE  To send your worries up in smoke.

BACKGROUND  If you need a dramatic way to get rid
of troubles that are hanging over you, you are looking at the
right spell. Rather than fend off worries, this spell destroys
the ones that are already bothering you. Needless to say, the
spell does not sort out all of your problems for you but works
by ritually naming and burning them in a magical fire,
known as a balefire.

### HOW TO CAST THE SPELL

#### YOU WILL NEED

One large bundle of dry wood

One tea-light in a lantern or jar

Matches or a lighter

One ink pen, with red ink

Sufficient slips of paper to represent
each worry

One large bundle of dry weeds

One large bundle of dry yarrow

Dried orange peel from five oranges

**TIMING** After dark, on a waning moon, on
any day—warn your neighbors to get their
washing in from the yard, as the fire will
create a good deal of smoke!

#### CASTING THE SPELL

1 Put together and light a bonfire using dry
wood outdoors.

2 Visualize a circle of white light all around
the bonfire and the area in which you will be
working.

A balefire is any fire made for magical purposes and therefore eminently suited for burning ingredients assembled for a spell. The destruction of what is named in a magical circle is a very powerful act, and you gain the most benefit from this spell if you keep it simple. Try to name your worries by summing them up in a single word. If it is a troublesome person, just write their name. Don't worry—you won't be harming them. It is the intent that counts here, and the intention of this spell is to obliterate the worries, *not* the person who causes them (however tempting).

3 Light the tea-light, and by its light, write your worries, one on each paper slip.

4 Throw the weeds on the fire, saying:
*By this bane, I root you out.*
Throw on the yarrow, saying:
*By this boon, I cancel.*
Naming each worry as you do so, throw the slips of paper in one by one, and watch them burn.
Cast in the orange peel, saying:
*Troubles begone*
*Sweetness anon.*

**3**

5 Stay outdoors until the fire is completely burned down.

6 Remove the ashes, and bury them away from the house.

# WEDJAT EYE CHARM
## TO KEEP ANXIETY AT BAY

PURPOSE  To exorcise anxiety and keep it away.

BACKGROUND  Wedjat Eye is the healed eye of the Egyptian god Horus, said in ancient mythologies to represent the powers of the moon. It has long been used as a protective charm, if worn as an amulet about the body or drawn on the outside of your home. In this spell the Wedjat Eye is used to raise the power to protect against evil from others, be that evil envy, wishing ill, or other ill feeling. Before this power can be effectively invoked, however, it is necessary to dispel all causes of anxiety from your life.

## HOW TO CAST THE SPELL

### YOU WILL NEED

One large white plate

One fine artist's brush

One tube of black oil paint

One charcoal disk in a fireproof dish

One teaspoon of frankincense gum anointed with honey and geranium essential oil

One black candle, 6–8"/15–20 cm in length

One silver candle, 6–8"/15–20 cm in length

Matches or a lighter

One small, plain tea-plate (or flat dessert-plate)

**TIMING** This working should be performed on the dark of the moon, on any day of the week, after dark.

### CASTING THE SPELL

1 Prior to the circle, and allowing enough time for the paint to dry, paint the following words onto the inside of the plate:

*Every evil word, every evil speech, every evil slander, every evil thought, every evil plot, every evil fright, every evil quarrel, every evil plan, every evil thing, every evil dream, every evil slumber.*

This is achieved symbolically by using an Egyptian spell, dating back approximately four thousand years.

In order to perform this charm, you should find an expendable plate on which to paint the words prescribed for the spell, as you will need to smash it immediately after the words are spoken in the circle. You will also need to purchase a plate-hanging bracket for the hanging of the Wedjat Eye amulet onto the outside of your home. Prior to casting the spell, it would be wise, provided your health will allow it, to fast during the day.

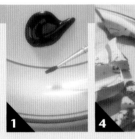

4 Light the black candle, and speak the words on the plate aloud. Smash the plate immediately after you finish speaking.

5 Light the silver candle, and paint the Wedjat Eye, on the center of the tea-plate (dessert plate).

6 Allow it to dry; then hang it on the outside of your building to protect you from anxiety. Bury the broken plate deep in the earth, away from your home.

2 Cast a circle in accordance with the guidelines on pages 32–35.

3 Light the charcoal disk, and burn the incense.

# OUROBORUS SPELL
## TO AID PHYSICAL BALANCE

**PURPOSE** To achieve physical balance and thereby pave the way to good health.

**BACKGROUND** This spell is based on an ancient principle that makes good sense for us today, the principle prescribing "moderation in all things" as the basis for sound health. This is not just a warning about excess, but a positive encouragement to ensure that we are balanced in all essentials, and that no one physical desire or need should overrule the well-being of our other physical requirements.

## HOW TO CAST THE SPELL

### YOU WILL NEED

One charcoal disk in a fireproof dish

Matches or a lighter

Benzoin granules

One black candle, 6–8"/15–20 cm in length

One white candle, 6–8"/15–20 cm in length

One pen with green ink

One 1" x ½"/2.5 cm x 1 cm strip of paper

Nine 18"/45 cm lengths of thick-stranded cotton embroidery thread, three each of black, red, and white

One 18"/45 cm length of thick-stranded gray cotton embroidery thread

**TIMING** This should be cast on a waxing half-moon to draw positive balance. Any day of the week is suitable, with Monday being especially powerful.

### CASTING THE SPELL

1 Cast a circle in accordance with the guidelines on pages 32–35.

2 Light the charcoal, and sprinkle on benzoin.

3 Place the black candle to the left of the white candle, and light both, saying:

> *Hermes, magus of the eternal*
> *Grant this boon*
> *Of perfect elemental balance.*

The symbol used in this spell is that of the ouroborus, the "serpent that swallows its own tail." It is an ancient alchemical sign that represents oneness, wholeness, and the nature of universal balance. There is a well-established link, throughout the Near East and northern and western Europe, between snakes and healing, as they have evolved as an image of earth wisdom. Brigid, an Irish goddess associated with healing wells, is closely associated with serpents, as are many other goddesses of the healing arts.

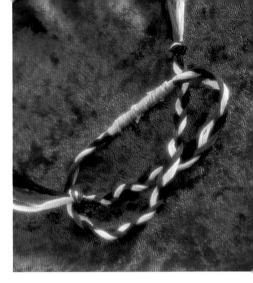

4 Using the pen, draw on the strip of paper the symbol of the ouroborus—the curved serpent swallowing its own tail.

5 When the ink has dried, pass the paper through the incense smoke. Place it to one side, and tie and braid a wristband to fit your left wrist from the black, red, and white threads.

6 Prior to tying this onto your wrist, roll the strip of paper with the ouroborus inscribed on it around the bracelet, and cover it by rolling the gray thread over it until it is completely used up; then fasten it firmly. Wear your ouroborus bracelet until it falls off.

# SUNFLOWER SPELL
## TO ENCOURAGE A HAPPY DISPOSITION

PURPOSE  To invoke happiness.

BACKGROUND  The secret of true happiness differs according to whom you ask and where they are in their lives. Those who have walked the earth for many years and who have meditated greatly on the matter may claim that happiness lies in finding peace within. People who have suffered, or witnessed suffering through privation, claim with equal validity that happiness resides within the simple things needed for physical and spiritual survival: food, warmth, clothing, shelter, freedom, companionship, and love. Most often, the secret of true happiness lies within those who ask the question.

This spell is based on the power of our friend the sun to generate warmth, health, and joy on the earth. The powers of Sol can sometimes be found concentrated in certain herbs and plants, and perhaps nowhere more so than in the seeds of the sunflower. Nutritionally speaking, sunflower seeds contain a concentrated property of sunlight—they are a good source of vitamin D. Vitamin D aids calcium absorption and helps regulate our metabolism. Since sunflowers in magical tradition represent the powers of the sun, the seeds carry in concentrated form Sol's ability to bestow health and happiness.

## HOW TO CAST THE SPELL

### YOU WILL NEED

One charcoal disk in a fireproof dish

Matches or a lighter

Frankincense

One orange candle, 6–8"/15–20 cm in length

Fifteen sunflower seeds

One small pouch with a drawstring mouth

One 26"/65 cm length of thong or fine cord

**TIMING** Work on a waxing moon to attract happiness, and on a Sunday, ruled by glorious Sol.

### CASTING THE SPELL

1 Cast a circle in accordance with the guidelines on pages 32–35.

2 Light the charcoal disk, and burn the frankincense. Light the candle, saying:

*Sol Invictus*
*You are honored here*
*Shine your blessings*
*Upon your child.*

3 Take five sunflower seeds and cup them in your left hand, then raise your right hand, saying:

*Your power*
*To pass to me.*

Eat the seeds.

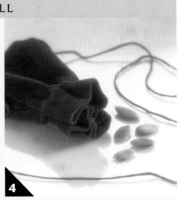

4 Take five more sunflower seeds and place them in the pouch, saying:

*Your strength to*
*Abide with me.*

Fasten the pouch, attach it to the cord, and place it around your neck, saying:

*Happiness reside within me*
*Happiness reside around me.*

5 Carry the incense around the circle *deosil* (clockwise) three times. Bow your head to the candle flame, saying:

*Sol Invictus*
*Blessed be*
*May I give*
*As I receive.*

6 Plant the remaining five seeds in the spring, approximately 1/4"/5 mm below the surface of finely tilled soil.

# LAVENDER SPELL
## TO AID RESTFUL SLEEP

PURPOSE  To aid relaxed and untroubled sleep.

BACKGROUND  Lavender is known as one of the great universals among scented herbs. Noted for its antiseptic qualities, its essential oil is also wonderful for curing headaches, healing scalds, and treating eczema and other troublesome skin conditions. It is a great relaxant and often used in dream pillows—sachets stuffed with soporific herbs to aid restful and natural sleep. Drops of the essential oil, either placed in a warm bath before bedtime or placed on a pillowcase, are used to bring on drowsiness.

## HOW TO CAST THE SPELL

### YOU WILL NEED

One lavender-scented pillar candle, any size

Matches or a lighter

One white candle, 6–8"/15–20 cm in length

One pliable whip of willow of a length to fit over a person if it is hooped

One 36"/90 cm length of strong twine

One large bunch of dried camomile

One large bunch of dried lavender

One roll of florist twine

**TIMING** Work on a waxing moon to bring rest, and on any day of the week save Saturday, ruled by restrictive Saturn.

### CASTING THE SPELL

1 Cast a circle in accordance with the guidelines on pages 32–35.

2 Light the lavender-scented candle, and carry it around the space deosil (clockwise) to scent it.

3 Light the white candle, saying:
*The purity of light*
*Guide the way to gentle sleep*
*Hence may I be known*
*For the peace that I keep.*

This spell uses a magical technique that has a venerable history in the annals of magical practice. It requires a hoop to be passed over the entire body of the person for whom the spell is being cast. The technique of passing someone through an opening or hole is very old—ancient holed standing stones have long been used for the purpose of blessing those passed through them. The flower hoop used in this spell has a similar principle—that once one has passed through a sacred space, its passing is irreversible, and so the blessing is sealed.

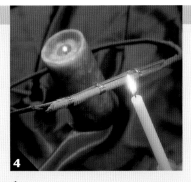

4 Bend the willow into a hoop, and fasten it firmly using the strong twine. Fasten the camomile and lavender onto it with florist's twine until the willow is entirely covered by the dried flowers.

5 Hold up the hoop vertically before the white candle, saying:

*Through this circle*
*I will pass*
*On the road to*
*Morpheus*
*So my spell for sleep*
*Is blessed.*

Pass the hoop over your entire body, head to toe, and step out of it.

6 Hang the hoop above your bed.

# SPIDER SPELL
## TO BRING HAPPY DREAMS

PURPOSE   To bring happy, wholesome dreams.

BACKGROUND   Native American dream catchers act as nets, letting good dreams through the net but catching and holding bad dreams at bay—until the morning light melts them away. But different types of nets can be used for different purposes, and in this spell a spider's web is used to catch happy dreams to nourish your imagination and grace your nights.

This spell is inspired by the magical and spiritual symbolism of the spider, which has at times been falsely associated with evil and deceit. In fact, many cultures honor the spider as a symbol of creativity and spirit energy. In Western magical traditions, their webs are likened to the patterns of magic, spirit, and connection. The spider is a truly amazing creature, and its weaving abilities are proverbial. Wonderful webs which join leaf to concrete, gateposts to trees—nature to the built environment— announce the turning of dreaming's tides. After the equinox in September, we pass into the darker days and so into our more creative selves, which are often revealed through the rich and vivid dreams we experience at this time of year.

## HOW TO CAST THE SPELL

### YOU WILL NEED

One oil burner with a tea-light

Two teaspoons of water

Six drops of poppy essential oil

Matches or a lighter

One white candle, 6–8"/15–20 cm
in length

One small nugget of pyrite (fool's gold)

One spider's web

One white drawstring pouch

One 24"/60 cm length of thin white
ribbon

**TIMING** To be cast on a waxing moon, with
Monday, dedicated to the moon, who rules
our dreams, as the most auspicious day.

### CASTING THE SPELL

1 Cast a circle in accordance with the
guidelines on pages 32–35.

2 Light the tea-light, placing the water
and poppy oil in the oil burner.

3 Light the white candle, saying:
  *Lady of the moon*
  *Grandmother spider*
  *Weave your magic*
  *Into my dreams.*

4 Wrap the pyrite nugget inside the
spider's web, and place it in the pouch.

5 Fasten it firmly halfway down the
length of ribbon. Then, enclosing the
pouch in your cupped hands, chant the
following over again for the space of at
least sixty heartbeats:
  *Grandmother spider*
  *Weave your threads*
  *Wrap all beauty*
  *In your web.*

6 Hang the pouch over your bedpost
or above your bed. Every night until
the next full moon, touch your hand
to it when you retire saying the
following words:
  *Happy themes*
  *Enter my dreams.*

# CYCLAMEN CHARM
## TO GUARD AGAINST NIGHTMARES

**PURPOSE**  To defend against bad dreams.

**BACKGROUND**  Everyone has the occasional bad dream; after all, dreams act as a safety valve, so it is not surprising that bad feelings come out as nightmares. However, if nightmares are frequent and there is no underlying trauma that can be discerned, a little magic may be used to good effect.

This particular magical charm is based on an old spell to cure night frights in children and is suitable for adults and children alike. Cyclamen is noted, by those who specialize in such things, as a great defense against bad vibes. Keeping the plant in the bedroom at night is said to reduce the occurrence of nightmares, and the flowers are sometimes carried to ease grief. The cheering nature of cyclamen is perhaps reflected in the fact that it is happiest growing in shaded parts of gardens and woodland, where it brings color and brightness to the darker places of each.

You should note that the blood used in this spell should be drawn from the person for whom the spell is intended—the directions opposite are written as if for the person casting the spell.

## HOW TO CAST THE SPELL

**TIMING** It is best to work at the dark moon to enhance protection, on any day of the week, with Saturday, ruled by Saturn the banisher, especially auspicious.

### CASTING THE SPELL

1 Cast a circle in accordance with the guidelines on pages 32–35.

2 Light the charcoal, and sprinkle on incense.

3 Light the black candle, saying:

*Hecate dark*
*Venus bright*
*Drive out the bad*
*Bring in the light.*

4 Use the needle to prick your forefinger, and squeeze out a drop of blood onto the potting soil in which the cyclamen is standing, saying:

*Guard what lives in this house of skin*
*Protected without, and held within.*

5 Pass the entire length of the ribbon through the incense smoke, saying:

*That which is pure*
*Shall aye endure.*

Tie the ribbon around the plant pot, and fasten into a bow.

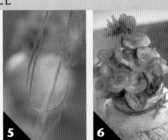

### YOU WILL NEED

One charcoal disk in a fireproof dish

Matches or a lighter

Blended incense of equal parts copal gum, juniper berries, and dried cyclamen flowers

One black candle, 6–8"/15–20 cm in length

One sterile needle

One healthy cyclamen plant, any color

One 24"/60 cm length of red satin ribbon

6 Keep this potted plant in your room day and night, and nurture and care for it always if you wish to keep bad dreams at bay.

# CANDLE WAX SPELL
## TO BANISH UNHEALTHY HABITS

**PURPOSE** To get rid of unhealthy habits once and for all.

**BACKGROUND** Have you ever wanted to kick smoking, nail-biting, thumb-sucking, or hair-twisting? Look no farther—this is the spell for you! A little bit of magic and a confidence boost will go a long way toward ridding yourself of an unhealthy or unwanted habit. You will need to ask yourself, however, whether the need that is encouraging your habit is going to be answered in some other way once that habit has

gone. If it is not, you may end up back at square one, so it is worth taking time to prepare for this spell.

Begin by identifying the cause of the habit (for example, nervousness, lack of confidence, anxiety) and then working out what the consequences of banishing your unhealthy habit may be. If you are a nail-biter, you won't wish to become a smoker or a thumb-sucker instead, so ensure that what is being banished is replaced with something healthy— a new outlook, for example. Ask yourself searching questions, and answer them honestly. Then you will be ready to consign your bad habit to the garbage can!

## HOW TO CAST THE SPELL

**TIMING** Work this spell on a waning moon to aid banishment, and on a Saturday, ruled by disciplinarian Saturn.

### CASTING THE SPELL

1 Cast a circle in accordance with the guidelines on pages 32–35.

2 Light the charcoal disk, and sprinkle on incense. Light the brown candle, saying:
*Saturn, witness and empower this spell.*

3 Heat the point of the nail in the candle's flame; then use it to carve the name of the habit you want to banish down the side of one white candle, from the bottom to the wick.

4 Hold this candle before the candle flame, saying:
*Burn it away.*
Pass it through the incense smoke, saying:
*Let it fly out.*
Hold this candle between your palms, saying:
*The habit that's in me*
*Fly into you*
*The fire burn it out.*
Light the candle.

### YOU WILL NEED

One charcoal disk in a fireproof dish

Matches or a lighter

Black copal incense

One brown candle, 6–8"/15–20 cm in length

One sharp 6"/15 cm iron nail

Two white household candles, approximately 6"/15 cm in length

5 Using the same method, carve into the side of the second white candle, from the wick to the bottom, "HEALTH."

6 Light the second candle, and allow both candles to burn down completely within the circle.

# CELTIC STONE SPELL
## TO GUARD AGAINST FREQUENT HEADACHES

**PURPOSE**  To banish frequent tension headaches.

**BACKGROUND**  There are many old remedies for
frequent headaches; herbal remedies include the application
of feverfew for migraines and good old aspirin or willow bark
to kill pain. If you are plagued by frequent tension headaches,
and you have checked with your doctor that there is no serious
underlying condition, try this ancient cure.

## HOW TO CAST THE SPELL

### YOU WILL NEED

One black candle, 6–8"/15–20 cm
in length

Matches or a lighter

One sharp piece of flint (or one sharp nail)

One gray or white egg-shaped stone

Pure water, 2 fl oz/50 ml

Red wine, 2 fl oz/50 ml

One salt dispenser

**TIMING** Cast on a waning moon to dispose
of the ailment, and on any day of the week.

### CASTING THE SPELL

1 Cast a circle in accordance with the
guidelines on pages 32–35.

2 Light the black candle, saying:
*Let this sickness shrink with this lamp*
*Let it shrink with the moon*
*Let it be cast away with this stone.*

3 Using the flint or the nail, scratch onto
the stone the shape of an oval; then strike it
through with an X-shaped cross.

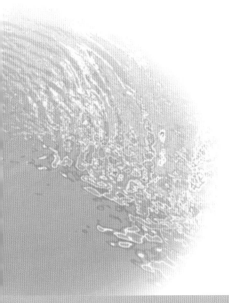

This spell relies on the transference principle of sympathetic magic—the belief that an ailment can be transferred from a person into an object, which is then symbolically acted on or placed where it cannot contaminate anyone. This spell employs a stone as the object and follows the practices of the nature-revering Celts, who often cast sacred or magical objects into deep water.

Here, the curative and concealing properties of water are brought into play to ensure that the transference of the headaches into the stone is sealed, and the headaches themselves are healed.

4 Rub the stone three times on the part of your head that gives you the most pain, saying:

*Place my headache in this stone*
*That I may have no cause to moan*
*Until its flesh be shrunk to bone.*

Pour the water over the stone. Hold up the wine, saying:

*I name you my pain.*

Pour the wine over the stone.

5 Place a circle of salt on the ground around the stone, saying:

*Shrink and wither,*
*Come not hither.*

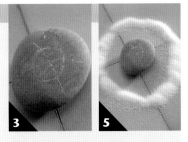

6 Cast the stone into the deepest local natural water source.

# SUN SPIRIT CHARM
## TO GUARD AGAINST SORROW

PURPOSE  To prevent you from falling into melancholy.

BACKGROUND  Here is a charm to help you to remember to look on the sunny side, especially if you are prone to fits of melancholy or pessimism. The power of the sun to raise our spirits is recognized in the sayings we have that refer to a generally happy person as having a "sunny" nature or always walking on the "sunny side of the street." In this spell, the spirit of the sun is called on to empower a charm that will ensure you resist the tendency to dwell on sorrow. If you are suffering from depression, do seek counseling or medical advice.

### HOW TO CAST THE SPELL

**YOU WILL NEED**

Four white candles, 6–8"/15–20 cm in length

One yellow candle, 6–8"/15–20 cm in length

One cinnamon incense stick in a holder

Matches or a lighter

One pen with brown ink

One small disk of oak wood cut from a severed branch

One can of clear varnish

One 24"/60 cm length of thong or cord

**TIMING** Cast this spell on a waxing moon, and on a Sunday, ruled by the sun, patron of health and happiness.

**CASTING THE SPELL**

1 Cast a circle in accordance with the guidelines on pages 32–35.

2 Place the candles in a row, with the yellow candle in the center.

3 Light the incense stick and all the white candles.

It is worth considering the power of the sun in dispelling gloom if you are considering casting this spell. In temperate climates, it is now generally acknowledged that the lack of sunlight during winter can cause severe depression. Even if this does not apply to you, it is worth increasing the amount of time you spend outdoors each day. If lack of sunlight can make us sick, it follows that a reasonable amount of daylight can raise our spirits. To complement this spell, engage in more outdoor activities in order to maximize the effect that the sun's many gifts will bring to you.

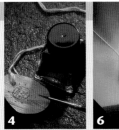

4 Using the pen, draw a circle in the center of the disk, surrounded by points to represent the rays of the sun. In the center of the circle, write:

> SALVE
> SOL.

5 Light the yellow candle, saying:

> *I invoke the powers of the life-giving sun*
> *I invoke the powers of the sun's fires*
> *That sorrow be burned away*
> *And happiness revealed.*

Allow the ink to dry in the light of the candles until all are burned down.

6 After the circle, drill a hole near the edge of the disk. Varnish it to protect the ink markings, then thread through it with the thong and wear it around your neck at all times.

# RASPBERRY LEAF SACHET
## FOR EASE IN CHILDBIRTH

PURPOSE  To provide a tonic for late pregnancy and to work toward ease in delivery.

BACKGROUND  For centuries, those with herbal and midwifery knowledge were village wisewomen whose knowledge was passed from mother to daughter. During the witchcraft persecutions of the sixteenth and seventeenth centuries, this knowledge condemned many women as "witches." Thankfully, their herbal wisdom and knowledge did not entirely die out with the witch-hunts, and many witches today still claim the historical link between witches and midwifery. It would be unthinkable, therefore, if this *Spells Bible* did not include a spell reflecting this tradition.

## HOW TO CAST THE SPELL

### YOU WILL NEED

One pale blue candle, 6–8"/15–20 cm in length

Matches or a lighter

Nine dried raspberry leaves

One 6" x 3"/15 cm x 7.5 cm oblong piece of white cheesecloth

One sewing needle

One 18"/45 cm length of white thread

Scissors

One small container of dried loose raspberry leaves

Cups for drinking tea

**TIMING** Perform this spell at the full moon, symbolic of all things coming to fruition. Any day of the week is suitable.

### CASTING THE SPELL

1 Cast a circle in accordance with the guidelines on pages 32–35.

2 Light the candle, saying:
*Full moon*
*Fruitful womb.*

3 Hold the raspberry leaves between your palms, and chant the following, at least nine times:
*Mother of all*
*Mother of earth*

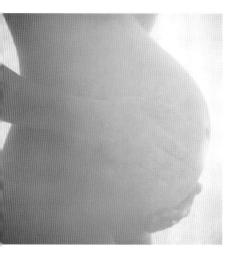

This spell, probably more than any other in this book, is as much based on the health-giving properties of the ingredients as it is on the magical nature of the spell casting. Raspberry leaf is commonly acknowledged to be helpful to women in the later stages of pregnancy. It contains an ingredient that relaxes the uterus, which is thought to aid contractions during labor.

For this spell, you can either purchase the dried leaves from a reputable herbalist or harvest and dry your own thoroughly, to ensure no toxins are present.

*Grant me ease*
*When I give birth.*

4 Place the leaves in the cheesecloth, which should be doubled over and sewn up. As you fasten off the thread, cut it with the scissors, saying:
*So mote it be.*

5 Keep the sachet in the container until your delivery day; then remove it to take with you into the delivery room.

6 Drink between two and four cups a day of a tea made from two teaspoons of raspberry leaf to one cup of boiling water.

**WARNING** Do not take raspberry leaf sachet tea if you have a history of miscarriages, or before the twenty-eighth week of pregnancy. Always consult your doctor for advice before taking any herbal remedy during pregnancy.

**175**

# GOODWIFE'S TISANE SPELL
## FOR GENERAL GOOD HEALTH

PURPOSE  To engender good health and to indicate where health problems are likely to come from.

BACKGROUND  For centuries, wisewomen's brews have bestowed cures and general good health. The brews are assembled from herbal and magical knowledge and are health-giving physically as well as spiritually. But teas—for this is what a *tisane* is— also have a reputation as divinatory tools, through the dregs, or leaves, that are left after they have been drunk. This spell combines the two functions in order to bestow good health and provide an early warning system of where health may be compromised in the future.

There is an entire science to go with tea leaf readings, and there is very little space here to explore all of the traditional meanings of all the shapes you are likely to encounter at the bottom of your cup. However, it is possible to give a few hints that will aid you if this is the first time you have "read" the tea leaves; the rest is up to you and your powers of intuition—and of research, should you need it! On the purely herbal front, you may be interested to know that the ingredients of this tisane provide plenty of vitamins, settle the digestion, and aid sleep—all basic ingredients of general good health.

## HOW TO CAST THE SPELL

### YOU WILL NEED

One pale blue candle, 6–8"/15–20 cm in length

Matches or a lighter

One large freshly chopped dandelion leaf

Three dried camomile flower heads, chopped

Five large freshly chopped mint leaves

One teacup and saucer

Boiling water

**TIMING** Work on a waxing moon, and on a Monday, day of the Moon, to honor the wisdom of the wisewoman or cunning man within!

### CASTING THE SPELL

1 Cast a circle in accordance with the guidelines on pages 32–35.

2 Light the candle, saying:
*By sun, wind, and rain*
*I bless this tisane.*

3 Place the ingredients in the cup and pour on the boiling water, then place the saucer over the cup to keep the heat in. While the tisane is brewing, chant the following:
*By the goodness in this brew*
*Sickness slay and life renew.*

4 Leave it for five minutes, then uncover it, and when it is cool enough, drink it.

5 Tip the residue onto the saucer.

6 The following shapes indicate associated areas to look out for in the future:

| | |
|---|---|
| *HORSESHOE OR CUP:* | *kidney or bladder* |
| *ANIMAL:* | *thighs or hips* |
| *FACIAL FEATURES:* | *the head* |
| *LINES AND ANGLES:* | *joints or arms/ hands/legs/feet* |
| *FIGURE EIGHT:* | *chest or sinuses* |
| *WAVES:* | *stomach or bowels.* |

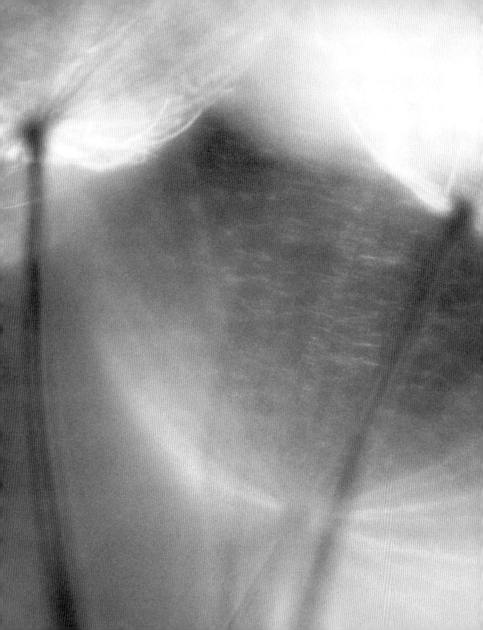

# FAMILY, FRIENDS, AND HOME SPELLS

# INTRODUCTION TO FAMILY, FRIENDS, AND HOME SPELLS

This section contains spells that operate close to home, focusing on family, roommates, neighbors, friends, and your home environment. Domestic harmony is so important in busy modern life; we need the peace and sanctuary of home in order to stay healthy and to go out into the world to work and socialize with ease. When the stability of our home "base" is compromised, these essential aspects of our lives are also under threat. Being happy and settled in our home space, then, is crucial to the balance of our lives and health.

The spells in this section recognize the importance of certain key elements in maintaining a happy household. Clearly, frequent disagreements are not going to add to anyone's sense of security, so keeping the peace while recognizing the justice of some complaints is crucial in keeping a balanced and restful home life. Here you will find spells to keep housemates and relatives sweet, to help mend quarrels on

the home front, and to keep unwelcome relatives at arm's length. In recognition of the importance most of us place on entertaining at home, there is also

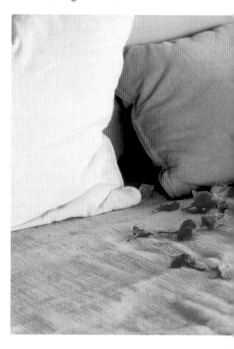

a spell to draw more welcome visitors. You could, if casting a spell to fend off disruptive relatives, follow this by casting one to attract sociable and welcome friends to prove that you are not unsociable, just choosy!

You will find in this section a number of spells that focus on the physical and emotional home environment. These include ways of protecting your living space, dispersing a bad atmosphere

following quarrels or other forms of household tension, and promoting communication within the home. Magical recipes to protect your territory and make your garden fruitful and productive are also found here.

Before considering using magic to enhance your home, you should ensure that the basic means for a nurturing and supportive home life are in place. Practical issues such as the fair division of housework and responsibilities are not resolved by magic but by negotiation, honesty, and fairness; a spell for harmony won't alter the atmosphere if there are genuine grievances to be answered! Similarly, material contributions in the way of money or equivalent input should be taken into consideration; ask yourself whether the wealth coming into the household is being distributed fairly. Consider also whether other forms of contribution, such as housework or home maintenance, are being properly recognized and appreciated. This way it is easier to identify when someone is being unreasonable or quarrelsome without fair cause, and consequently, the situation is easier to deal with, magically or otherwise! Magic works best with a practical basis.

# PLANT SPELL
## TO PROMOTE HARMONY WITHIN THE FAMILY

PURPOSE  To bring a harmonious atmosphere to family situations.

BACKGROUND  Plants are used in a number of spells in this book, and this reflects their popularity as magical ingredients generally. Often, the common name of a plant directs us toward its magical use, and nigella, the flower recommended for this spell, is no exception. *Nigella damascena*, a beautiful blue flower that nestles among delicate fronds, is commonly known as love-in-a-mist.

## HOW TO CAST THE SPELL

### YOU WILL NEED

One charcoal disk in a fireproof dish

One pale green candle, 6–8"/15–20 cm in length

Matches or a lighter

One teaspoon equal parts chopped orris root and white sandalwood

One wineglass containing one packet of loose *Nigella damascena* seeds

One wineglass containing 5 fl oz/150 ml of water

**TIMING** This spell should be cast indoors on a new moon, in early spring, on any day of the week except Saturday, which is dedicated to stern Saturn. The first part of this spell should be undertaken indoors at sunset, and the planting should take place outdoors, preferably in your garden.

### CASTING THE SPELL

1 Cast a circle in accordance with the guidelines on pages 32–35.

2 Light the charcoal disk, then the green candle, saying:

*Spirit of the green earth*
*Make fruitful the wishes I plant in you.*

Its use refers not only to romantic love but also to ties of kinship and affection.

This spell involves a bit of gardening. Planting and harvesting Nigella is particularly rewarding; this annual grows well in poor soil and is extremely reliable. When the flowering is over, attractive seed heads are left, from which seeds may be harvested and dried, then packed up as gifts or kept for next year's crop. Harvesting seeds can be fun for all the family, although it is recommended that rubber gloves be worn in case some people are sensitive to the seeds.

3 Sprinkle incense onto the charcoal disk, with a pinch of Nigella seeds, saying:

*Love in a mist*
*Seeds in sweetness*
*Carried in earth*
*Born of richness.*

4 Hold the bowl of the glass containing the seeds in both hands, and close your eyes to envisage scenes where your family members interact happily and in harmony. Take a deep breath and breathe your out-breath onto the seeds.

**4**

5 Take the seeds outside and plant them evenly in finely tilled soil; then sprinkle the water from the wineglass onto them, saying:

*Blessed be!*

# NEW MOON SPELL
## TO FIND NEW FRIENDS

PURPOSE  To help people moving to a new area and seeking friends or to help those wishing to broaden their social horizons.

BACKGROUND  Wishing on a star, especially a shooting star, is a widely established custom, but the lesser-known tradition of wishing on the moon has an equally long history. There are a number of superstitions relating to the first sight of a waxing moon, including the imperative to turn over any silver coins you have in your pocket when you see the first sliver of the moon's crescent, in order to wish for money luck. Another superstition is a prohibition relating to the first sight of the waxing crescent, that one should never observe it through glass—such as a closed window.

The latter practice appears to relate to the importance of marking time according to the cycles of the moon: looking for it outdoors in order to retain a contact with the rhythms of nature—a very wise superstition indeed! The moon rules over various natural tides and cycles, including the movement of the seas and the habits of much animal life on the planet. In magic, we observe that among other things, the moon presides over matters of dreaming, psychic abilities, and mysteries. Just as the moon reflects the sun's light, magically it is a mirror of the soul and our deepest desires—therefore an appropriate celestial body on which to wish!

**184**

## HOW TO CAST THE SPELL

### YOU WILL NEED

One tablespoon of granulated sugar

Six cherry stones from cherries you have eaten, bleached in the sun

One small bowl

One sewing needle

One white tea-light in a jar

Matches or a lighter

**TIMING** This spell should be cast on or within three days of the new moon, when the moon is visible in the sky, in the open air, preferably on a hill or high place.

### CASTING THE SPELL

1 Place the sugar and the stones in the bowl together.

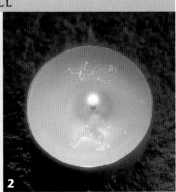

2 Using the needle point, on the right side of the wick inscribe a waxing crescent moon, and to the left, the planetary sign for Venus (the circle with a conjoined cross at the bottom).

3 Light it, and then looking up at the moon, say:

*I fire an arrow from your bow*
*And sweetness add that sweetness flow.*

4 Place your right palm on the stones and the sugar, and say:

*I cast you to the east wind, to the south*
*The west, the north*
*To summon friends and companions*
*    forth.*

5 Bow to the moon, then scatter the sugar and stones to the four directions.

# HOUSE GUARDIAN SPELL
## TO PROTECT YOUR HOME

PURPOSE   To create a guardian to protect your living space.

BACKGROUND   Guarding the home by magical means is a practice that goes back thousands of years in the history of human societies. Prehistoric figurines thought to be house guardians have been found all over the world. Considering the universal importance of shelter and protection, it is not really surprising that the practice of setting up magical safeguards for the home is so ancient and so widespread.

It is likely that the humanoid figures were favored as substitutes for, and replicas of, the householder, or a representation of them in a stronger and more powerful form—as a god or goddess renowned for protective abilities, for example.

Charging a magical figure with your protective intentions is very straightforward and comes from some of the very oldest traditions of magic. It can be imbued not only with our own wishes but also with the influence of any protective deities that we might wish to invoke. All the goddess names used in this spell refer to particularly fierce and protective deities.

Although the practice of making wax figures is one of the popular stereotypes associated with "curses," it is used here as a guardian and protector of your household.

**186**

## HOW TO CAST THE SPELL

**TIMING** Work on the night of the dark moon.

### CASTING THE SPELL

1 Prior to casting your circle, place the household candles in the jar. This should be placed in a pan of boiling water on a burner on the stove until the wax is liquid.

2 Cast a circle in accordance with the guidelines on pages 32–35.

3 Light the black candle, saying:
*May Hecate, Black Annis, and Kali Sekhmet, and Lilith witness and empower my spell.*

4 Make a human-shaped hollow, approximately 4"/10 cm tall, in the modeling clay, and place it on a heatproof plate.

5 Fill this mold with the molten wax. Place in the liquid wax the thorn, nail, bay leaf, and juniper berry, saying:
*Defend this home by tooth and claw Let no evil pass my door.*

6 When the figure is set hard, peel away the modeling clay, and bury your guardian outside to the front or rear of your home, close to a door.

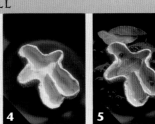

**4**   **5**

### YOU WILL NEED

Three white household candles

One empty glass jar

One pan

Boiling water

One black candle, 6–8"/15–20 cm in length

Matches or a lighter

One heatproof plate

One tennis ball-size piece of soft modeling clay

One bramble thorn

One iron nail

One dried bay leaf

One juniper berry

# KNITBONE POUCH SPELL
## TO MEND QUARRELS

PURPOSE  To calm quarrels in homes where this pouch is hung.

BACKGROUND  Comfrey, or *Symphytum officinale*, is known as knitbone partly because of its medicinal properties. Historically, its leaves have been used in poultices and leaf teas to speed the mending of sprains, breaks, and muscular pain as well as treatment for various skin complaints. Contemporary herbal use is based on its high levels of allantoin, calcium, potassium, and phosphorus, which encourage the renewal of cells in bone and muscle damage, so it certainly lives up to its folk name. In its magical usage it is renowned as an herb that soothes anger and induces peace.

### HOW TO CAST THE SPELL

**YOU WILL NEED**

One charcoal disk in a fireproof dish

Matches or a lighter

One teaspoon equal parts frankincense and cinnamon

One blue candle, 6–8"/15–20 cm in length

Two dried eucalyptus leaves

Two cloves

Root, leaves, and flowers of comfrey

One 3"/7.5 cm square red velvet pouch, sewn on three sides and attached to

a 24"/60 cm cord handle

**TIMING**  Pick the comfrey on the waxing moon, close to full, but cast the spell at any phase thereafter.

**CASTING THE SPELL**

1 Cast a circle in accordance with the guidelines on pages 32–35.

2 Light the charcoal disk, and sprinkle on the incense.

3 Light the blue candle, saying:
   *Let peace be amongst us now and always.*

There are sometimes good reasons why people should air their views or express their disappointment or anger with each other at home, however, a prolonged bout of unpleasantness between relatives or friends should be avoided for the sake of all concerned.

This spell will help calm things down and bring a little peace to your home.

For this spell, you will need leaves, flowers, and the root of a plant, so be certain to thank the earth for its sacrifice by leaving out a small coin and a piece of bread soaked in red wine. It would be wise to replace the comfrey used, too.

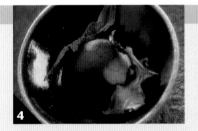

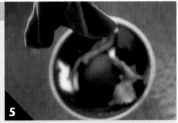

4 Place the eucalyptus leaves and cloves on the charcoal, saying:

*Let healing be amongst us now and always.*

5 Put the root, leaves, and flowers of the comfrey into the pouch, and sew it shut. Hold it over the incense smoke, and chant the following at least eight times,

visualizing a reconciliation after a quarrel.

*May quarrels mend*
*And hurts amend*
*And each heart shall*
*Be whole again.*

6 Hang the pouch by its strap on a wall in the heart of your home.

# ELF-SHOT SPELL
## TO KEEP TROUBLESOME RELATIVES AT BAY

PURPOSE  To keep relatives from interfering in your life and to discourage them from dropping by unannounced.

BACKGROUND  Flint arrowheads have been identified in different locations around the globe, dating back more than twenty-five thousand years. They are still found in large quantities in Britain and Europe, most of them dating from the Neolithic era.

These prehistoric artifacts are still discovered on farmland after plowing, heavy rains, or floods. So common are these finds that country folk have a name for them—*elf-shot*—and a rather unusual idea about their origins.

As the country name indicates, elf-shot was deemed to be the remnants of fairy weaponry. It was thought that elf darts, or *saighead sidhe* as they are known in Scotland, were from arrows fired at humans or animals by the fairy folk when they were displeased or feeling particularly mischievous. They were also deemed to have magical qualities and were used as talismans or amulets. One of their chief virtues was that of protection—a merit used in this spell to protect you against troublesome relatives.

If you are not lucky enough to have access to a genuine Neolithic flint arrowhead, you should obtain a small, thumbnail-size piece of pointed flint, either by going out into a flinty area to pick one up or from a rock and crystal dealer.

## HOW TO CAST THE SPELL

### YOU WILL NEED

One charcoal disk in a fireproof dish

Matches or a lighter

One black candle, 6–8"/15–20 cm
in length

One red candle, 6–8"/15–20 cm in length

One small piece of flint

Fire tongs or tweezers

One teaspoon of dried juniper berries

One 2" x 2"/5 cm x 5 cm black drawstring
pouch

**TIMING** Prepare this charm on a dark or
waning moon, with Tuesday, day of fiercely
protective Mars, as the favorite.

### CASTING THE SPELL

1 Cast a circle in accordance with the
guidelines on pages 32–35.

2 Light the charcoal disk, then the black
candle, saying:
> By the dark of the moon.

Light the red candle, saying:
> By the fierce light of Mars
> This spell is made.

3 Hold the flint between your palms.
Close your eyes and visualize it as an
arrowhead pointing at troublesome
relatives who attempt to enter your home.

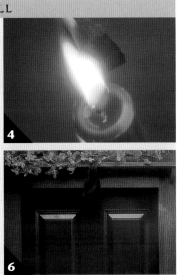

4 Using the tongs, hold it in the flame of
the red candle, saying:
> In fire I forge thee
> My intent will harden thee.
> As I will it, so mote it be!

5 Sprinkle juniper berries onto the
charcoal, and pass the flint through
the smoke.

6 Place it in the pouch, and hang it above
your front door.

# HARMONY INCENSE SPELL
## TO PROMOTE DOMESTIC HARMONY

PURPOSE  To bring a sense of peace and concord to your home.

BACKGROUND  Incense is put to many uses in magic. It can be used to psychically "cleanse" a space, to carry messages into the ether, and to help alter your state of consciousness. Apart from the magical vibrations it raises, its ingredients may key into systems of symbols and other psychic correspondences, such as a relationship to a deity or planetary influence. The incense used in this spell is really a mixture of many of these functions, as its ingredients are known for their powerful cleansing and calming energies as well as for their magical symbolism. Raising and releasing magical

### HOW TO CAST THE SPELL

#### YOU WILL NEED

One charcoal disk in a fireproof dish

One pink candle, 6–8"/15–20 cm in length

Matches or a lighter

One teaspoon of orris root powder

One teaspoon of dried lavender

One teaspoon of saffron

Mortar and pestle

Two teaspoons of finely chopped dried orange peel

One airtight jar

**TIMING**  Work with a waxing moon to draw harmony, and on a Friday, day of peace-loving Venus.

#### CASTING THE SPELL

1 Cast a circle in accordance with the guidelines on pages 32–35.

2 Light the charcoal disc, then the candle, saying:
> Star of love
> Star of peace
> Witness and empower
> The work of this hour.

intentions through incense can be very powerful, so censing your entire home with this blend will have quite an impact.

The key components of this mixture are found in a variety of spells. Lavender is widely used in love, healing, and cleansing rituals and in spells for better communication—a quality that helps to bring harmony to any home. Orris root is frequently used in love magic, and dried orange peel is known to help foster amity and raise spirits. Saffron is included to enhance insight and intuition. The properties of these ingredients will "lift" the heaviest atmosphere.

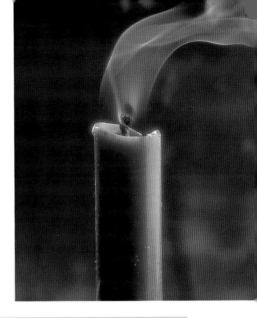

3 Place the orris root, lavender, and saffron in the mortar, and grind them thoroughly, chanting the following as you work:
*May all changes come with love*
*May love come with all change.*

4 Add the orange peel; then sprinkle some onto the charcoal, saying:
*The circle is open*
*The spell unbroken.*

5 Carry the incense clockwise around each and every room of your house, adding incense liberally when required.

6 Return to extinguish the candles, and thereby seal the spell. If sealed tightly in a jar, the incense will keep well for some time, so you might consider doubling or trebling the amounts in order to keep a store for censing the house whenever trouble is brewing!

# POTATO SPELL
## TO BANISH A BAD ATMOSPHERE

PURPOSE   To banish bad atmospheres, whatever their origins.

BACKGROUND   If you are scouring this book for a spell to remove a bad
atmosphere, then you probably already know the sort of situation this spell refers to.
Sometimes you may get a vague feeling of unease in a particular room in your house
or feel that a certain spot in your home has a "bad" or "cold" feeling. This is similar to
the sensation of walking into a room where an argument is taking place or where there
is hostility or tension in the company. Some people are so spooked by this sort of
experience that they become convinced that their home is "haunted."

The ability of humans to decide
whether a space feels good or bad
is a little mysterious. As a species,
we certainly can be observed to
become very attached to certain
places for no other reason than
we feel at home or peaceful when
we visit or live in them. Suffice it
to say that this same ability may
also enable us to detect a less than
pleasant atmosphere—it does not
matter whence it came—and desire
it to be removed. Once you have
banished a bad atmosphere, replace
it with a better one, for example
using the Harmony Incense mixture
found on pages 192–193.

**194**

## HOW TO CAST THE SPELL

**TIMING** Perform the spell on a waning or dark moon, on a Saturday, sacred to Saturn the banisher.

### CASTING THE SPELL

Twenty-four hours before casting the circle, cut the potato in half, and place the halves in the north and south of the affected room. Just before casting this spell, light a match in the east, south, west, and north of the same room, allowing each to burn down before extinguishing it. Bring the potato halves and burned matches to the circle, which should be cast in another room.

1 Cast a circle in accordance with the guidelines on pages 32–35.

2 Light the black candle, saying:
*I call upon Saturn the banisher*
*To lend power to this spell.*

3 Rejoin the potato halves by inserting several burned matches in one side and impaling the other on them.

4 Place the potato in the cheesecloth with the burned matches, and tie the corners together.

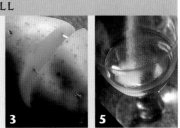

### YOU WILL NEED

One large potato

One box of matches

One black candle, 6–8"/15–20 cm in length

One 12"/30 cm square piece of white cheesecloth

One teaspoon of salt in an eggcup

One wineglass of water

5 Pour the salt into the water, saying:
*Conjoined these bring forth purity.*
Go into the affected room, and sprinkle the water all around it, saying:
*This room is cleansed*
*May only goodness enter.*

6 Bury the cheesecloth parcel away from the house.

# SUGAR SPELL
## TO DRAW WELCOME VISITORS TO YOUR HOME

**PURPOSE** To help those who enjoy entertaining at home.

**BACKGROUND** Many of the spells in this book have a push-me pull-you element in that they are about attracting or repelling people or influences. This is a particularly appealing one that is specifically designed for sociable souls who wish to attract a welcome flow of visitors to their home. It works by using the sometimes very literal symbolism of sympathetic magic in offering a magical sugar trail into your front door. This should entice some interesting visitors.

### HOW TO CAST THE SPELL

**YOU WILL NEED**

One purple candle, 6–8"/15–20 cm in length

Matches or a lighter

Granulated sugar, 4 oz/115 g

One pinch of saffron

One teaspoon of ground dandelion root

Three drops of orange essential oil

One bowl

One wooden spoon

One sheet of newspaper

One airtight jar

**TIMING** Work on a waxing moon to attract visitors, and on a Thursday, day of fun-loving Jupiter.

**CASTING THE SPELL**

1 Cast a circle in accordance with the guidelines on pages 32–35.

2 Light the candle, saying:
> Mighty Jove
> Bringer of cheer
> Bring good company
> Here.

Using magical "powders" in this way is a familiar feature of very traditional magic from all around the world. Some magical powders are specifically blended to send enemies far away, whereas others are created to attract lovers or bring money or fortune. This powder is designed to draw good company toward you so that you can experience the blessings that frequent, good-humored gatherings can bring.

This spell requires a little patience to carry it out. Note that the directions recommend that the powder should be left undisturbed to dry in the sun.

3 Place the sugar, the saffron, the dandelion root, and the oil in the bowl, and mix them together, chanting the following:

*Come bee to honey*
*Come sun to flower*
*Come tide to shore*
*Come joy to share.*

4 As you are stirring, let your mind drift with the chant, and try to visualize a golden line going from your front door out into the world. Imagine lots of friends and welcome family members traveling along that line to your front door, and continue to chant and stir until the mixture is quite even.

5 Sprinkle the mixture flat on the newspaper, and place it in the sun to dry.

6 Store the mixture in the jar, and spoon in a line outside your front door whenever you have need of visitors or company.

# MAGIC JAR SPELL
## TO PROTECT YOU FROM TROUBLESOME NEIGHBORS

PURPOSE   To fend off spite.

BACKGROUND   Given the store that we set by a secure home life, any disruption to it can result in our health and peace of mind being compromised. When neighbors behaving badly or inconsiderately cause such disquiet, it can feel that it is out of our control and that our peace is being invaded. Such situations can seriously damage our quality of life and even our health. The business of negotiation is a tricky one, but sometimes compromises can be reached, and it is worth trying to reach a reasonable agreement with your neighbors before casting this spell.

   The custom of burying containers of magical ingredients goes back centuries, and they have been used for a variety of purposes, including safeguarding those in danger and warding off evil. There are several versions of this spell in circulation at the present time, and the one used here is found in several places around the globe.

   The deity that you call on to empower your spell is Annis, a goddess of the traveling people, known for her protective powers. She guards those who are being oppressed by others, so ensure that your cause is just and that you are not being unreasonable in your dealings with neighbors.

## HOW TO CAST THE SPELL

**TIMING** Cast this on a waning moon, close to its dark phase. Saturday, with its saturnine associations, is favored.

### CASTING THE SPELL

1 Cast a circle in accordance with the guidelines on pages 32–35.

2 Light the candle, saying:
*Saturn of the stern visage*
*Bless this spell and bear its message*
*All who wish us ill are spurned*
*With all evil thrice returned.*

3 Place the thorns inside the jar, saying:
*Throw yourself upon this thorn*
*And only your blood shall be drawn.*

4 Add the chiles, saying:
*Every spite that shall be given*
*For each bite you shall be bitten.*

### YOU WILL NEED

One black candle, 6–8"/15–20 cm in length

Matches or a lighter

Nine thorns from a blackthorn tree

One airtight jar

Three red baby chiles

One teaspoon of chili powder

One square of cheesecloth to cover the jar

5 Place the chili powder inside, saying:
*Fire from the south*
*To fly into the spiteful mouth.*
Fasten the jar.

6 Pass the jar three times counterclockwise over the candle flame, saying at each pass:
*I abjure thee.*
Wrap the jar in the cheesecloth, and bury it close to your front door.

# MERCURY SPELL
## TO ENHANCE COMMUNICATION IN THE HOME

PURPOSE  To help communication flow easily within your home.

BACKGROUND  The ability to communicate effectively is an essential skill in all areas of our lives, but it is never so important as when it applies to our personal relationships. People who live cheek by jowl in the same living space particularly need to be able to communicate their needs and wishes to each other. Otherwise, misunderstandings among families or roommates can be terribly upsetting and disruptive to home life.

### HOW TO CAST THE SPELL

**YOU WILL NEED**

One charcoal disk in a fireproof dish

One yellow candle, 6–8"/15–20 cm in length

Matches or a lighter

Two teaspoons equal parts lavender, pine needles, and lemongrass

One white household candle

One plastic or metal coaster

One small pine twig for inscribing wax

One 2"/5 cm square black drawstring pouch

**TIMING**  Work on a waxing moon, and on a Wednesday, sacred to Mercury the messenger.

**CASTING THE SPELL**

1 Cast a circle in accordance with the guidelines on pages 32–35.

2 Light the charcoal disk, then the yellow candle, saying:

*Hail Mercury*
*Swift messenger*
*Empower and bless this spell*
*Grant me favor in my labors.*

200

Mercury, the planet associated strongly with communications of all sorts, is the key correspondence called on in this spell. The malleable substance mercury is also sometimes called *quicksilver*, as it was thought to be "alive." It is poisonous, so it is represented here by molten wax, into which you will imprint the symbol that stands both for Mercury, the planet, and the mercury the metal. This will form a talisman to ensure ease of communication, so that your household can function effectively and the chance of misunderstandings amongst its members is minimized.

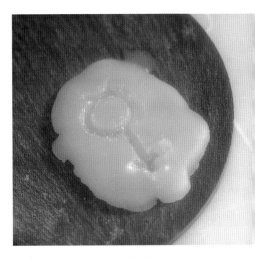

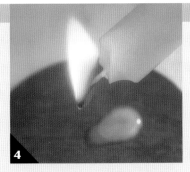

3 Sprinkle the incense onto the charcoal, and cense the circle traveling clockwise. Add more incense, and light the white candle.

4 Allow wax from this candle to drip onto the coaster to form an oval tablet about 1"/2.5 cm in diameter. While the wax is still soft, inscribe the symbol for Mercury (the circle with the conjoined cross at the bottom and "horns" at the top).

5 Allow it to cool; then remove it intact from the coaster. Place it in the pouch and seal. Breathe on the pouch, saying:
*I seal you by my breath*
*I charge you by my desire.*

6 Place the pouch over the doorway to the most frequented room of the house.

# EARTH DRAGON SPELL
## TO ENSURE A FERTILE AND BEAUTIFUL GARDEN

**PURPOSE** To make your garden grow.

**BACKGROUND** Folkways, customs, and traditions of ancient origin are replete with "superstitions" concerning the spiritual management of fields and harvests and the changing of the seasons, indicating that magic has long been used to ensure future growth. One very old custom, after the harvest was brought in, was for a couple to make love in the field, symbolically reproducing the crop in preparation for the next year. You will no doubt be reassured that this spell does not require you to follow suit in full view of the neighbors—but instead works on the principle of representing the transformation of the earth from barren to fruitful in symbol.

The key ingredient to be used here is an empty chrysalis, the universal symbol of transformation. Obtaining one should not be too difficult—particularly if you are ecology-conscious and grow plants attractive to butterflies—but in the event that none are available, contact a local butterfly conservation center to see if they can oblige.

This charm calls on the powers of the great dragon who represents the enormous natural energies of the earth. Acknowledging and respecting Earth Dragon energies enables us to step into the magical realm, where the laws of nature and the life force are all-powerful.

## HOW TO CAST THE SPELL

### YOU WILL NEED

One charcoal disk in a fireproof dish

One green candle, 6–8"/15–20 cm in length

Matches or a lighter

Sandalwood

Three drops of patchouli essential oil

One pen with green ink

1" x ½"/2 cm x 1 cm strip of paper

One empty chrysalis

One teaspoon of mustard seeds

**TIMING** This spell should be worked in early spring, on the day after the new moon, to ensure maximum growth.

### CASTING THE SPELL

1 Cast a circle in accordance with the guidelines on pages 32–35.

2 Light the charcoal, then the candle, saying:

*Within me and around me*
*The power of the earth*
*Come creature, eating fire*
*Come through the air*
*Come by water*
*Make this good earth your home.*

3 Sprinkle the sandalwood and patchouli onto the charcoal.

4 Write in green ink, on one side of the paper strip, the following words:
*Draco*
*Erce*
*Venit.*
Roll it into a tiny scroll, and insert it into the chrysalis. Insert the mustard seeds into the chrysalis.

5 Pass the chrysalis through the incense smoke, chanting the words written on the scroll three times over.

6 Bury the chrysalis and its contents in the center of your garden.

# SEASONAL SPELLS

# INTRODUCTION TO SEASONAL SPELLS

All of the festivals in the sacred wheel of the year carry their own magical power and meaning, and many witches and magicians notice that different times of year are particularly auspicious for certain types of spell. Unsurprisingly, these spells are as linked to the needs of humans in given seasons as they are to the powers that prevail at that time. Thus for example, at Yule, when we are most likely to feel the need for the sun, we are able to draw on the energies of the season of sun return in order to strengthen us in the winter. Similarly, at Eostre, as we tip over into the lighter part of the year, we are likely to need physical and mental balance to carry us forward now that a new season, requiring our more outgoing energies, is upon us. Because Eostre is a time of outer balance, between light and darkness, we can draw on this to inspire inner balance.

On pages 22–31, there are explanations of the eight main festivals of the year, their main foci, and their respective traditions. These are not

exhaustive—indeed, any of the festivals could justify a whole book on their history, customs, and magical meaning—but they do provide a framework for what follows in this section of the

*Spells Bible*. In the following pages, you will find spells bent to purposes most suitable to the time of year with which they are associated, numbering three to a festival. By way of example, under the heading of Imbolc—the time of early seed sowing after thaw—you will find spells for new projects. As Imbolc is sacred to Brigid, a Celtic fire and healing goddess, there is also a spell for healing or to bring general good health. Imbolc is also associated with justice and change, so a spell to obtain justice is included.

This is the case for each of the spells in this section—they all have associations with the time of year or the customs that correspond with festival traditions. Accordingly, they are designed to be performed within a circle cast especially for the appropriate festival. All of the spells for Beltaine should be cast at Beltaine in a circle to celebrate May Day, and all the spells for Litha should be woven in a circle that celebrates the summer solstice, and so on. The spells appear as rituals to be performed as part of a seasonal celebration, which makes them versatile enough to use in group situations and thereby enable some powerful, collective energy raising. "Merry Meet!" (a greeting for a group), as the pagans say.

# YULE—FIRE ASH SPELL
## TO ENSURE PROSPERITY IN THE COMING YEAR

**PURPOSE** To bring prosperity in the next solar cycle.

**BACKGROUND** The tradition of the Yule log dates back to pagan times in northern Europe and is believed to be associated with the nature-based religions that existed for millennia before the coming of Christianity. Our ancestors held that all things contained the life force and that trees, in particular, were the abode of spirit people, gods, and goddesses. Certain trees, therefore, were regarded as especially sacred, and if felled to build a special fire—at Yule for example—the ash was thought to be particularly powerful.

## HOW TO CAST THE SPELL

### YOU WILL NEED

An open fireplace or outdoor bonfire

One section of any branch, complete with bark

One sharp knife

Six dried holly leaves

One green candle

**TIMING** Cast this spell at Yule—see pages 22–31 for details.

### CASTING THE SPELL

1 The night before your Yule celebrations, make a roaring fire in your fireplace or with an outdoor bonfire.

2 With the knife, carve into the side of your "Yule log" the word "PLENTY."

3 Place the log on the fire, and crumble the dried holly leaves over it. When it is reduced to ash, remove it from the fire. As part of your Yule celebrations, and in a properly cast circle, work as follows:

We know that the tradition of the Yule log originally came from Scandinavia, as did the naming of the midwinter season as *Yul* (meaning "wheel"), which took place in the early eleventh century C.E. That the winter solstice was already a well-established part of the ritual year in prehistoric Britain and Ireland is evident from the alignment of many prehistoric monuments; invaders from Denmark simply overlaid this tradition with some of their own.

The Yule log carried an especially potent magic if it was of oak, reflecting the power invested in this tree, but it is clear that other woods were used, too.

4 Carve your first name along the side of the green candle, and light it, saying:
*You are named for me*
*That blessed you be.*

5 Sprinkle half of the ash in a circle around the candle, saying:
*Though storms come*
*None shall remove you.*

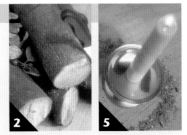

6 Keep a pinch of ash to place in next year's Yule fire, and place the rest on your doorstep to ensure that prosperity finds its way to your home in the coming year.

# YULE – MISTLETOE SPELL
## TO LEND STRENGTH IN THE WINTER

PURPOSE To help you gather strength for the rest of the winter.

BACKGROUND The mistletoe, or *Viscum album*, has a venerable place in herb lore as the plant sacred to the Druids. Perhaps because of its semiparasitic habit, it was associated with fertility, and the Yuletide custom of kissing beneath it is a pale reminder of this. It was associated with potency for another reason—its milky berries, which surround its seed, were thought by our ancestors to resemble semen, and the life-giving properties of this fluid lent its reputation to the plant. In magic, mistletoe represents power and strength in many forms, and the one referred to in this spell comes from its association with the sacred oak—tree of the sun.

Bringing the sun back in the midst of darkness is part of the purpose of Yule celebrations; in the darkest hour we not only celebrate the prospect of the return of the sun's strength, but we positively encourage it! In short, when we celebrate, we are trying to bring the sun back. This is less a human tendency to believe that we control nature than an atavistic fear that the sun will not rise on the most important of days. It is important to acknowledge that we not only celebrate the sun's return; we *encourage* light in darkness by using a kind of latter-day sympathetic magic, otherwise known as fairy lights, tinsel, and shiny baubles. This spell draws on the potency of the sun just as the mistletoe draws on that power from the oak, the sun tree itself.

## HOW TO CAST THE SPELL

### YOU WILL NEED

Six white candles, 6–8"/15–20 cm in length

One bunch of hung and dried mistletoe

Mortar and pestle

Three 3"/7.5 cm square pieces of white paper

One pen with green ink

One fireproof dish

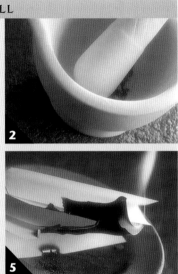

**TIMING** Cast this spell at Yule—see pages 22–31 for details.

### CASTING THE SPELL

As part of your Yule celebrations, and in a properly cast circle, work as follows:

1 Place the candles in a circle, and light every other one, saying:
*Here in the season of sun return*
*May life return and strength return.*

2 Using the mortar and pestle, grind the dried mistletoe to dust.

3 Choose up to three areas in your life where you need strength, and write them as a single word on each square of paper. For example: HEALTH, ENERGY, EMOTIONS, and so on.

4 Sprinkle mistletoe dust on each one of them, then fold them and set them alight using lit candles.

5 Place them in the fireproof dish to burn, and light the remaining candles.

6 Bury the ash under an evergreen.

# YULE – YULE FRUITCAKE SPELL
## TO FIND THE KEY TO THE COMING YEAR

**PURPOSE**   To help you spot major influences for the new solar cycle.

**BACKGROUND**   Yule has traditionally been a time for looking back over the year, as it comes at the time of the *solstice* (literal translation: "sun stands still"). In the darkest season, it affords a pause in which to weigh up events since the last winter solstice. It is also a time for looking forward, and this spell aims to help you do just that.

In Victorian England, the custom of putting silver charms into the Christmas or "figgy" pudding was played out in middle-class households, while poorer households

## HOW TO CAST THE SPELL

### YOU WILL NEED

Self-rising wholewheat flour, 6 oz/175 g

Brown sugar granules, 4 oz/115 g

Butter, 4 oz/115 g

Mixed dried fruit, 2 oz/55 g

One teaspoon of allspice

Wooden spoon

Twelve baking cases

Twelve 2" x ½"/5 cm x 1 cm strips of paper

One pen

Twelve 3" x 2"/7.5 cm x 5 cm strips of aluminum foil

**TIMING**   Cast this spell at Yule—see pages 22–31 for details.

### CASTING THE SPELL

1 Mix the edible ingredients with a spoon, or by hand, until they are smooth, adding the fruit last. Spoon the mixture into the cake cases, and bake them prior to the circle at 400°F/200°C until firm and golden.

As part of your Yule celebrations, and in a properly cast circle, work as follows:

would place a coin in the pudding. This is an echo of an older tradition in which revelers dining on rich cake or bread baked at Yule hoped to draw a plum or other fruit from it—a prediction that the year ahead would be good for the lucky recipient. The older tradition seems a far safer one, given the potential for choking, cutting gums, or breaking teeth on coins or metal charms!

You will be happy to note that this version of the Yule fruitcake divination is safer by far—and also very tasty! It also honors a custom that goes back many centuries.

2 Write the following words, one to a paper strip:

| | |
|---|---|
| *HEALTH* | *TRAVEL* |
| *WEALTH* | *SPIRIT* |
| *HOME* | *FRIENDS* |
| *LOVE* | *BEGINNINGS* |
| *CHILD* | *ELDERS* |
| *WORK* | *TIME* |

3 Roll the strips and secure them separately in foil, then mix them up. Insert the foil "bullets" into the cakes from underneath.

4 Choose a cake and break it open to remove the message. Eat the cake; then read the message.

5 Distribute the remaining cakes to friends, explaining their purpose. Ensure that the friends remove the messages before eating the cakes.

6 The word you select provides the key to life developments in the coming year.

213

# IMBOLC—SEED SPELL
## TO GROW WISHES AND BRING SUCCESS IN NEW PROJECTS

**PURPOSE**  To bless wishes and favor new projects.

**BACKGROUND**  Seasonally, Imbolc is linked to the appearance of the first spring flowers—snowdrops—an early sign in Europe that winter is retreating and spring is approaching. This is the time of early seeding, and in temperate climes, farmers keep their eye to the soil to see if it is warm enough to sow crops. It is a good time for sowing other "seeds" as well—ideas that you wish to come to fruition and plans and projects that you have for the coming year.

 The following spell is based on a first principle of sympathetic magic—symbolizing "like with like." The seeds you plant now represent your wishes for the coming months.

 In the Imbolc circle, you enact on the seeds what you wish for these plans. In short, you plant them in good soil and promise to feed, nourish, and care for them, trusting to nature—just as we entrust our wishes to magic—to help them to grow. As you minister to these seeds, so will magic minister to the wishes they represent. For this reason, you will need to take care of them when Imbolc has passed to ensure that they yield results!

 There are plenty of seeds available at this time of year. Resourceful gardeners may have some stored from last year. The genus of the plant is immaterial. What matters most are the intentions with which you magically charge the seeds and that the seeds themselves are large enough to handle separately.

## HOW TO CAST THE SPELL

### YOU WILL NEED

Three white candles, 6–8"/15–20 cm
in length

Matches or a lighter

Nine seeds of any variety

One pen and some paper

Good seeding soil or potting soil

One small garden trowel

One indoor planter

**TIMING** Cast this spell at Imbolc—see
pages 22–31 for details.

### CASTING THE SPELL

As part of your Imbolc celebrations, and in
a properly cast circle, work as follows:

1 Light the candles, saying:
*Triple Brigid, you are welcome*
*Thrice you are welcome.*

2 Name each seed as a wish or project
you hope will take root and grow in the
next year. Write these wishes down, to be
reviewed next Imbolc.

3 Place the seeds in your right hand, and
cup your left hand over them, saying:
*Now her breath is upon the earth*
*Her warmth will bring new seeds to birth*
*Holy Brigid, bless all that lives*
*Between my right hand and my left.*

4 Plant the seeds in the soil or potting
soil according to the directions for the
seeds you are planting.

# IMBOLC—BRIGID'S WELL SPELL
## TO HEAL OR BRING GENERAL GOOD HEALTH

**PURPOSE** To ease ill health or bring well-being in the coming year.

**BACKGROUND** Imbolc is also known as the Feast of Brigid, a well-beloved Irish goddess renowned as a patron of healing. Many springs and rivers are sacred to her, bearing features of her name, in Brittany, England, Ireland, Scotland, and Wales, but her strongest association with the healing power of waters is with wells.

In pre-Christian times, people venerated the *genii loci*, or "spirits of place," of natural locations that were considered particularly sacred. Springs and wells, sources of water that came up from the earth, were considered very special, and healing properties, including cures for eye and skin problems, became attributed to many of those associated with Brigid. In this spell, you will be recreating Brigid's Well in symbol, in the form of a pottery or stone bowl or cup. Since Brigid's Healing Well is a spiritual symbol, this recreation is just as valid as if you had applied to the spirit of a well in Kildare, in Ireland, or a river in Wales. You may make up to three requests for healing, including one for general good health, as appropriate.

## — HOW TO CAST THE SPELL

### YOU WILL NEED

Six white candles, 6–8"/15–20 cm in length

One stone or pottery cup or bowl

Three small beach pebbles

One small cup of salt

Spring water

Matches or a lighter

**TIMING** Cast this spell at Imbolc—see pages 22–31 for details.

### CASTING THE SPELL

As part of your Imbolc celebrations, and in a properly cast circle, work as follows:

1 Place the candles all around the cup.

2 Name each stone as an ailment you wish healed, as appropriate, sprinkling a pinch of salt over each. Breathe onto them, saying:

*By my breath.*

Cover them with your hands, saying:

*By my flesh.*

Place them in the cup, and cover them with water, saying:

*By the living waters of Brigid*
*May health prevail and good reside.*

3 Light each candle, saying:

*Hail, lady of fire.*

4 Hold your palms toward the flames and close your eyes, then visualize dark stains on the stones dissolving in the water, rising to the surface to be burned away in the candle flames.

5 Chant the following until you feel the energies in the circle rise:

*Earth, water, flame*
*Work in her name*
*Earth, water, fire*
*Work my desire.*

Discharge the energy raised by raising your hands into the air and mentally releasing it.

6 Return the stones to a beach as soon as possible after Imbolc night.

# IMBOLC–CLOUTIE SPELL
## TO OBTAIN JUSTICE

**PURPOSE**  To help those who have a just cause to plead.

**BACKGROUND**  Imbolc's patron goddess, Brigid, is a famous protector of women, children, and animals and has a reputation as a firebrand for justice and equality. It is fitting that this aspect of Brigid is celebrated at this time of year; just as the growing light makes visible the dust and grime hidden by winter, Brigid's bright sun can also shine light on dark deeds. Spring cleaning with a mop and bucket can clean away dust, but answering injustices requires something special. Happily, magic pertaining to matters of justice and fairness is favored at this time.

## HOW TO CAST THE SPELL

### YOU WILL NEED

One charcoal disk in a fireproof dish

Matches or a lighter

One teaspoon of myrrh

One white candle, 6–8"/15–20 cm in length

One purple candle, 6–8"/15–20 cm in length

Thirteen 12" x 3"/30 cm x 7.5 cm strips of white cotton cloth

One dead branch, propped up

**TIMING** Cast this spell at Imbolc—see pages 22–31 for details.

### CASTING THE SPELL

As part of your Imbolc celebrations, and beginning in a properly cast circle and progressing outdoors toward a tree where your spell will remain undisturbed as long as possible, work as follows:

1 Light the charcoal disk, and sprinkle on myrrh.

2 Light the white candle, saying:
  *Brigid is here.*

3 Light the purple candle, saying:
  *And justice will come.*

Tree dressing, the old custom of tying clouties, or "strips of cloth," to trees above sacred wells, was originally done to leave tokens of requests for healing and mercy where the spirit of that place was strongest. Here, the custom is used to send your plea for justice via the sun, wind, and earth into the great web of spirit, where all things are balanced out. Blessed by fiercely protective Brigid, your spell is not about revenge, but about redressing a grievous imbalance. Imbolc is a time for rendering all things anew. Redeeming balance is a part of this process.

4 Speaking your anger, fear, or despair at the injustice you wish redressed into each strip of cloth, seal them by passing them separately through the incense smoke.

5 Hang them loosely on the dead branch, and placing your hand on the topmost twig, say:

*Brigid, pity this branch*
*For it is as dead as my enemy's cause.*

6 Go out to the tree, and as you tie each cloutie loosely to its lower branches, say:

*May the earth hear me in the roots*
*of this tree*
*May the air carry my cry*
*May the sun take up my plea*
*And the moon decry it*
*For with Brigid on my side*
*My cause is carried.*

# EOSTRE–HARE SPELL
## TO AID FERTILITY

PURPOSE  To help when there is no known medical reason why a pregnancy cannot succeed.

BACKGROUND  The long association between hares and fertility is partly due to a fact of nature and partly to the hare's symbolic link to moon goddesses all around the world. The fertility of hares is proverbial—a doe can produce forty-two young in a single year—so it isn't surprising that they came to be associated with the fertility of the earth, and of humans. Hares are seen to race about madly in the fields at mating time, around Eostre—sacred to the Teutonic fertility deity Oestra, or Ostar.

### HOW TO CAST THE SPELL

**YOU WILL NEED**

One green candle, 6–8"/15–20 cm in length

Matches or a lighter

One pencil

One 12"/30 cm square sheet of white tissue paper

Scissors

One 12"/30 cm square sheet of black tissue paper

One free-range egg

One 18" x 1"/45 cm x 2.5 cm length of wide yellow ribbon

**TIMING** Cast this spell at Eostre—see pages 22–31 for details.

**CASTING THE SPELL**

As part of your Eostre celebrations, and in a properly cast circle, work as follows:

1 Light the green candle, saying:
*Let Ostara come now*
*Let her people drum the earth awake*
*Let Ostara come.*

2 Draw a circle roughly 9"/22.5 cm in circumference on the white paper, marking the outline of a hare's head in the center, and cut it out.

The association, across several cultures, and a variety of moon goddesses has a certain logic to it! One likely explanation is that lunar features seen from earth sometimes resemble a hare. As the cycles of the moon were seen to coincide with women's menstruation and reproductive cycles, the two became synonymous. Goddesses of the moon were seen as patrons of fertility, pregnancy, and childbirth. Thus the hare has become a totem of many goddesses, including Andraste in Britain, Maia in Italy, Chang O in China, Freya in Scandinavia, and Harfa in northern Europe.

**3** Place the hare's head on the black paper. Put the egg in the center of the white disk; then bunch the white tissue over it, saying:

*Sent from the moon.*

**4** Bunch the black paper up over this, then say:

*Grown in the womb.*

**5** Fasten it with the yellow ribbon.

**6** Take it outside, and place it in a hole approximately 12"/30 cm deep, saying:

*When hare leaps*
*And moon peeps*
*Let us grow big together!*

# EOSTRE – DOORPOST SPELL
## TO BALANCE YOUR PHYSICAL AND MENTAL HEALTH

PURPOSE  To aid balance in all areas of your life.

BACKGROUND  Alongside the fertility aspects of Eostre, the astronomical event of the spring equinox is also celebrated. At this point, when daylight and darkness are of equal length, we are about to spill over into the light side of the year, when light will prevail. This makes it an especially fortuitous time to ensure positive balance around and within us. Eostre is therefore a good time to look to health and consider whether our current lifestyles are supportive of mental and physical balance.

## HOW TO CAST THE SPELL

### YOU WILL NEED

One charcoal disk in a fireproof dish

Matches or a lighter

Incense blended from equal parts of frankincense and myrrh

One black pillar candle, 12"/30 cm high

One white pillar candle, 12"/30 cm high

Two teaspoons of almond oil in a saucer

One eggcup of salt in a dish

**TIMING** Cast this spell at Eostre—see pages 22–31 for details.

### CASTING THE SPELL

As part of your Eostre celebrations, and in a properly cast circle, work as follows:

1 Light the charcoal, and add incense.

2 Light the black candle, saying:
   *The pillar on my left is night*
   *All things within it are held in potential.*

3 Light the white candle, saying:
   *The pillar on my right is light*
   *All things within it are brought to fruition.*

4 Anoint your feet, knees, breast, mouth, and forehead with oil, saying:
   *I make myself sacred to enter a sacred space.*

The space of equilibrium, of perfect balance between light and darkness, may be represented in Eostre circles by a white and a black candle. These are the posts of a doorway through which we pass into the season of light. To stand between these posts is to enter a magical realm where neither darkness nor light rule, but both hold excess in check. In this spell, you will step into this space to find the source of that same balance within. Prior to the circle, therefore, spend some time thinking about priorities and superfluities within your life and the possibilities for balance within it.

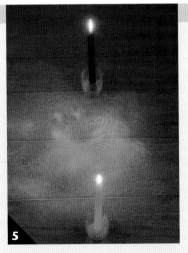

5 Throw salt onto the ground between the candles and step onto it, saying:
*I make myself pure to enter a pure place.*
Recite the following:
*In the doorway of the year*
*Between the gate of night and day*
*I have a word to leave: BALANCE*
*And beg a word to take.*

6 Close your eyes and wait for a word to come to you. This will provide the key to attaining balance throughout the coming year.

# EOSTRE–DAFFODOWN DILLY SPELL
## FOR GROWTH IN ALL AREAS OF YOUR LIFE

PURPOSE  To make wishes concerning all areas of life.

BACKGROUND  This time of year is suitable for planting wishes that will come to fruition in the summer. Using plant ingredients for magic is a well-established custom, and casting a spell using flower bulbs is simple, fun, and most of all, effective. Charging bulbs—which are life in potential—with a wish is a favorite magical method in many working circles. Staggered planting, however, is a method more usually favored by gardeners than magicians, so this spell is a little different in that respect!

## HOW TO CAST THE SPELL

### YOU WILL NEED

One green candle, 6–8"/15–20 cm in length

One yellow candle, 6–8"/15–20 cm in length

Matches or a lighter

Summer-flowering bulbs, one to a wish

Soil or potting soil in a medium-size indoor planter

**TIMING** Cast this spell at Eostre—see pages 22–31 for details.

### CASTING THE SPELL

As part of your Eostre celebrations, and in a properly cast circle, work as follows:

1 Light the green candle, saying:
*By the shoot.*

2 Light the yellow, saying:
*By the flower*
*I invoke Ostara's power.*

3 Take each bulb, and separately name it after the wish you seek to achieve.

The daffodil is a spring flower that generally appears in March in England, and this spell is named for an old English term for it. The bulbs used for this spell, however, are not daffodils, as by the time Eostre comes, these are already in bloom. The idea here is to trade on the fertility of the daffodils by empowering summer-flowering bulbs and planting them close by. The summer bulbs will get the general idea from the flowering daffodown dillies and, charged with your wishes, hurry to grow and flower.

Choose from the many summer-flowering bulbs available. Choose a hardy variety, as it would not do for your "wish" to be eaten by slugs or bugs!

**3**

4 Hold them in your hands, and chant your wish into them with the following words:

*As the nights shrink down
And this bulb goes underground*

*As the days grow long
So the thing I wish grows strong.*

5 Bury the bulbs in the soil or potting soil. Place your hands palms down on the soil, and visualize the growth you have wished for coming to pass.

6 Keep the bulbs inside until the threat of frost is passed; then plant outside next to the spring-flowering bulbs.

# BELTAINE — NUT SPELL
## TO KEEP FIRM PROMISES

PURPOSE   To boost your willpower by helping you keep a promise to yourself.

BACKGROUND   In some pagan mythologies, Beltaine celebrates the marriage of the Green Man and the earth goddess. The time when the May blossom bursts into flower is known, for this reason, as the *Goddess's Bridal*. This marriage requires that the Lord of the Greenwood and the pregnant goddess declare their commitment to each other and to the child of their union. For this reason, Beltaine is a good time for making promises and celebrating and honoring commitments.

It is an ideal time, in fact, to make a pledge and commit to keeping faith with it for the remainder of the year—or longer, if appropriate. Prior to casting your Beltaine circle, think carefully about the implications of any promises you are considering. Ask yourself whether it is necessary or realistic; consider any sacrifices it might entail. Your promise to yourself can relate to a habit, a behavioral trait, or a desire to improve an area of your life. Whatever it is, ensure that it is genuinely required and that you are not trying to fulfill someone else's idea of health, beauty, conformist behavior, and so on.

The pledge is represented by a nut— a common fertility symbol of Maytime. Eating it seals the spell and causes you to absorb literally the promise that will nourish your life.

## HOW TO CAST THE SPELL

### YOU WILL NEED

| |
|---|
| One broomstick |
| Two green candles, 6–8"/15–20 cm in length |
| Matches or a lighter |
| One fresh almond for each promise |
| One nutcracker |
| The juice of a lemon |
| One saucer of sugar |

**TIMING** Cast this spell at Beltaine—see pages 22–31 for details.

### CASTING THE SPELL

As part of your Beltaine celebrations, and in a properly cast circle, work as follows:

1 Place the broomstick across your path.

2 Place the candles at either end of the broomstick, and light them, saying:
*Here's to Marion in the wood*
*Here's to Jack so green and good.*

3 Hold the nut between your palms. Envisage the promise you wish to keep, and speak your pledge to the nut.

4 Crack the nut open, and dip one end in lemon juice, saying:
*Bitter though it prove*
*I plight my troth.*

5 Dip the same end into the sugar, saying:
*Sweetness to who*
*Holds fast and true.*

6 Place the nut between your teeth, and jump over the broomstick. Eat your nut immediately, and repeat the process for each promise you wish to make.

# BELTAINE –RIBBON SPELL
## TO ATTRACT AN EXCITING LOVER

**PURPOSE**  To attract a new lover.

**BACKGROUND**  Beltaine rightly has the historical reputation of being an erotic time of year. Much of the sixteenth-century English church's objection to Beltaine rites was based on the nature of the entertainments and the custom of staying out all night on April 30 to "bring in the May." Given the opportunity this offered youngsters to indulge in lovemaking away from the watchful eyes of their elders and the local priests, it is little wonder that churchmen who preached against the "sin" of sex outside of marriage sought to ban it.

Happily, some rural communities have managed to hold onto the old ways and Maypoles are still seen in England.

### HOW TO CAST THE SPELL

**YOU WILL NEED**

One oil burner with a tea-light

Two teaspoons of water

Six drops of ylang-ylang essential oil

Matches or a lighter

One green pillar candle, 12"/30 cm high

One rubber band, to fasten around candle

Two 18"/45 cm strips of red ribbon

One 18"/45 cm strip of green ribbon

**TIMING**  Cast this spell at Beltaine—see pages 22–31 for details.

**CASTING THE SPELL**

In a properly cast circle, work as follows:

1 Place the oil and water in the burner and light the tea-light.

2 Press the candle in both hands, saying:
  *This Maypole I endow*
  *With my fond vow*
  *He/She that would seek me*
  *Find me now!*

A latter-day entertainment inspired by these historical fun and games is known as the Beltane love chase. This custom, which lets everybody be a little crazy, involves a form of hide-and-seek, with the men tying bells onto ribbons that they attach to their clothing and the women pursuing them into the woods. Once caught, a man surrenders a kiss to his captor, and they come back to the party to drink each other's health. Needless to say, there are variations on this for same-sex couples or groups— and it's all innocent fun! This spell uses ribbons, seen at Beltaine in the love chase and on Maypoles, to lead an as-yet-undiscovered lover toward you.

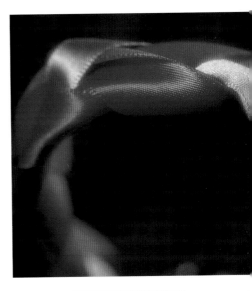

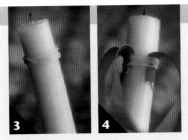

*An he/she be kind*
*I'll not repine.*
Repeat, using the green ribbon, saying:
*An he/she is saucy*
*Send him/her to me.*

5 Tuck in the remaining red ribbon, saying:
*An he/she bring love*
*I'll not remove.*

6 Light the candle, then remove the ribbons and weave them together to wear on your wrist until a lover appears.

3 Place the rubber band around the candle, approximately 1"/2.5 cm from the wick.

4 Tuck the end of a red ribbon into the band, saying:

# BELTAINE – MAY TREE SPELL
## TO COMMUNICATE WITH THE SPIRITS OF THE GREENWOOD

PURPOSE  This spell is for those who wish to commune with nature and explore a new spiritual path.

BACKGROUND  In the cycle of the festivals, there are two that stand face to face across the circling seasons, sharing much in common, although they have many oppositional aspects. Both Beltaine and Samhain are renowned as times when the veils between the worlds are thin. At Samhain, the worlds of the living and the dead come close together, and at Beltaine the border between the world of humans and the world of faerie is narrowed. This makes Beltaine a good time to make a spiritual link with the natural world and the spirits of the greenwood.

Many superstitions relate to this time of year, including the custom of avoiding bringing greenery and may into the house. This reflects a much older fear of the fairy folk, also known as "the sidhe," "the gentry," "the little people," "the shining ones," or "the hill folk" in parts of Europe. Modern-day pagans now consider it lucky to bring greenery and May blossom into the house for May Day, to honor the growth of greenery outdoors and to bring this natural fertility magic into our homes. Some of us even leave out a saucer of milk to show our goodwill toward the nature spirits, although I suspect many of these nature spirits take the form of grateful cats and hedgehogs.

## HOW TO CAST THE SPELL

### YOU WILL NEED

A private spot beneath a tree

One charcoal disk in a fireproof dish

Matches or a lighter

One tea-light

One clean jar

Two tablespoons of dried mugwort

TIMING Cast this spell at Beltaine—see pages 22–31 for details.

### CASTING THE SPELL

As part of your Beltaine celebrations, work outdoors as follows:

1 Find a spot beneath a tree, and light the charcoal.

2 Sitting with your back to the tree, light the tea-light in the jar.

3 Sprinkle mugwort onto the charcoal; inhale, and say aloud:

*Spirits of the greenwood*
*I come in love and trust to*
*Learn what you will teach*
*I wish no mischief*
*And ask for none.*

4 Close your eyes, and meditate on the life force of the tree against which you are leaning. Allow yourself to daydream, occasionally adding mugwort to the incense.

5 When you are ready to leave, take a leaf, twig, stone, or feather from that place, to be kept under your pillow until after the next full moon.

Happy dreaming . . .

# LITHA—FLAME TALISMAN SPELL
## TO DRAW ENERGY AND STRENGTH FROM THE SUN

**PURPOSE** To gain energy that you can carry right through to the winter solstice.

**BACKGROUND** Litha, or the summer solstice, celebrates the sun at the height of its powers. On the longest day, we honor the strength of the sun just before the days begin to shorten again. It is generally well known that the sun has some positive physiological effects on humans: at this time of year we are generally more outgoing, happier, and healthier. This spell enables you to capture some of that sun power to carry

## HOW TO CAST THE SPELL

### YOU WILL NEED

One red candle, 6–8"/15–20 cm in length

One white candle, 6–8"/15–20 cm in length

Matches or a lighter

One sharp iron nail

One plain copper disk with a hole through it

One 24"/60 cm length of fine cord

One tea-light in a jar

**TIMING** Cast this spell at Litha—see pages 22–31 for details.

**CASTING THE SPELL**

As part of your Litha celebrations, work the first part of this spell indoors in a properly cast circle prior to going out overnight to await the Litha sunrise.

1 Light both candles.

2 Using the nail, inscribe on the disk a circle divided by eight lines meeting in the center and overlapping at the edge.

with you throughout the summer and all through the shorter days of the fall and early winter to the winter solstice.

The sun is fire in its most elemental form—encapsulating even a little of its energy on the magical plane can provide great strength to those who invoke it. This talisman uses the powerful symbol of the sun's rays to magically embody that power. It should be prepared just prior to going outdoors into the open overnight in order to greet the sunrise on the longest day. As dawn breaks, place the talisman on a stone or rock so that the first rays of the sun will shine down and charge it with strength.

4 Thread the pendant, and take it with you to greet the sunrise.

5 Place it on a rock next to the tea-light, which should be lit as dawn breaks. As sunlight strikes the pendant, raise your arms and say:

Ignite the sacred
Fire within.

3 Hold the disk in your left hand, then cover it with your right and close your eyes. Focus on the afterimage of the candle flames behind your eyelids. Visualize it moving through your body to your solar plexus and through your hands into the disk.

6 Wear it until the winter solstice.

# LITHA—SPIRAL SPELL
## TO PRODUCE OPPORTUNITIES TO TRAVEL AND MEET NEW PEOPLE

PURPOSE  To create travel options and lead the way to new friendships.

BACKGROUND  At Litha, in the center of the light half of the year, we tend to spend more time out of doors. Many of us make travel plans in the summer, either for relaxing vacations or visits to friends and family. Humans tend to be more gregarious generally in the lighter half of the year, perhaps because the outdoors offers us more flexibility in our travel and social arrangements, or because we simply have more energy when the sun is at the height of its powers. Whatever the reason, it is a good time to get out and about, and an even better time to cast a spell for travel opportunities and new friendships.

The spiral shape used here is an ancient symbol of the mysteries of life, death, and regeneration—a symbol of spirit, or connection. In this spell, we are working so that connection manifests as opportunities for travel and meeting new people. You will need a sandy beach to work on, which may not afford you a great deal of privacy from vacationers at this time of year, but you won't look out of place among fellow beach visitors if you wear a swimsuit and carry a towel!

## HOW TO CAST THE SPELL

### YOU WILL NEED

A sandy beach

One fallen twig at least 18"/45 cm
in length

Five pebbles of equal size

**TIMING** Cast this spell at Litha—see
pages 22–31 for details.

### CASTING THE SPELL

As part of your Litha celebrations, work
this spell on a sandy beach as follows:

1 Using the side of your twig, smooth
a 5 ft./1.5 m square area of sand.

2 Visualize a circle of white light entirely
surrounding you and this area.

3 Standing outside the smoothed area,
beginning in the center, use the twig to
draw a clockwise spiral of at least five
parallel curves, ending at the edge of
the area.

4 Walk around the spiral clockwise,
depositing the five pebbles equidistant
from each other.

5 Imagine a line of light emanating from
each pebble and meeting in the center
to make a five-legged wheel. Watch it
spinning faster and faster until it rises up
from the ground and disappears skyward.

6 Step into the center of the spiral, taking
care not to disturb its shape, and spend
a while meditating on why you wish to
travel and what new friendships would
mean to you.

# LITHA—SEA SPELL
## TO BRING GOOD HEALTH

PURPOSE   To bestow good health—and the power of healing.

BACKGROUND   This is another Litha spell to be performed on a beach next to the sea. One of the joys of the warmer days is that traveling is easier, as is getting out into nature. Many of us are drawn to seaside locations at this time of year where we can enjoy being near the element—water—that produced the cells which millions of years ago developed and evolved into life as we know it. In the magical circle, water is the element of love, balance, natural justice, and healing, and it is with this latter aspect that this spell is concerned.

As Litha celebrates the glory of the midsummer sun—a symbol of health and well-being in its own right—it is possible to combine these aspects of its fiery power with the healing energies of water in a special blessing ceremony. You should be at the waterside at sunrise on the longest day to perform this ritual, which calls on Yemana, goddess of the sea, to bestow good health—and the power of healing. To honor this much-beloved lady of the sea, carry turquoise, pearl, or mother-of-pearl, to remind you of her blessing.

## HOW TO CAST THE SPELL

**TIMING** Cast this spell at Litha—see pages 22–31 for details.

### CASTING THE SPELL

As part of your Litha celebrations, work this spell next to the sea as follows:

1 At dawn, walk to the water's edge and use the twig to draw a triangle measuring 6 ft x 6 ft x 6 ft/1.8 m x 1.8 m x 1.8 m in the sand.

2 Place lighted tea-lights at each corner.

3 Stand in the center holding the goblet, and facing the water, say:

*Yemana, goddess of the waves*
*Know me as your child*
*And grant me the power of healing.*

4 At sunrise, carry the goblet to the sea, and fill it.

5 Return to the center of the triangle, and using the shell, scoop water onto your feet, saying:

*Let me walk in health.*
Scoop the water over your head, saying:
*Let me be healed.*
Then scoop water onto both hands, saying:
*As I heal myself*
*So might I heal others.*

### YOU WILL NEED

A sandy beach by the sea

One fallen twig at least 12"/30 cm in length

Three tea-lights in jars

Matches or a lighter

One wine goblet

One large watertight seashell

6 Pour the remainder of the water into the center of the triangle, and extinguish the candles, saying:

*By the grace of Yemana*
*So mote it be!*

# LUGHNASADH– WINNOWING SPELL
## TO CAST OFF BAD HABITS

PURPOSE  To help banish unwanted habits.

BACKGROUND  Lughnasadh falls in the period of the grain harvest, and one of the activities undertaken when reaping corn is the separation of the wheat grain from the chaff—known as winnowing. This act carries over into the symbolic "harvest" of our lives, and at this time we consider all of the good things that have come to fruition, gather them to us in appreciation, and decide what needs to be cast aside. Lughnasadh is therefore a good time for getting rid of bad habits.

You will need to spend some time considering what your personal harvest has been this year in order to acknowledge and appreciate the material and spiritual features of your life that have sustained and rewarded you. It is possible to consider life events as a part of that harvest—for example, a cherished plan that blossomed into success, the attainment of good health, or a valuable experience. Your pleasure in the things that are gathered in will enable you to identify those things that need to be cast out, particularly those within your control, such as tendencies of behavior. Shedding what is no longer needed is as much a part of the harvest as the celebration of abundance.

## HOW TO CAST THE SPELL

**TIMING** Cast this spell at Lughnasadh—see pages 22–31 for details.

### CASTING THE SPELL

As part of your Lughnasadh celebrations, work the first part of this spell in a properly prepared circle; then repair outdoors to a bonfire as follows:

1 Light the candles, saying:
*Come the harvest*
*Come the fruit*
*Those I need and*
*Those I don't*
*Some I'll keep and*
*Some I won't.*

2 Write down, one to each paper strip, the good things that have come to you and the habits you wish to lose.

3 Light the papers bearing these bad habits, and drop them into the fireproof dish to reduce to ash.

4 Sprinkle the ash onto the papers bearing the good things that have come, and fold each one tightly.

5 Go out to the bonfire, and cast them in one by one, saying:
*Blessings and curses*
*Come from the harvest*
*Return to the earth*
*To nourish next year's.*

### YOU WILL NEED

Three orange candles, 6–8"/15–20 cm in length

Matches or a lighter

One pen with brown ink

Sufficient 3" x 1"/7.5 cm x 2.5 cm strips of paper for each harvest blessing and each bad habit

One fireproof dish

# LUGHNASADH–HARVEST BLESSING SPELL
## TO SHARE GOOD FORTUNE AND RECEIVE A BLESSING

PURPOSE  To distribute magical gifts from the harvest to friends.

BACKGROUND  The custom of harvest home—a community feast at the end of the harvest—has been kept since before medieval times in Europe. Many historical customs are attached to this meal, including the crowning of the last sheaf of corn (called "wheat" in the U.K.) at the feast. In some places, the dinner was partial payment from a farmer to the harvesters, but whatever its intention, the harvest home meal ensured that at least some of the harvest was distributed among the laborers. Lughnasadh, likewise, is a time for celebrating abundance *and* a time for sharing it.

This spell uses the principle of distribution and the custom of the last corn sheaf to magically pass blessings to friends. You will need to work with at least one other person, and the more of you there are, the more effective the spell. Prior to the circle, get everyone to think how they might sum up in one word the greatest blessing they have received this year. Those who have been helped through difficult times by a friend might put "friendship," while those who benefited from a material blessing—say, a car—might write "mobility," and so on. Remember: blessings shared are never halved!

**240**

## HOW TO CAST THE SPELL

### YOU WILL NEED

Six orange candles, 6–8"/15–20 cm in length

Matches or a lighter

Nine stems of ripe corn (wheat) per person

One 9" x 1"/22.5 cm x 2.5 cm length of wide red ribbon per person

One 3" x 1"/7.5 cm x 2.5 cm strip of paper per person

Writing pens

One large basket

**TIMING** Cast this spell at Lughnasadh—see pages 22–31 for details.

### CASTING THE SPELL

As part of your Lughnasadh celebrations, and in a properly prepared circle, work as follows:

1 Light the candles in the center of your circle, saying:

*Harvest time, harvest time, all gathered in
The labor has ceased, and the feast
shall begin.*

2 Distribute nine stems of ripe corn (wheat) to each participant. Each should weave these into braids and loop them, then fasten them with ribbon, chanting as they work:

*We weave you and hail you
As queen of the corn
When all's gathered in and
When you are sown.*

3 Each person should write the word signifying their chosen blessing (for example, FRIENDSHIP, MOBILITY) on paper, keeping it secret. Fold it, and attach it to the hoop.

4 All corn (wheat) hoops should be placed in the basket. All are then invited to close their eyes and pick one.

5 When all the papers are distributed, they may be opened and read.

6 Hang the hoop indoors until Imbolc; then burn and sprinkle the ashes in your garden.

# LUGHNASADH— CORN SPIRIT SPELL
## TO ENSURE BOUNTY IN YOUR LIFE DURING THE FOLLOWING YEAR

PURPOSE  To keep abundance in your home all year.

BACKGROUND  Corn dollies—shapes and figures woven from corn (wheat)—are nowadays sold as good luck charms. Keeping them in the home was originally a way to capture the spirit of the corn and thus ensure an abundant crop the next year. Given the importance of the harvest in cultures where wheat is a staple food, it is not surprising that the custom of the corn dolly, with all its pagan associations, has endured for so long. The corn dollies that we now see in shops are the descendants of a craft that honored the spirit of the fields, and their intricate shapes are testimony to the skill of the weavers and the importance of the task they undertook.

You may be pleased to know that this spell does not require the expertise of a seasoned corn weaver, but it does draw somewhat on the original reasons for making corn dollies. Here, you will weave a spirit cage—which is not as cruel as it sounds, incidentally— to capture your own corn spirit, which will ensure abundance in your home throughout the next year. This will enable you to mark your appreciation of the blessings that have come to you and your household and magically reserve a little of it to "seed" abundance for the coming solar cycle.

**242**

## HOW TO CAST THE SPELL

### YOU WILL NEED

One green candle, 6–8"/15–20 cm in length

Matches or a lighter

Twenty-four stems of ripened corn (wheat)

One embroidery needle

One 4" x 4" x 4"/10 cm x 10 cm x 10 cm triangle of cardboard

One 9" x ½"/22.5 cm x 1 cm length of wide green ribbon

**TIMING** Cast this spell at Lughnasadh—see pages 22–31 for details.

### CASTING THE SPELL

As part of your Lughnasadh celebrations, and in a properly prepared circle, work as follows:

1 Light the candle, saying:
*I call upon the element of earth to bless this circle.*

2 Using the needle, pierce holes in the cardboard, one at each corner. Add seven along each side, between the corner holes.

3 Thread the corn (wheat) through root first, knotting it beneath the triangle and leaving 6"/15 cm of stem below the ear above the surface of the triangle.

4 Tie the stems together with ribbon just below the ears.

5 Hold up your spirit cage, saying:
*Come spirit of the corn*
*Live within this home*
*Stay content twixt turf and roof*
*And have no cause to roam.*

6 Hang it in your kitchen, and burn it at Imbolc to release your corn spirit into the fields for seedtime.

# MABON—
# POMEGRANATE SPELL
## TO GAIN WISDOM

PURPOSE  To advance spiritual development and attain wisdom.

BACKGROUND  At Mabon, the hours of daylight and darkness are balanced before darkness prevails. Around this time, many trees shed leaves, fruits, and seed, and nature prepares for the deep cold of winter. There are numerous world myths to explain this seasonal change, many involving a descent into the underworld, to the land of the dead.

One such myth recorded in ancient Sumer almost four thousand years ago is the tale of Inanna's visit to the underworld. In this, Inanna's descent and eventual return account for a season of barrenness. This bears an uncanny similarity to the Greek legend of Persephone, whose disappearance from the earth causes her mother, the earth goddess Demeter, to mourn, thereby causing the first winter. Read more closely, both tales may be interpreted as adventures where both divine heroines go into the dark to gain wisdom. In fact, Inanna's slow striptease at each of the seven gates to the land of the dead is thought by anthropologists to represent the stripping away of ego in order to assume spiritual power.

In Persephone's tale, her consumption of six seeds while in the land of the dead binds her to remain there for six months out of every year. In this spell, you will eat six pomegranate seeds to help you explore the darkness of the winter and the quiet time within you, in order to gain spiritual wisdom.

## HOW TO CAST THE SPELL

**TIMING** Cast this spell at Mabon—see pages 22–31 for details.

### CASTING THE SPELL

As part of your Mabon celebrations, and in a properly prepared circle, work as follows:

1 Light the charcoal disk, then the candle, saying:

*I call upon Inanna, queen of heaven*
*Earth, and the land of the dead*
*Wise beyond reckoning*
*To bless my spirit quest*
*And guide my footsteps*
*Through the darkness.*

2 Sprinkle the dittany onto the charcoal.

3 Slice open the pomegranate, then extract six stones and eat them.

4 Close your eyes. Imagine yourself sinking into the darkness behind your eyelids, going deep into the dark, where there is nothing but silence. Remain there for as long as possible; then slowly return to the circle.

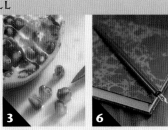

### YOU WILL NEED

One charcoal disk in a fireproof dish

One purple candle, 6–8"/15–20 cm in length

Matches or a lighter

Two tablespoons of dried dittany of Crete

One whole pomegranate

One sharp knife

5 Blow out the candle, and burn it for an hour at each sunset until it is gone.

6 Bury the pomegranate deep in your garden, and keep a dream diary throughout the winter.

# MABON—WILLOW BARGE SPELL
## TO CAST OFF SORROW

**PURPOSE**  To help you to stop dwelling in the past.

**BACKGROUND**  In the wheel of the year, Mabon is in the west, the element of water. As the memories of the summer fade with the light, many of us are prone to sadness. Spiritually, we are in the time of water—a place of emotion and sometimes of sorrow. It is also a place of departures—the sun sets in the west, and for our ancestors, that was where the dead went. At Mabon, we can cast melancholy thoughts aside—and indeed, send them "across the water" to the sunset in fine style.

## HOW TO CAST THE SPELL

### YOU WILL NEED

Five willow switches 12"/30 cm in length

One reel of natural twine

One thin twig 8"/20 cm in length

One 4"/10 cm square piece of white paper

One 3" x 1"/7.5 cm x 2.5 cm strip of paper for each sorrow

One white candle, 6–8"/15–20 cm in length

Matches or a lighter

**TIMING**  Cast this spell at Mabon—see pages 22–31 for details.

### CASTING THE SPELL

As part of your Mabon celebrations, conduct this ritual outdoors as described above, as follows:

1 Construct a "long ship" shape by bending and fastening the switches, using two to form the rim of the hull and the others to shape the rest of it.

2 Secure the 8"/20 cm twig "mast," and thread the square paper "sail" onto it.

3 Write one sorrow per strip of paper, and fasten them to the mast.

For this spell you will need to be outdoors by a tidal river or sea in order to send your sorrows on their way. The idea here is to prepare a "Viking funeral," such as that prepared for Baldur in Nordic legend, and such as was witnessed in Rus by the Arab traveler Ibn Fadar in 920 C.E. The construction of the willow barge is very simple, and the remains will not cause any pollution or leave any dangerous rubbish at the waterside.

You will need to think about the causes of your sadness, as you must be able to identify these in order for the spell to work.

4 Place your boat next to the water. Plant the candle in the sand, and light it, saying:

> Set sail into the west
> Across the water
> Away from my heart
> All sorrows named.

5 Place your right hand on the mast, and mentally send all anguish and regrets you have named into the boat.

6 Drip candle wax onto your willow barge, and set it alight. Watch until the tide carries off the remains.

# MABON–APPLE SEED SPELL
## TO OBTAIN ARCANE KNOWLEDGE

PURPOSE  To improve your magical abilities.

BACKGROUND  Mabon coincides with the apple harvest, and apples and apple trees feature quite strongly in world mythologies, both in relation to gaining knowledge and to entering another realm. In the Judaic myth of Adam and Eve, consumption of a single fruit that grows on the Tree of Knowledge results in the first man and woman passing through the gates of Eden into another world. In the Arthurian legend, Avalon, sometimes called the Isle of Apples, is part of a Celtic otherworld. In this spell, you use apple seeds to travel into the realm of magic and gain arcane knowledge to aid your spiritual development and magical abilities.

There is a message hidden inside the apple; cut in half horizontally, it reveals the shape of a five-pointed star, symbol of humanity and the five sacred elements. The free-standing star, or pentagram, represents spirit; depicted in a circle, as a pentacle, it represents the planet earth. As spirit is the element that joins all things together, and many magical folk honor the earth as sacred, the pentacle is much loved by witches. If you wish to attain the knowledge of the *Wicce*, or "wise ones," create an apple seed talisman using this spell.

## HOW TO CAST THE SPELL

**TIMING** Cast this spell at Mabon—see pages 22–31 for details.

### CASTING THE SPELL

As part of your Mabon celebrations, and in a properly prepared circle, work as follows:

1 Light the candle, saying:
*Old one of the apples*
*Waiting with your sickle*
*Give me the courage*
*To grow in your knowledge.*

2 Halve the apple horizontally, then place all the seeds in the pouch and tie it around your neck.

3 Eat half of the apple, and close your eyes.

4 Imagine you are walking in an orchard of apple trees. In its center stands an ancient tree and below it, an old woman. Approach her and repeat the last two lines of the rhyme you have spoken. Mark carefully all that she does and says, and when she is finished, return from your inner journey to your circle.

5 Bury the remaining half apple outdoors.

6 Wear the apple seed talisman for one lunar cycle, keeping a dream diary, and note any "coincidences" that happen around you—it is now for you to interpret these symbols and their meaning.

### YOU WILL NEED

One black candle, 6–8"/15–20 cm in length

Matches or a lighter

One seeded apple

One sharp knife

One white 2"/5 cm square drawstring pouch

One 24"/60 length of fine cord

# SAMHAIN–CRONE SPELL
## TO PRODUCE PSYCHIC DREAMS

**PURPOSE** To aid all-around psychic development.

**BACKGROUND** Samhain is the season of the crone—the "old woman" aspect of the goddess, the divine midwife who brings us into life and helps us cross over into death. A guardian of sacred thresholds, she also spins, weaves, and cuts our life threads. Because of this, she is sometimes depicted as a spider or represented by a web. Sometimes known as the "hag," or Cailleach, the crone is strongly connected with psychic abilities and the ability to walk between the worlds—the capacity to traverse the borderland between everyday reality and other realities such as faerie or the land of the dead.

## HOW TO CAST THE SPELL

### YOU WILL NEED

Two teaspoons of dried mugwort

One teaspoon of powdered elder leaves

Six drops of cypress essential oil

Mortar and pestle

One charcoal disk in a fireproof dish

One black candle, 6–8"/15–20 cm
in length

Matches or a lighter

**TIMING** Cast this spell at Samhain—see pages 22–31 for details.

### CASTING THE SPELL

As part of your Samhain celebrations, and in a properly prepared circle, work as follows:

1 Blend the mugwort, elder leaves, and cypress oil in the mortar and pestle.

2 Light the charcoal, then the black candle, saying:

*Hecate, goddess of the crossroads,*
*Direct me.*
*Weaver, guide my thread into*
*The spaces between.*

Shamans are said to walk between the worlds when they engage in magical acts, follow their intuition, or enter a lucid dreamtime in order to bring back important information or expand their spiritual understanding.

Being psychic is less about foretelling the future than it is about learning to inhabit this "between space" in order to grow. Hecate, one of the many names of the crone, as the guardian of thresholds and spinner and weaver of the great magical web, is the ideal goddess to appeal to if you wish to improve your psychic abilities. You will need to visualize the crone for this spell.

3 Sprinkle the incense onto the charcoal, and inhale the scent.

4 Close your eyes. Visualize yourself walking from the east to a crossroads at sunset and stopping to face north. From this direction, a dark figure approaches. This is the crone. When she stops, she will beckon you to follow her. She will lead you to a gateway; do not pass through this time, but note what it looks like and any symbols that are written on it. This is the gateway through which you must pass before you can walk between the worlds—and you will need to look out for it, or its symbols, in lucid dreams during this winter.

5 Keep careful note of your dreams between now and Imbolc.

# SAMHAIN—
# GATEWAY SPELL
## TO COMMUNICATE WITH THE DEAD

**PURPOSE**  To speak with our beloved dead.

**BACKGROUND**  Samhain is the time of year when the veil between the realms of the living and the dead are thinnest. This is when we remember and honor our ancestors as well as the recently dead, and in many circles we build a gateway to the

west—the quarter of death—through which the dead might come and visit just for that one night.

Giving ourselves this special time to acknowledge our sorrow at being separated through death from friends or family is a healthy approach. Western society generally discourages too much contact with death, and just as the bodies of our loved ones are tended to away from home by professional funeral directors, so our feelings are filed away so as not to cause embarrassment in public.

At Samhain, we can let ourselves feel sad at departures and acknowledge the importance to us of those who have died. The Samhain circle is a safe space in which to grieve—and remember on our own terms—those we have lost.

## HOW TO CAST THE SPELL

### YOU WILL NEED

Two blue candles, at least 12"/30 cm in length

One white candle, at least 12"/30 cm in length

One charcoal disk in a fireproof dish

Matches or a lighter

Two teaspoons of dried Solomon's seal

Approximately 25 seaside pebbles

**TIMING** Cast this spell at Samhain—see pages 22–31 for details.

### CASTING THE SPELL

As part of your Samhain celebrations, and in a properly prepared circle, work as follows:

1 Place the blue candles at the western quarter of the circle and place the white one to your left.

2 Light the charcoal, then the blue candles, and face the "gateway," saying:

*Ancestors of blood, ancestors of spirit*
*You are honored here*
*I call my beloved dead to this gateway*
*Only those who wish me well may enter*

Sprinkle incense onto the charcoal.

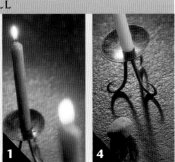

3 Name friends or relatives who have died in the last year:

*I remember [name] who ...*
*I want to say this to you...*

4 For each person, place a pebble near the white candle. Next, remember those who have passed away before this year, and then groups of people you wish to commemorate.

5 When you have finished, and the pebbles are heaped around the white candle, light it, saying:

*All are mourned, remembered, and*
*honored.*

6 Say farewell, and close the gateway before the circle is closed. Return the pebbles to the sea.

# SAMHAIN—THARF CAKE SPELL
## TO PREDICT YOUR FORTUNE IN THE COMING YEAR

**PURPOSE**   To gain insight into your fortune for the next solar cycle.

**BACKGROUND**   There are many recipes for tharf cake, all associated with this time of the year and all including the basic ingredient of oats. Tharf cake eaten at Samhain reputedly has the special quality of foretelling the fortune of those eating it. This may be related to a much older custom in which flat cake with a little darker dough mixed in would forecast the death in the next year of the one unlucky enough to receive a slice with the fateful "shadow" on it. The purpose of this tharf cake is much less morbid; it predicts, instead, where your fortune will lie in the next twelve months.

   The methodology employed here is very similar to that of reading tea leaves, in that it involves interpreting patterns from the dregs or leavings of a drunk or eaten substance. Here, crumbs from a tharf cake are tossed into a small bowl that is overturned and removed, and the formation of crumbs is read according to the guidance below. Tharf cake (*tharf* comes from a word meaning "unleavened" in Old English) has been eaten at this time of year since before Anglo-Saxon and Viking times.

**254**

## HOW TO CAST THE SPELL

### YOU WILL NEED

One black candle, 6–8"/15–20 cm in length

Matches or a lighter

Butter, oats, and wholewheat flour, 4 oz/115 g of each

Sugar, 2 oz/50 g

One teaspoon of allspice

Chopped apple, 2 oz/50 g

One tea plate per person

One small bowl

**TIMING** Cast this spell at Samhain—see pages 22–31 for details. Bake your tharf cakes prior to casting the circle.

### CASTING THE SPELL

1 Mix all the ingredients, adding the apple last; roll them and cut them into round cakes, and bake at 350°F/180°C until firm.

2 As part of your Samhain celebrations, and in a properly prepared circle, work with friends as follows:

3 Light the black candle, saying:
*Hail to the cake*
*Hail to the baker*
*Hail to the coming year.*

4 Distribute one cake each. Eat half and crumble the other half onto another plate.

5 Taking turns, tip the crumbs of each person into the bowl, then pour them back onto their plate and read the crumb patterns as follows:

| | |
|---|---|
| MAINLY TO THE EDGE: | *you will work for your bread* |
| MAINLY TO THE CENTER: | *necessities will come easily* |
| TO THE LEFT: | *fortune leaving* |
| TO THE RIGHT: | *fortune coming* |
| TO THE TOP: | *you will triumph over adversity* |
| TO THE BOTTOM: | *guard your health* |
| SPIRALS, CURVES, OR CIRCLES: | *what is owed will be repaid* |
| STRAIGHT LINES, ANGLES: | *a steady income* |
| HORSESHOES: | *a journey will bring luck* |
| ANIMAL SHAPES: | *guard your home.* |

6 Place the crumbs outside for the birds after the circle.

# GOOD FORTUNE
## SPELLS

# INTRODUCTION TO GOOD FORTUNE SPELLS

Magicians have been associated with luck or fortune since magic was first practiced, and the interest it provokes today is evident from the popularity of astrology columns in newspapers and the advertised services of tarot readers and fortune-tellers. We are all conscious of the chances that make a difference in our lives, even those of us who are wise enough to know the huge part that our social situation plays and who do not necessarily subscribe to the idea of a set "fate." Coincidence, synchronicity, or luck—whatever we choose to call it— can set us down paths that lead to life changes. The continued human fascination with these connections stems partly from the notion that magic can manipulate them and contrives to ensure that they manifest in a way favorable to the petitioner.

To a certain extent—the extent to which magic is based on connections, including the synchronicity and coincidences sewn into the great web of life itself—magic can alter the pattern being woven. The spells in this section reflect the ways in which it is possible to weave change to include favorable chance. Many of them are based on very old tools and techniques of magic from around the world. Here you will find traditional spells to help wishes come true or to win your "heart's desire." The customary concerns are also catered to,

with spells to bring material prosperity and to ensure an ongoing supply of basic needs. There are enchantments to bless new enterprises and to persuade fortune to smile on myriad undertakings. You will find in this section spells to bless a new home or a newborn baby and to bestow health, wealth, and happiness.

There are also a number of spells that deal specifically with the issue of luck—both good and bad. These are designed to attract good luck and carry it with you, to "lend" your luck to another—a quaint but time-honored principle of sympathetic magic—and to rid yourself of a run of ill luck. Predictably, there are charms in this section to deal with being *ill-wished*, a folk belief that finds resonance in cultures the world over.

Whatever your needs in the line of fortune, you will find something in this section to suit you. Many of the spells here are based on folk practices from around the world; most of them are eminently adaptable and can be customized to match more specific needs, provided they are based on a similar premise to the original. It is often noted that we make our own fortunes, and to a degree, and for some, this may be true. But sometimes it is good to give ourselves the magical edge to make this possible.

# PALINDROME SPELL
## TO MAKE A WISH COME TRUE

PURPOSE   To secure a favorite wish.

BACKGROUND   Palindromes—words that read the same backward as forward—have been used in magical work since ancient times. Remnants of this tradition are found in early Christian magic, which in the first to the third centuries C.E. incorporated many earlier pagan references and traditions. The word ABRACADABRA, invoked by stage conjurers when something amazing is about to happen, actually comes from this

## HOW TO CAST THE SPELL

### YOU WILL NEED

One charcoal disk in a fireproof dish

Matches or a lighter

Incense made from equal parts orris root, cinnamon, and nutmeg

One dark blue candle, 6–8"/15–20 cm in length

One feather, sharpened to a nib

One bottle of purple ink

One 4"/10 cm square piece of yellow paper

TIMING   Perform this working on a waxing moon to draw the wish toward you, on any day. Thursday, ruled by fortunate Jupiter, is the most auspicious day, however.

### CASTING THE SPELL

1 Cast a circle in accordance with the guidelines on pages 32–35.

2 Light the charcoal disk, and sprinkle on the incense.

3 Light the candle, saying:
   *Abraxas, great mage*
   *Mage of mages*
   *Grant me, grant me favor.*

tradition and is a mishmash of an earlier palindrome—ABLANATHANALBA. Neither is a true palindrome, but both seem to have been used with good effect for over eighteen hundred years, so this spell will stick to the original!

The principle of the palindrome is not that the word in itself carries any meaning—although remnants found in the late classical period suggest that some may be misspelled deity names—but that the strange quality of the word secures for it a mysterious power. On this basis, palindromes can be used in the form of concrete writing, which shapes words to represent the thing you wish to happen.

In this spell, because we desire something to come to us, we use the palindrome in an increase format—as seen in the early non-true palindrome in the steps below.

*When palindromes are used to diminish something, the shape shown is of diminution:*

> *ABRAXARBA*
> *BRAXARB*
> *RAXAR*
> *AXA*
> *X*

4 Dip the nib of feather into the ink, and write on the page, in perfectly uniform block letters, the following, while thinking all the while of your wish:

> TH
> ATHA
> NATHAN
> ANATHANA
> LANATHANAL
> BLANATHANALB
> ABLANATHANALBA

5 Hold the paper over the incense smoke, and say the lines out loud, beginning with the sound "TH" and working your way down to "ABLANATHANALBA," over and over until the ink is dry.

6 Roll the paper into a scroll, then set it alight by the candle flame and place it on the incense dish to burn, saying:
*So my wish is carried to the ether.*

# LANTERN SPELL
## TO OBTAIN YOUR HEART'S DESIRE

**PURPOSE** To set in motion events that will eventually secure your heart's desire.

**BACKGROUND** The use of natural ingredients in spells is well established, but sometimes nature surprises us by providing formations that we can exploit for magical means. The physalis (*Physalis peruviana*), sometimes known as Cape gooseberry or Chinese lantern, is one example, producing a beautiful natural formation around its fruit that resembles a lantern. These are buoyant in water and able, if required, to carry and transport small items.

This spell uses the empty lantern of the physalis—which requires removal of the fruit. The physalis "cherries" inside are delightfully scented and taste delicious, so consider this a bonus! The lanterns should be kept as intact as possible in order to keep their buoyancy, because they are to be placed in naturally running water, such as a river or stream, once the spell has been cast.

There is a saying in magic: "Be careful what you wish for." This warning comes because magic may work in unexpected ways, with surprising results. Magic cast upon water is particularly powerful, so ensure your heart's desire is both good and needful.

## HOW TO CAST THE SPELL

### YOU WILL NEED

One stick of jasmine incense in a holder

Two pale blue candles, 6–8"/15–20 cm in length

Matches or a lighter

One sewing needle

One teaspoon of almond oil

Seven physalis lanterns

**TIMING** Cast on a waxing moon to draw your heart's desire, on a Monday, ruled by the moon, patron of our deepest desires.

### CASTING THE SPELL

1 Cast a circle in accordance with the guidelines on pages 32–35.

2 Light the incense, then one of the candles, saying:

> To the moon
> All honor
> Pearl of the sky
> Lamp of pale fire
> Hear me and grant
> My heart's desire.

3 With the point of the needle, write on the other candle, from the base to the wick, your heart's desire.

4 Anoint the candle with the oil from the base to the tip and back again twice, then base to tip and halfway down again—avoiding the wick.

5 Light this candle. Open the physalis lanterns, then place a single drop of wax from the candle into each center, once the wax melts around the letter nearest the wick.

6 After the circle, on a waxing moon, launch the lanterns onto natural running water to bear your wishes to the great waters, saying as you launch each:

> So shall it be.

# FORTUNA'S WHEEL
## TO TURN INDIFFERENT
## OR BAD LUCK INTO GOOD

PURPOSE  To reverse a run of bad luck.

BACKGROUND  In medieval Europe the Wheel of Fortune was used to illustrate the fickleness of fate. Sometimes depicted with a king at one side and a beggar at the other, its moral function seems to have been to persuade the poor that their position was divinely ordained. The symbol was actually a corruption of the sacred insignia of a goddess of change, known to the Etruscans as Vortumna, to the Greeks as Tyche, and to the Romans as Fortuna. Her wheel represented the shifting stars, planets, tides, and seasons.

## HOW TO CAST THE SPELL

### YOU WILL NEED

Five dried basil leaves

One pinch of dried mint

One pinch of saltpeter

One charcoal disk in a fireproof dish

One purple candle, 6–8"/15–20 cm in length

Matches or a lighter

Four long household cook's matches

One 6 ft/1.8 m length of thick purple cotton embroidery thread

**TIMING** Cast this spell on a waxing moon to move the wheel of Fortuna forward, and on a Thursday, sacred to Jupiter, planet of fair fortune.

### CASTING THE SPELL

1 Prior to casting the circle, grind the basil, mint, and saltpeter together.

2 Cast a circle in accordance with the guidelines on pages 32–35.

3 Light the charcoal disk, then the candle, saying:

*Lady Fortuna*
*Silver-eyed goddess*

In Wales, the moon, which represents the mysterious powers of nature and magic, was known as Arhianrhod's Wheel—Arhianrhod being a powerful goddess said to weave the fates and fortunes of all. In what is now Germany, pictograms of wheels were carried for luck. The wheel is still used in Hindu and Buddhist iconograph, and is an almost universal symbol of changing fortune.

All of us experience periods in our lives when everything appears to go wrong. If your circumstances seem to be the result of bad luck more than anything else, then this spell is for you.

*Turn your wheel for me*
*And my fortunes bless.*

4 Lay the matches across each other at their center to form an eight-spoked wheel with struts of equal length, and fasten them together with one end of the thread.

5 Weave the thread over and under the struts until all the thread is used, beginning from the fastening at the center, chanting:

*Weaver, weave in what is best*
*By the warp and by the weft.*

6 Leave sufficient thread by which to hang your wheel above the hearth, and seal it by sprinkling the incense mixture onto the charcoal and censing the wheel in its smoke.

# GOLDEN MINT SPELL
## TO BRING MATERIAL PROSPERITY

PURPOSE  To attract prosperity when it is required for material need.

BACKGROUND  Pineapple mint (*Mentha rotundifolia variegata*) is a delightfully scented and delicious member of the mint family. Its variegated leaves, with creamy flecks, lend it a slightly striped effect when it grows en masse in the garden, and its appearance lends variety to the usual greens of mints found in standard herb patches. All varieties of mint are useful in prosperity spells, but pineapple mint, with its golden appearance, is particularly suitable for bringing prosperity from unexpected sources.

As with all prosperity spells, you should be certain to ask for material things for need— this spell will not work if you are lusting after a new model of car or designer clothes. It works on the principle that there is material need involved and will manifest to answer need rather than greed.

Tradition has it that a house with mint growing around it is a house where true riches reside; to pre-industrial peoples this meant, as one old Nordic blessing tells us, food, clothing, shelter, and love. This is perhaps a clue to how this spell works.

## HOW TO CAST THE SPELL

### YOU WILL NEED

One green candle, 6–8"/15–20 cm in length

One tablespoon of almond carrier oil

Six drops of mint essential oil

Matches or a lighter

One 6"/15 cm length of fine golden cord or ribbon

Six pineapple mint leaves

**TIMING** Work on a waxing moon to draw prosperity forth, and on any day of the week except Saturday, when restrictive Saturn rules.

### CASTING THE SPELL

1 Cast a circle in accordance with the guidelines on pages 32–35.

2 Anoint the candle with the blended carrier and mint oils, avoiding the wick. Cover it from the base to the tip and back six times, then from the base to the tip and halfway back down.

3 Light the candle, saying:
*May I prosper as truth prospers*
*May my fortunes wax as the moon waxes*
*May my needs be answered as the sea*
*    answers the shore*
*May food, clothes, shelter come as my*
*    breath comes*
*I implore this by the blood of my body*
*    and the flesh of my bones.*

4 Using the cord or ribbon, fasten the mint leaves together firmly at the stem, and hold them before the candle, saying:
*May my vittles, cloth, and roof tiles be as*
*    plentiful as Mentha in a garden!*

5 Keep your mint leaves in your purse or wallet at all times.

6 Grow mint around your home to maintain the power of this spell.

# SPELL OF THREE
## TO BLESS A NEW VENTURE

PURPOSE  To bring good fortune to a new venture

BACKGROUND  Triplicities, or things that come in "threes," have always had
an important place in magic. In some cultures, the number three is associated with
spirituality. Researchers of the occurrence of the number three in fairy tales have
suggested that there may be a strong psychological reason for this. Saying something
once awakens the conscious mind; saying it twice makes it unmistakable; and saying it
a third time knocks on the subconscious, enabling a thing to be truly known. Repeating
things three times in stories must have been a good memory aid for storytellers and

## HOW TO CAST THE SPELL

### YOU WILL NEED

One yellow candle, 6–8"/15–20 cm
in length

Matches or a lighter

One large feather, naturally shed

One small flat disk, 3"/7.5 cm in diameter,
of soft self-hardening clay

Three sprigs of fresh rosemary

One 6"/15 cm length of thin red ribbon
or wool

One stick of lavender incense in a holder

**TIMING**  To be carried out on a waxing moon
and on a Wednesday, day of enterprising
Mercury, also associated with the number
three.

### CASTING THE SPELL

1 Cast a circle in accordance with the
guidelines on pages 32–35, in the place
where the new venture will be based.

2 Light the candle, saying:
*Earth, water, fire combine*
*Bring blessings to this*
*[project/shop/business] of mine*
*Good fortune in your wheel enshrined.*

bards in mainly oral cultures, so there may be something to this theory. In magic, the number three has a particular meaning for the purpose of blessing.

The triskele, on which this spell is based, is found in many Celtic cultures. The one used here comes from Brittany, now a province in northwestern France. Considered to represent the intersection of earth, fire, and water, the triskele is thought to bestow blessings. Druids in North America have based a logo on this design, which sometimes comes with the words: *Beannaithe ag Draoith*, meaning "Blessed by Druids."

3 Using the hard root of the feather, draw the triskele symbol (pictured, right), onto one side of the clay disk.

4 Bind the rosemary sprigs together at the root end with the ribbon or wool.

5 Cense the whole area by carrying the incense and directing the smoke with the rosemary. Now cense the disk in the same way, and set it down to dry hard by the candle.

6 Just before dawn the next day, place the clay triskele disk above the doorway to the premises.

# LUCKY HAND SPELL
## TO ENSURE GOOD FORTUNE IN ALL YOUR UNDERTAKINGS

PURPOSE   To ensure good luck.

BACKGROUND   This is a general good luck spell for those who simply want to wish themselves luck, perhaps before setting out on a journey or undergoing a life change. It is based on a blend of traditions—remnants of the medieval Hand of Glory charm and an old English witch custom of "measures." Each are compatible with the aims and methods of sympathetic magic, on which most of the spells in this book are based, and both bring their own powers to bear on this magical working.

The rather grisly Hand of Glory was originally a hand severed from a hanged felon, anointed with gall and fat from specified animals. If lit, this charm would enable a robber to enter a house undisturbed. Should a digit sputter out, this signaled that someone in the house was awake, enabling thieves to escape the fate of the hand's original owner. Later representations of the Hand of Glory in wax were reputed to bring luck and, in a complete turnaround of their original purpose, guard against theft!

In this spell, you "take a measure" by drawing an outline of your right hand. Witches' measures are still taken by matching cord lengths against a person's own body rather than via a measuring tape, so you are in good magical company if you use this spell!

## HOW TO CAST THE SPELL

**TIMING** Cast this spell on a dark moon, all ready for the growth of the new moon, and on a Thursday, the day of Fortuna, goddess of fortune.

### CASTING THE SPELL

1 Cast a circle in accordance with the guidelines on pages 32–35.

2 Light the candle, saying:

> *Lady Fortuna,*
> *Bless this spell*
> *And my fortune*
> *As well.*

3 Rest your right hand, palm down, on the paper. With the pen, draw around the outline of your hand.

4 Write across the paper palm the following:

ROOT<br>TO<br>CROWN

Then say:

> *All held in this palm*
> *Keep from harm,*
> *All here enclosed*
> *Let fortune choose.*

5 Cut around the hand outline. Then, say:

> *I send my wish forth*
> *In smoke*

### YOU WILL NEED

One dark blue candle, 6–8"/15–20 cm in length

Matches or a lighter

Scissors

One sheet of paper, for drawing around hand

One ink pen with purple ink

One fireproof dish

Set fire to the digits with the candle flame, and place the burning "hand" in the dish to burn completely.

6 Bury the ash in earth, under the night sky, saying:

> *This wish*
> *In ash*
> *By new moon*
> *Bloom.*

# MOJO LUCK SPELL
## TO ENSURE THAT YOU TAKE LUCK WITH YOU WHEREVER YOU GO

**PURPOSE** To provide a charm to carry with you at all times.

**BACKGROUND** The word *mojo* is thought to have come from a word in an African language meaning "magician" or "shaman." A mojo bag is a pouch containing magical items; it may be either a talisman to attract particular powers or an amulet to ward off unwanted energies. Mojo bags and their items are placed together for specific reasons—for example, to turn away the wrath of an enemy or to win the attention of one who will help. Although the mojo bag originates from Afro-American magical

## HOW TO CAST THE SPELL

### YOU WILL NEED

One charcoal disk in a fireproof dish

Matches or a lighter

Dried juniper berries

One teaspoon of honey

One cream pillar candle, approximately 12"/30 cm high

One spool of red cotton thread

One 3" x 3"/7.5 cm x 7.5 cm red velvet drawstring pouch

One small white pebble

One bunch of dried white sage

**TIMING** Weave this charm on the sixth night after a new moon, when the moon is visible in the night sky.

### CASTING THE SPELL

1 Cast a circle in accordance with the guidelines on pages 32–35.

2 Light the charcoal disk, and sprinkle on the juniper berries.

3 Smear honey onto the top 2"/5 cm of the candle, avoiding the wick. Light the candle saying:

customs practiced in the United States, variations of it exist all over the world. Whether called a mojo, a *gris-gris,* or a charm bag, pouches containing lucky ingredients amount to pretty much the same thing—humans intuitively capturing their luck and carrying it with them.

In this spell, the ingredients are traditional magnets for good luck, based on herbal and craft knowledge, and they should be kept well sealed in your mojo bag, which should be carried with you at all times. The mojo bag makes a good gift for a friend who needs a little luck.

*Hear me*
*I stand between the light and the dark*
*Between a high place and a low place*
*And none that inhabit these places*
*May gainsay or cross the luck I seal within.*

4 Measure the circumference of your right wrist with the thread. Knot it into a "bracelet" and place it in the pouch.

5 Cense the stone in juniper smoke, and place it in the pouch. Put three sage leaves in the pouch. Light the remaining sage with the candle, and allow it to smolder.

6 Using sage smoke, cense the mojo bag, saying:
*All within is pure and safe*
*That within is that without*
*That without is that within*
*Let the charm begin.*
Seal the bag immediately.

# MOUNTAIN ASH "GOD" SPELL
## TO LEND LUCK TO ANOTHER

**PURPOSE**   To be used when you appear to have an excess of good fortune and a friend has none.

**BACKGROUND**   If you consider yourself lucky or blessed, and a friend could use some good luck, this is the spell for you. Obviously, practical advice and material help should come first, but if it genuinely seems that your friend is star-crossed rather than feckless, it is time for magical action. It should be emphasized that casting this spell doesn't mean that your own luck is forfeited. On the contrary, luck, like love, is multiplied when it is shared, and for this reason the recipient should pass on the charm to someone who would benefit from it when their luck turns for the better.

You may have heard people say, when they hear of someone who has been lucky or fortunate, "Maybe their good luck will rub off on me!" In fact, this sort of reaction is the remnant of an old folk belief regarding the ability to pass on luck. The wood of mountain ash (rowan) used in this spell is traditionally referred to as a "god"—itself an indication of much older European beliefs that venerated the spirits and deities of nature within particular trees.

## HOW TO CAST THE SPELL

### YOU WILL NEED

One green candle, 6–8"/15–20 cm in length

Matches or a lighter

One sharp black-handled kitchen knife

One slim 2"/5 cm length of mountain ash, (rowan) with a fine hole drilled through its side approximately ½"/1 cm from the top to enable a cord to pass through

One 24"/60 cm length of fine cord

**TIMING** Work on a waxing moon, and on a Thursday, sacred to Jupiter the generous.

### CASTING THE SPELL

1 Cast a circle in accordance with the guidelines on pages 32–35.

2 Light the candle, saying:
*God of the earth,*
*Whose roots drink of water and rock*
*Whose arms touch the clouds*
*Bestow your gifts upon [friend's name]*
*As you have bestowed them upon me*
*By water, rock, sky, and tree.*

3 With the knife, carve into a side of the bark that is at right angles to the drilled hole an X-shaped cross.

4 Spit onto the carved rune, saying:
*I gift you by my essence.*
Breathe onto it, saying:
*I gift you by my breath*
*I gift you by this god*
*Good fortune.*

5 Pass the mountain ash (rowan) god through the flame, to dry the spittle and seal the spell.

6 Pass the cord through the hole, and wear it as a necklace until you can pass it directly over your friend's head, with a kiss.

# EGG SPELL
## TO RID YOURSELF OF ILL LUCK

PURPOSE  To enable you to cast away bad luck.

BACKGROUND  The symbol of the egg has represented, for millennia and across many civilizations, the mysterious essence of life and regeneration. Here, it is used as a symbol of containment and as a way of casting away from you a run of bad luck.

This spell refers to situations that are not of your own making but were arrived at seemingly through a series of chances that have led to a detrimental state of affairs. We sometimes talk of having "a run of bad luck" when we have been relying on luck a little too much. It is important, before casting this spell, that you examine recent events carefully to ensure that it is not a dereliction of responsibility which is responsible for this bad "luck." Otherwise, the spell will be worse than useless, and your bad run will continue.

In the case of circumstances that are genuinely beyond your control and seem to have piled up of late, some magical intervention is entirely legitimate, and the centuries-old tradition behind the Egg Spell is particularly apt to the purpose. It is considered particularly lucky to pass this spell to a friend in need once you have benefited from it.

## HOW TO CAST THE SPELL

**TIMING** Cast this spell on a waning moon, preferably on a Saturday, sacred to Saturn the diminisher.

### CASTING THE SPELL

1 Cast a circle in accordance with the guidelines on pages 32–35.

2 Light the black candle, saying:
*Your powers that banish*
*Make ill luck vanish.*

3 Bathe the egg in the water, saying:
*Your house is clean*
*When mine is mired*
*Work ye unto*
*My desire.*

4 Using the needle, make a hole in the narrower end of the egg. Blow into the egg and say:
*Ill luck forthwith*
*From my house*
*Into thine*
*From hall of bone*
*To path of stone,*
*Get thee hence*
*From my home*
Sprinkle saffron over the hole to seal it.

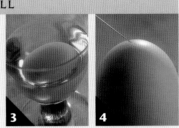

### YOU WILL NEED

One black candle, 6–8"/15–20 cm in length

Matches or a lighter

One free-range chicken egg

Half a wineglass of fresh spring water

One sharp sewing needle

One pinch of saffron

One small-denomination bronze or gold-colored coin

One fresh sprig of yew

5 Take the egg to the garden and dig a hole at least 12"/30 cm deep, then cast in the coin and the sprig of yew. Throw the egg down to smash on them, and cover it quickly with earth.

6 Your luck should change for the better within one moon cycle.

# CLOCK SPELL
## TO REVERSE THE FORTUNES OF AN ILL-DOER

**PURPOSE** To frustrate an evildoer in their plans.

**BACKGROUND** There are many spells in existence that are known as binding or banishing spells (see pages 362–383), and these are often mistaken for "curses." In the sense that they are designed to thwart the nasty ambitions of those who do harm to others, they are; but in the Hollywood B-movie sensationalist media sense, they are not. Bindings and banishings are not performed from spite or for revenge, but to stop harm

### ≡ HOW TO CAST THE SPELL

**YOU WILL NEED**

One functioning analog (not digital) clock

One mantelpiece

One black candle, 6–8"/15–20 cm in length

One white candle, 6–8"/15–20 cm in length

Matches or a lighter

One black ink pen

One 4" x 4"/10 cm x 10 cm square piece of black paper

One 81"/202.5 cm length of thick black cotton thread

**TIMING** Use this spell on a waning moon, on a Saturday, and ensure that it culminates exactly on the stroke of midnight.

**CASTING THE SPELL**

1 Cast a circle in accordance with the guidelines on pages 32-35.

2 Place the clock in the center of the mantelpiece, the black candle to the left and the white candle to the right.

3 Light the black candle, saying:
   *May ill deeds be wiped out.*
Light the white one, saying:
   *And good take their stead.*

being done. Those doing harm need to learn lessons from their bad behavior, and an adroitly timed spell can do much to bring the consequences of that behavior to their attention.

This spell is a reversal type spell, based on an Anglo-Saxon binding spell. Although it uses the technique of winding the clock backward, its aim is not to turn back time, but to frustrate the designs of an ill-doer. This spell is dedicated to my nephew Joshua Wright, who gave me the idea. The wisdom of children is sometimes beyond measure.

4 Write a large "O" in the center of the paper. Fold it twice, and wrap it with the thread, saying:

> The spell I intone
> Shall see thee undone
> By circle and line
> By flesh and by bone
> By sea and by sky
> By sun and by moon.

5 Turn back the arms of the clock one hour, saying:

> For each ill thought
> I set thee back.

Turn them back another hour, saying:

> For each ill word, I set thee back.

Turn them back another hour, saying:

> For each ill deed, I set thee back.

Turn the clock face to the wall.

6 Bury the bound paper deep in your garden, saying:

> There you stay until you pay
> May wisdom grow
> Till good you show.

**279**

# OAK TREE SPELL
## TO ENSURE CONTINUED MATERIAL PROSPERITY

PURPOSE   To ensure the continuance of material fortune.

BACKGROUND   In Druidic tradition, the oak, closely associated with the element of earth, is also connected with the cycle of the sun. From a magical point of view, these correspondences also coincide with matters of security, fertility, wealth, and health. This makes the oak the ideal tree to call up when you wish to ensure the continued flow of material fortune to your home.

This spell works its magic by means of a magical staff that should be placed at the main doorway to your home. One of the symbols you will carve on it resembles the reverse of the rune known as ken. This rune represents the power of the oak and is set alongside others that magically spell out a charm of security and plenty. This staff should not be fooled around with or handled by anybody outside of your household, or its power will be sapped. Keep it, therefore, out of reach, perhaps on hooks above the doorway. This will ensure that your good work does not go to waste if curiosity gets the better of a visitor to your home!

## HOW TO CAST THE SPELL

**TIMING** Work on a waxing moon, and on a Sunday, ruled by the sun, whose power is embodied by the mighty oak.

### CASTING THE SPELL

1 Cast a circle in accordance with the guidelines on pages 32–35. Light the candle, saying:

> *Power of the oak,*
> *Mighty Duir I invoke.*

2 Using the white-handled knife, carve on one side of the staff, about 1 ft/30 cm from the bottom, the symbol *V*, saying:

> *That which is given*
> *None shall shrink.*

3 Carve the symbol of a downward pointing equilateral triangle 6"/15 cm above it, saying:

> *Fortune flowing*
> *None shall sink.*

4 Carve a diamond shape 6"/15 cm above the triangle, saying:

> *Safety in which*
> *To eat and drink.*

5 Finally, 6"/15 above the diamond, carve a stave resembling the reverse of the rune ken, saying:

> *Duir forfend*
> *That any send*

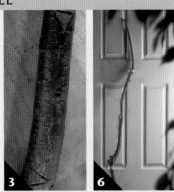

### YOU WILL NEED

One green candle, 6–8"/15–20 cm in length

Matches or a lighter

One sharp white-handled knife

One staff of oak, 36"/90 cm in length

One 9 ft/2.7 m length of natural twine

> *A blow or blight*
> *To any wight*
> *That dwells in sooth*
> *Twixt earth and roof.*

6 To seal the magic into the staff, bind it about with twine 2"/5 cm from the top, above the ken rune. Do the same 6"/15 cm from the bottom, below the *V* stave. Hang the stave from your doorway.

# TRIANGLE SPELL
## TO OBTAIN AN ITEM THAT YOU NEED

PURPOSE  To obtain something you genuinely need. This spell will not work if you use it frivolously.

BACKGROUND  If you are considering using magic for your own gain, you should always think about what is needful before reaching for your spell book. This is not because of some benighted idea that we should never ask for anything for ourselves, but because in magic, as in any other area of your life, you need to exercise common sense. Expending your energy on spells for things you do not really need means that you are focusing in an imbalanced way on possessions, or people, or invitations that are

## HOW TO CAST THE SPELL

### YOU WILL NEED

One charcoal disk in a fireproof dish

Matches or a lighter

Dried holly berries

One purple candle, 6–8"/15–20 cm in length

Three x 5"/12.5 cm holly twigs

One 18"/45 cm length of red cotton thread

One 18"/45 cm length of red woolen thread

**TIMING** Cast on a waxing moon, between the seventh and fourteenth day after the new moon, on any day of the week.

### CASTING THE SPELL

1 Cast a circle in accordance with the guidelines on pages 32–35.

2 Light the charcoal disk, and sprinkle on the berries; then light the candle, saying:
   *Spirit of the holly tree,*
   *Come forth as I call to thee.*
   *Witness all, and let it be.*

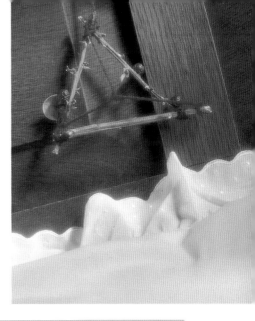

not, in an essential way, going to do you any good. Besides paying too much attention to these things, the magic itself will not work, except in the sense that bringing an obsession into a magical circle will simply magnify truths about the place it occupies in your life until you deal with it. If you are certain that a thing is both needful and good and that you lack the practical means to obtain it in the usual way, take a chance on this spell. It does yield some unusual results, so be ready for anything! Holly is associated with gifts so your item may come from an unexpected source.

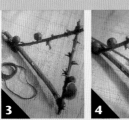

3 Tie the three holly twigs together with cotton thread to form an equilateral triangle with 3"/7.5 cm sides, with the twigs overlapping.

4 Fasten the end of the woolen thread to a corner, then draw it loosely over to another corner and fasten it off. Tie a new length to the third corner, and tie this to the middle of the loose thread to form an equal-armed Y shape in the center.

5 Hold the triangle over the incense, visualizing what you wish for, chanting:

*Gift of gifts*
*Need of need*
*Leave my dreams*
*And come to me*
*As I will it*
*So mote it be!*

6 Hang the triangle from your bedroom ceiling until the wish is fulfilled; then burn it.

# LODESTONE SPELL
## TO INCREASE MONEY FORTUNE

PURPOSE  To attract money wealth.

BACKGROUND  The lodestone, or the mineral magnetite, was used
historically to cure male sexual dysfunction, to prevent a lover from straying,
and to attract money or fortune. It is still used today all over the world for
a number of different types of spells, including the very traditional uses already
mentioned. Widely available now from crystal and gemstone dealers,
lodestones are sometimes painted a color associated with the use to which
one wishes to put them. In the United States, for example, it is painted green
to attract money—dollar bills being green—in a latter-day variation
on sympathetic magic which represents like with like.

In this spell, the lodestone acts as a talisman to attract material
fortune in a specifically monetary sense. Generally, spells should
focus on final outcomes rather than means to achieve
things, and money would normally come under this
heading. However, given how often such spells are
requested, and in the light of the comprehensive
nature of this *Spells Bible*, it would be churlish to
leave out such a traditional charm. Suffice it to say
that the magical "health" warning of "need, not
greed" applies fully here, as elsewhere.

## HOW TO CAST THE SPELL

### YOU WILL NEED

One green candle, 6–8"/15–20 cm in length

Matches or a lighter

One small lodestone

One saucer of spring water

One teaspoon of iron filings

One teaspoon of almond oil

One 2" x 2"/5 cm x 5 cm brown draw pouch

One 24"/60 cm length of fine cord

**TIMING** Cast on a waxing moon to attract money, and as lodestones are sacred to Venus, work on her day, Friday.

### CASTING THE SPELL

1 Cast a circle in accordance with the guidelines on pages 32–35.

2 Light the candle, saying:
> Venus, look well
> Upon my spell.

3 Hold the lodestone before the candle flame, saying:
> Venus, behold one of your children.

Place the lodestone in the water, saying:
> Drink well and be strong.

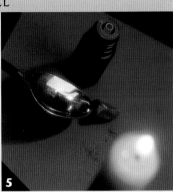

4 Blow onto the stone to dry it; then spoon on the iron filings, saying:
> Eat well and be stronger.

5 After about a minute, brush off the filings, and anoint the stone with the almond oil, chanting at least nine times the following rune:
> Here is want
> Of bright trove
> Bring it forth
> With your love.

6 Slip the lodestone into the pouch. Fasten it tightly and use the cord to tie into a necklace. Wear the lodestone charm until the needed money appears; then hang it on your bedpost until need arises again, when the spell should be repeated.

# LUCKY SHOE-DUST SPELL
## TO LEAD YOU INTO GOOD LUCK

PURPOSE  To enable luck to walk with you and guide your steps.

BACKGROUND  There are many charms that stipulate that they should be placed in someone's shoe, and considering many of the traditions of magic, this is not really surprising. There are many metaphors in Western culture that provide vital clues as to how important feet are considered to be. For example, if we wish to speak of someone putting things into perspective before judging us, we say, "Walk a mile in my shoes, and then judge." When someone takes on the role of another, we speak of them as "stepping

into someone else's shoes." We also speak of life directions as "pathways" and of "putting our best foot forward" when we set out on them.

Even though such metaphors appear to be aimed at non-disabled people, those of us who are wheelchair users might wish to note that the importance of the feet from a magical point of view does not begin and end with walking.

Our footprint, whether in sand, or in mud, or in ink, is connected with our "measure"—in witchcraft and magic, something that captures our essence. Accordingly, placing a charm in our shoes is a very powerful magical act.

## HOW TO CAST THE SPELL

### YOU WILL NEED

Three drops of peppermint essential oil

Thirty drops of carrier oil

One green candle, 6-8"/15–20 cm in length

Matches or a lighter

One yellow candle, 6-8"/15–20 cm in length

One pen with green ink

One sheet of office paper

One fireproof dish

Six dried mint leaves

Six dried basil leaves

**TIMING** Work on a waxing moon to lead you toward luck, and on a Wednesday, day of wayfaring Mercury.

### CASTING THE SPELL

1 Cast a circle in accordance with the guidelines on pages 32-35.

2 Blend the oils, then rub them onto the soles of your feet, saying:
   *Thus I am guided.*
Rub the green candle on your soles, avoiding the wick, and light it.

3 Light the yellow candle, saying:
   *Traveling in my way*
   *Fortune lead me not astray.*

4 Using the green ink, write in the center of the sheet of paper the following words:
   *Salve Fortuna Salve.*

5 Light the paper, using the flame from the green candle, and place it in the fireproof dish to burn completely to ashes. Add the crumbled mint and basil leaves to the cool ash.

6 Mix well by hand, and sprinkle the mixture in both shoes before you next leave your house. Allow it to dissipate naturally.

# UNCROSSING SPELL
## TO REVERSE BAD LUCK
## WISHED ON YOU BY ANOTHER

PURPOSE   To undo any bad vibes sent your way by the envy or spite of another.

BACKGROUND   It is common to hear people say that they are having a run of bad luck, but occasionally they become convinced that their ill fortune is the result of a curse or being wished ill by another. Curses are usually threats made by individuals on ego trips, who imagine that they have magical powers. Happily, the only power these deluded souls have is the power to inflate their own egos. However, envy, spite, and ill feeling carry their own energy, and sometimes you need to feel protected against them.

## HOW TO CAST THE SPELL

### YOU WILL NEED

One black candle, 6–8"/15–20 cm in length

Matches or a lighter

One small hand mirror

Salt in a pourer

Black cloth

**TIMING** Cast on the night of the dark moon, which is ideal for breaking spells and building a psychic shield of protection.

### CASTING THE SPELL

1 Cast a circle in accordance with the guidelines on pages 32–35.

2 Light the black candle, saying:
*What was full is now empty*
*What was empty is now full*
*In this time that is not a time*
*In this place that is not a place*
*In the world of spirit I stand.*

3 On the upward-facing mirror, pour salt in the shape of an X, saying:
*Thus I cancel out what is bad.*

If you feel you are being "crossed" by someone who wishes you harm, this spell will undo any effects that this ill will might exert, including the anxiety caused by knowing that someone thinks badly of you. It is based on a folk belief, found in many parts of the world, that mixing up your clothing—sometimes turning garments inside out or wearing them back to front—will confuse mischievous powers. After this spell is cast, you should go out of your house at least once a week for a full month with one of your garments either inside out or the wrong way round.

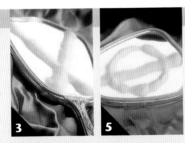

Blow the salt away, saying:
*Thus I share out what is good.*

4 Take off all your garments. Turn them inside out, and put them on back to front.

5 Pour on the salt in the shape of a circle, with a vertical line through its center, saying:
*This moon is empty*
*This moon is full*
*Who guesses which*
*Shall be a fool.*

6 Blow away the salt, and wrap the mirror in the black cloth to store in a dark place for a month.

# FLAGSTONE SPELL
## TO SEND BACK ILL WISHES
## TO THEIR ORIGINATOR

**PURPOSE** To send back ill wishes when you know for sure that a particular person is wishing harm to you or yours.

**BACKGROUND** In northern European folklore, the flagstone epitomizes all that home and shelter mean to us. These days, most of us have concrete or wooden floors rather than stones inside our homes, so for this spell you will need to find a small paving stone for temporary use. As these are readily available from most home improvement stores or garden centers, this should be neither difficult nor expensive.

Marking patterns on stones is a very old craft, which in parts of the world was once considered an essential part of housekeeping. Cultural historians discovered that the custom of marking front doorsteps with elaborate patterns continued into the twentieth century in Wales. Although pride in the home seemed to be the main motive for these elaborate markings, the curious patterns seem to hark back to the practice of using powerful symbols to protect the household and to claim and identify territory and boundaries. In this spell, you will be marking out boundaries and protecting territory—as well as sending all bad wishes straight back to their originator.

## HOW TO CAST THE SPELL

**TIMING** This spell is best wrought on a dark moon to turn aside bad intent. Renew it every three months for the first year by chalking over the markings on December 21, March 21, June 21, and September 21.

### CASTING THE SPELL

1 Cast a circle next to your front door in accordance with the guidelines on pages 32–35.

2 Stand the candle directly in the center of the stone, using molten wax to stabilize it.

3 Draw a chalk arrow appearing to go through the candle, pointing left.

4 Place the stone before your front door, saying:

*Thus have you injured.*

Turn it around so that the arrow points out the front door, saying:

*I put you to rout*
*As I turn you about.*

5 In the top left-hand corner, draw a small square, saying:

*Hearth.*

In the top right-hand corner, draw an X, saying:

*Love.*

### YOU WILL NEED

One black candle, cut down to 3"/7.5 cm in length

Matches or a lighter

One square paving stone, 8–12"/20–30 cm square

One thick piece of chalk

In the bottom left-hand corner, draw an upward pointing arrow, saying:

*Roof above.*

In the bottom right-hand corner, draw a circle with a dot in the center.

6 Allow the candle burn down, then cover the stone with a rug, and keep it by your front door.

# KITCHEN WITCH SPELL
## TO ENSURE THAT YOU AND YOURS WILL NEVER GO HUNGRY

PURPOSE   To create a lucky charm to ensure that your household will never go short of food.

BACKGROUND   The kitchen witches sold in shops in the United States and in parts of Europe are often figures of cute old grannies on broomsticks, which advertisers claim will ensure that your cooking does not get spoiled. In fact, the idea behind these wall charms originated in Europe, where salt dough figures were used to contain the spirit of the corn cut from the previous harvest. Preserving the flour in this way was

## HOW TO CAST THE SPELL

### YOU WILL NEED

One red candle, 6–8"/15–20 cm in length

Matches or a lighter

Household salt, one cupful

Plain white flour, one cupful

Water, one cupful

One large bowl

One egg white

One teaspoon of poppy seeds

One oven

One 12" x ½"/30 cm x 1 cm length of red ribbon

**TIMING** Cast this spell on a waxing moon, as near to full as possible.

**CASTING THE SPELL**

1 Cast a circle in your kitchen in accordance with the guidelines on pages 32–35. Set your oven to 100°F/38°C.

2 Light the red candle and, passing your hands on each side of the flame back and forth three times, say:

*I invoke the spirit of life,*
*I invoke the spirit of earth.*

thought to ensure the return of the corn spirit for the next crop. At some point, the dough came to be baked in the shape of good witches, ostensibly to frighten off so-called bad witches who might spoil the corn.

The salt dough figure of this spell will not demand much of your artistic abilities, as it invokes the original symbolism of the salt dough—to ensure plenty. Your kitchen witch may not have a pointy hat or broom, but rest assured that she is far more powerful than the "cute old lady" figures currently on the market!

4 Roll the dough into an even tube, and form it into a figure eight.

5 Coat it with egg white, and press the poppy seeds evenly into the surface. Place it in the oven. The dough is cooked if it sounds hollow when rapped. Cooking times differ from oven to oven, so check it frequently. When the cooking is complete, allow it to cool.

6 Dress it with a red bow, and hang it in your kitchen.

3 Place the salt and flour in the bowl and blend, then add water until the dough is smooth and pliant. Knead for at least three minutes, chanting the following words:

*Come wealth, come weal*
*Come plenty by.*

# ROMAN CORNUCOPIA SPELL
## TO BESTOW LUCK ON A NEW HOME

**PURPOSE**  To bring luck to a new home—ideal for blessing a couple moving into their first home together.

**BACKGROUND**  The symbol of the cornucopia, or "horn of plenty," appears from Renaissance times in Western art to signify abundance. It was originally an ancient Roman symbol of a magical horn that held an endless supply of food. This was usually seen carried by a goddess figure in Roman religious art and was so popular that a number of deities became associated with it: Abundantia (abundance), Spes (hope), Copia (wealth), Ceres (growth), Justitia (justice), and Concordia (peace) were all seen

with this symbol. The frequency with which it appears in ancient times—and its ongoing popularity as a necklace charm—perhaps reflects the perennial concerns of humans with ensuring a sufficiency of resources.

Another custom that the ancient Romans left us is closely connected with the cornucopia. This is the act of bestowing bread, oil, and salt on a new household in order to guarantee that none of these staples is lacking in the future. This spell is based on that ritual and uses the ancient symbol of the cornucopia to draw good luck to the home.

## HOW TO CAST THE SPELL

**TIMING** Work with a waxing moon to ensure that resources flow into your home, and on any day of the week apart from Saturday, domain of frugal Saturn.

### CASTING THE SPELL

1 Cast a circle in accordance with the guidelines on pages 32–35.

2 Light the candle, saying:
*I call upon Ceres*
*Goddess of the corn harvest*
*Of fertility and growth*
*To witness and bless this spell.*

3 Cut the roll in half, and spoon the oil into the center of one side, saying:
*May goodness flow here.*
Sprinkle the salt into the other side, and repeat the line above.

4 Tie the halves together again with twine, and fasten off, saying:
*All that is needful is sealed in this house.*
Fold the felt into an open cone, stitching with the thread to secure it.

5 Place the bread into the cone, and sew the top flap shut.

6 Keep this in your own home, or present it to friends when entering their home, saying:
*What abundance has made*
*Abundance will bless.*

**3**

### YOU WILL NEED

One green candle, 6–8"/15–20 cm in length

Matches or a lighter

One sharp knife

One small bread roll

One teaspoon of virgin olive oil

One pinch of salt

One 18"/45 cm length of twine

One 12"/30 cm square piece of red felt

One spool of red thread

One sewing needle

# RED BRACELET SPELL
## TO BESTOW GOOD FORTUNE ON A NEWBORN BABY

**PURPOSE**   To weave a charm to bring luck to a newborn.

**BACKGROUND**   Cords and threads are important in magic, never more so than when they represent life and destiny. In this spell, a variation on a custom found in various parts of the world, they signify the future fortunes of a newborn and are therefore to be treated with great respect. Anthropologists have often noted the emphasis placed on cords in various rites of passage in many cultures, and tying a lucky wristband on a newborn is a common custom all over the world. Traditions where a red thread is employed use the color to signify power, health, and long life, and these themes are taken up in this charm, which has a distinctly Celtic flavor.

In Celtic beliefs, the goddess Brigid is a protector of all newborn creatures. In her triple aspect, she is healer, bringer of fire, and inspiration of both poets and craftspeople. She is closely associated with triplicities—things that come in threes—and sometimes is seen depicted with braided knot work decorating her attire or framing her image. Here, she is invoked to bless and empower with good fortune a braided red bracelet to give to a newborn.

## HOW TO CAST THE SPELL

### YOU WILL NEED

One charcoal disk in a fireproof dish

Matches or a lighter

Three red candles, 6-8"/15–20 cm in length

Three 18"/45 cm lengths of 15-thread thick red embroidery skein

One pencil

Three teaspoons of frankincense

Scissors

One eggcup of water

One pinch of salt

**TIMING** Work on a waxing moon to attract good fortune, and on a Sunday, in honor of fiery Brigid.

### CASTING THE SPELL

1 Cast a circle in accordance with the guidelines on pages 32–35.

2 Light the charcoal disk.

3 Light three candles. After lighting each one, say the following in turn:

*Brigid, queen of healing wells.* (Candle 1)
*Brigid, queen of balefires.* (Candle 2)
*Brigid, queen of makers*
*Hail and welcome.* (Candle 3)

4 Tie the strands to a pencil, and weave a braid, chanting the following throughout:

*Your days be long*
*Your shadow great*
*Your heart be glad.*

Fasten, and cut when the braid is 4"/10 cm longer than the baby's wrist measurement.

5 Sprinkle incense on the charcoal, and pass the braid through the smoke, saying:

*Air to speed you fortune.*

Pass it through candle heat, saying:

*Fire to haste you power.*

Sprinkle it with water, saying:

*Water to bring you love.*

Sprinkle it with salt, saying:

*Earth to send you health*
*And Brigid walk with you in your*
*footsteps.*

6 Tie the bracelet around the baby's wrist; then remove it, and place it under the crib mattress.

# BERRY NECKLACE SPELL
## TO BRING HEALTH, WEALTH, AND HAPPINESS

PURPOSE  To bless you with health, wealth, and happiness.

BACKGROUND  Berries are versatile ingredients, used in incense blends and potions. Their traditional symbolism is employed in spell work, and they carry magical energies. They also look attractive when used in charms to be hung in the home! This charm draws on traditions associated with mountain ash (rowan), juniper, and holly berries and uses their magical vibrations in charm for health, wealth, and happiness.

## HOW TO CAST THE SPELL

### YOU WILL NEED

One red candle, 6–8"/15–20 cm in length

One green candle, 6–8"/15–20 cm in length

Matches and a lighter

One 48"/120 cm length of black thread

One sharp needle

One bowl

Dried juniper berries, 4 oz/115 g

Dried berries of mountain ash (rowan), 4 oz/115 g

Dried holly berries, 4 oz/115 g

**TIMING** Work on a waxing moon, and on Tuesday, sacred to protective Mars.

### CASTING THE SPELL

1 Cast a circle in accordance with the guidelines on pages 32–35.

2 Light the red candle, saying:
   *Health and heart prevail.*
Light the green candle, saying:
   *Wealth and weal, all hail.*

3 Thread the needle, doubling the thread.

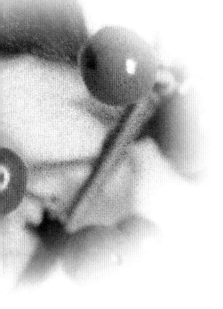

In tree lore, mountain ash (rowan) and juniper ward off evil, and their berries have particularly protective properties. They are used in purification and protection incense blends, and will ward off thieves when kept by the back door of a house. The holly tree has a similar reputation, although its berries are accredited with the power to bind oaths and seal lover's pledges. Among the more arcane properties of all three are the abilities to ensure health, plenty, and happiness. This spell calls on these lesser-known influences to empower a charm designed to attract all three.

4 Pour the juniper berries into the bowl, and with your hands palm down on them, say:

*Berries in your house of black*
*Never hold your bounty back.*

Repeat with the berries of mountain ash (rowan), saying:

*Mountain ash in your house of blood*
*Keep me hale and do me good.*

Repeat with the holly berries, saying:

*Holly berries, for my sake*
*Happy find and merry make.*

5 Thread the berries onto the thread in the order outlined above, chanting:

*Three bright things I would possess*

*Health, wealth, and happiness*
*Health show, wealth grow*
*Happiness all in this row.*

When the thread is full, tie the ends together, and pass it over your head. Walk to the heart of your house, and hang the necklace from the highest point.

# PROTECTION AND BLESSING SPELLS

# INTRODUCTION TO PROTECTION AND BLESSING SPELLS

The power to bless and protect has been both valued and feared in Western societies for several centuries. This is because the nature of magic itself has been largely misunderstood. Rituals and charms for blessings and protection have sometimes been assumed to be absolute: that a person or object once blessed is totally impervious to the harms of the world. This is a dangerous assumption to make, both for those who believe themselves invincible through magic and particularly for those who perform the spells, as they are consequently blamed when things go wrong. It is this latter tendency that has, in past times, led to accusations of "cursing" or even "killing" when the intention has been to protect or heal.

Fear and misapprehension about the magical ability to protect or bless arise from the mistaken belief that with the ability to bless comes also the ability to curse. This has encouraged fear and loathing of magical folk and, in times

gone by, persecution. Thinking of this type comes from a mindset—a very common one—that sees all aspects and principles of existence in black and white and divides the world into positive–negative opposites. Magic, however, does not operate according to such principles, and spells for protection and blessing are exactly what they say they are!

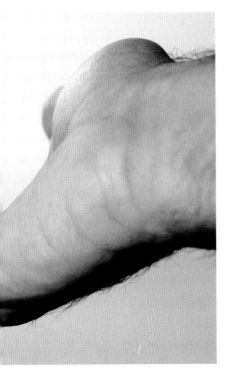

Rites for protection are not curses but ways of harnessing the power of magic to provide safeguards and to discourage the dishonest, spiteful, or deceitful from doing harm. Similarly, blessings are not fail-safe devices that keep the arrogant and foolish from harm. Rather, they should be seen as messages sent into the magical web by someone who respects the power of spirit and who wishes blessings to come to them or to another who is deserving.

Be reassured that the blessing spells in this section are not the flip side of another, more sinister aspect of magic, and moreover, that by invoking protection, you are not cursing anyone. The foci of the spells in this section should set your mind at rest on this count, as you will find spells to bless your home or a newborn baby and to wish a couple well in their life together. You will also find charms and magic to protect your home against intrusion and theft, to combat deceit in others, to fend off unwanted attentions, and to deflect spite.

To close this section, you will find a very special blessing, well known to witches, that helps you to gather your strength and face adversity in times of trouble.

# MEXICAN EYE SPELL
## TO GUARD AGAINST THE EVIL EYE

PURPOSE  To deflect ill wishes.

BACKGROUND  The *Ojo de Dios*, or "Eye of God," symbol used in this spell is a protective device of ancient origin. The Huichol people of Mexico wove this symbol as a means to fend off evil and invite supernatural protection. Similar artifacts for the same purpose have been found in other parts of South America as well as in Africa and the East. The Eye of God is depicted in different ways in art—one common depiction is a round eye with a horizontal iris surrounded by a sunburst—but the simplest and most common representation is seen in woven specimens similar to that created in this spell.

### HOW TO CAST THE SPELL

**YOU WILL NEED**

One charcoal disk in a fireproof dish

One orange candle, 6–8"/15–20 cm in length

Matches or a lighter

One teaspoon of frankincense

Two oak twigs 8"/20 cm in length

Balls of wool in the following colors: black; red; orange; yellow; green; turquoise; azure

One pinch of cinnamon

**TIMING**  Cast this spell on a Sunday to honor the patron of the spell, and on a waxing moon, to draw its strength.

**CASTING THE SPELL**

1 Cast a circle in accordance with the guidelines on pages 32–35.

2 Light the charcoal, then the candle, saying:

> Mighty Sol
> All-seeing eye
> Light upon all enemies
> Who dwell beneath sky
> Find them out,
> Put evil to rout.

Belief in *the evil eye*, or the ability to cause harm to someone by looking at them with ill intent, is found all over the world. Often it is the fear of such power that does the job of any curse or ill wish, as worrying and fretting about curses simply gives them a bigger space in your life. But it is easy to tell someone not to fret and hard for them to ignore their fears, so this spell concentrates the mind toward feelings of security by invoking the protection of the sun. While you are weaving your *Ojo de Dios*, try chanting or humming to raise the magical vibes and strengthen the spell.

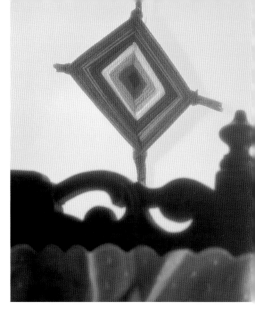

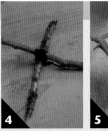 

3 Sprinkle the frankincense onto the charcoal.

4 Place the twigs across each other at right angles, and fasten them at the center with black wool.

5 Weave nine rounds of each color in the order outlined above, drawing the wool under and around each of the four struts in succession, so that the wool wrapped around the twigs stands out against that which is woven between.

6 When you are finished, fasten off securely. Place the cinnamon on the charcoal, and cense your Eye of God in the smoke, saying:

*I seal and proclaim you*
*Let none defame you.*

Hang it over your bed.

# SNAPDRAGON SPELL
## TO GUARD AGAINST SPITE

PURPOSE   To protect against the spiteful intents of others.

BACKGROUND   The snapdragon, or *Antirrhinum majus,* is a flower beloved of
children, who pinch the base of the blossoms to make the "dragon mouth" of the bloom
snap open and shut. It has the reputation of being highly protective of the pure in heart
and is particularly powerful in fending off the spiteful intentions of others. The flowers,
which are highly popular with bees, are diverse in color, and the most exciting hues are
perhaps the fiery yellows and reds—real dragon colors!

   As a child, I found this flower in the front gardens of houses I passed on the way
to one of the city parks. My friends and I would dare each other to pick blossoms from
the plants. I was pleased to discover, when I grew up to have children of my own, that
youngsters are still fascinated with snapdragons and can still be seen roaring around
and chasing each other with the snapping maws of the flowers. It seems that little
children know instinctively where magic lies!

## HOW TO CAST THE SPELL

**TIMING** Cast this spell on a waning moon to repel, and on a Tuesday, day of fierce and fiery Mars.

### CASTING THE SPELL

1 Cast a circle in accordance with the guidelines on pages 32–35.

2 Light the charcoal, then the red candle.

3 Heat the point of the nail in the candle flame; then use it to etch an upward-pointing equilateral triangle into the side of the candle 1"/2.5 cm from the wick.

4 Sprinkle the rosemary onto the charcoal.

5 Place snapdragon blossoms into the pouch one by one, reciting the following lines, one to each as you do so:

*Power of one, the mighty sun*
*Power of two, hold right and true*
*Power of three, sting of the bee*
*Power of four, all harm deplore*
*Power of five, voice of the hive*
*Power of six, all harm desist*
*Before the seven, all harm be driven.*

### YOU WILL NEED

One charcoal disk in a fireproof dish

One red candle, 6–8"/15–20 cm in length

Matches or a lighter

One sharp masonry nail

One teaspoon of dried rosemary

Seven snapdragon blossoms

One 2" x 2"/5 cm x 5 cm red drawstring pouch

One 24"/60 cm length of fine cord

6 Hold the pouch between your palms, and visualize its power as dragon fire, ready to blast all spite and unkindness that comes near. Pass the pouch through the incense smoke to seal it.

7 Attach the cord and wear the pouch around your neck for personal protection, or hang it in your home to guard your family or housemates.

# HERB GUARDIAN SPELL
## TO PROTECT YOUR HOME
## FROM BURGLARY AND THEFT

PURPOSE  To deter thieves.

BACKGROUND  Evidence of charms to guard against theft dates back centuries, and traditions relating to house guardians go back thousands of years. Many old spells relating to repelling thieves refer to herbal knowledge and magical and religious

symbolism. However, the principle of creating a guardian for the home is informed by a magical technique sometimes called god-making. This spell comprises both herbal and god-making techniques.

Juniper berries, well known in magic for their power to dispel evil intentions, are also regarded as safeguards against theft. Here, a berry is placed inside a small wax figure into which you will also place your intent to deflect all thieves. Since the juniper berry will form its "heart," you can be assured that the sole reason for the guardian you create will be to protect your home and property. For this spell you will need to construct a mold of modeling clay in which to cast the figure to be your Herb Guardian. Since one of the arms (the right) is to carry a miniature sword, you will need to make it thick enough to be pierced by a needle without actually breaking any of the arm away. This will mean some prior preparation and perseverance.

## HOW TO CAST THE SPELL

**TIMING** Perform your work on a waning moon, on a Saturday, dedicated to Saturn the banisher.

### CASTING THE SPELL

1 Before casting the circle, prepare the modeling clay by forming a mold for a humanoid figure approximately 4"/10 cm high, and place it on the plate. Prepare the wax by placing the jar in a pan of boiling water on a heated burner on the stove; put the candles in the jar and let them melt.

2 Cast a circle in accordance with the guidelines on pages 32–35.

3 Light the black candle, saying:
*As Saturn's rings surround the whole*
*My guardian protect this home.*

4 Pour the wax into the mold and sprinkle it with sage. Chant while you are waiting for it to solidify:
*Evil deed and evil word*
*All are banished by your sword.*

5 When the wax is almost set, place the juniper berry where the heart would be. Place the eye end of the needle into the "hand" of the figure, with the point jutting out.

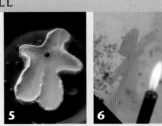

### YOU WILL NEED

One large ball of soft modeling clay

One heatproof plate

One glass jar

One pan of boiling water

Twelve household candles

One black candle, 6–8"/15–20 cm in length

Matches or a lighter

One teaspoon of chopped sage

One juniper berry

One sewing needle

6 When the figure is completely solidified, cease chanting. Extinguish the candle, and bury the guardian near your property, sword pointing outward with the candle by its side.

# SWORD SPELL
## TO PROTECT AGAINST ALL TYPES OF INTRUSION

PURPOSE   To defend against intrusion. This spell has long been used by witches to defend their homes and meeting places.

BACKGROUND   The central technique of this spell is one that is used to a greater or lesser extent in many spells: that of visualization. If you were ever accused of daydreaming when you were a child, there is a good chance that you will have a flair for visualization in a magical context. In magic, visualization techniques are valuable because they help you to focus on the purpose of the spell and at the same time to empower it with your intent. An advanced form of this technique is creating a thought-form to do your bidding.

When we use a thought-form that resembles ourselves (a feature of mirror magic) it is known as a *fetch*. However, in this spell, you are creating a body of energy in the form of an object—a sword, the archetypal symbol of defense. It is a simple technique, but it requires concentration and self-discipline. It would be a good idea, therefore, to spend some time practicing the technique of visualization in a cast circle until you are confident that you can hold your concentration for the purposes of this spell.

## HOW TO CAST THE SPELL

### YOU WILL NEED

One charcoal disk in a fireproof dish

Matches or a lighter

Nine tea-lights in secure holders

One teaspoon of mugwort

One teaspoon of dittany of Crete

**TIMING** Work on a dark moon to empower this spell.

### CASTING THE SPELL

1 Cast a circle in accordance with the guidelines on pages 32–35.

2 Light the charcoal.

3 Sit on the floor in the center of the circle, facing north, and place the tea-lights at equal points in a circle around you before lighting them.

4 Sprinkle mixed mugwort and dittany onto the charcoal, and breathe in the scent.

5 Close your eyes, slow your breathing, and allow yourself to drift into the darkness within. When you are ready, envisage in the north of the circle a shield; in the east a wand; in the south a sword; and in the west a chalice. Allow the shield, wand, and chalice images to merge into that of the sword. Envisage the sword passing over your head to the front of you, resting point downward. Now mentally instruct the sword to guard your home, and set it spinning in a vertical arc. Mentally move this spinning sword toward the front boundary of your home.

6 To ensure that its strength is continually renewed, envisage the sword spinning in this place prior to going to sleep each night.

# HERB CORSAGE SPELL
## PROTECTION AGAINST UNWANTED ATTENTIONS

PURPOSE   To fend off all uninvited attentions.

BACKGROUND   There are many spells to attract suitors, or the attention of influential work colleagues, and to make new friends. Because life is complicated, magical tradition also provides us with the magical means to deflect attention away from ourselves, when it is unwanted and uninvited. This spell, designed to repel unwanted notice, can be used for many purposes. It could be that you have an unwanted suitor or that you wish to escape the attentions of a bully or an unpleasant personality. This spell cannot render you invisible in given situations—let's face it, no one with a bunch of herbs in their lapel is ever going to be invisible—but the power of the herbs and your stated intentions are wielded to repel those you wish to avoid. Wearing the Herb Corsage charm created by this spell is to declare magically the wish

that the person or persons you are evading will pass by without invading your private space. "Wearing your heart on your sleeve" is a saying that applies to anyone who leaves themselves vulnerable by making obvious to all where their heart lies. Wearing these herbs on your lapel is to guard your own heart and your integrity and make your thinking clear on the matter:
*Stay away!*

## HOW TO CAST THE SPELL

### YOU WILL NEED

One red candle (for Mars) or one black candle (for Saturn), each 6–8"/15–20 cm in length

Matches or a lighter

One sprig of white heather

One sprig of thyme

One 9"/22.5 cm length of natural twine

One ball of absorbent cotton

One saucer of water

One twist of aluminum foil

**TIMING** A waning or dark moon is best for this spell, and Saturday, for stern Saturn, or Tuesday, day of fiercely defensive Mars, are the most favorable days.

### CASTING THE SPELL

1 Cast a circle in accordance with the guidelines on pages 32–35.

2 Light the candle, saying:
*[Mars/Saturn], you are honored here*
*Let no enemy near*
*Whose notice I fear.*

3 Bind the heather and thyme stems together with twine. Dip the absorbent cotton in the water and squeeze it out, then apply it to the roots of the thyme and heather. Cover the absorbent cotton with foil.

4 Hold the corsage before the candle flame, visualizing the person or persons you wish to avoid passing you by, as if they had been repelled.

5 Repeat the following incantation nine times over the corsage:
*Cardea*
*Ouvret*
*Allaya*
*Dixet.*

6 Wear the herb corsage on your lapel until it dies off; then dry the herbs and crumble them into an open fire to seal the spell.

# TRISKELION SPELL
## TO PROTECT A TRAVELER

PURPOSE  To protect you on your travels.

BACKGROUND  The word *triskelion* comes from the Greek and means
"three-legged." It is a very old symbol that has been ascribed many meanings through
the ages and that is inevitably bound up with the mysterious nature of triplicities.
The triskelion in this spell draws on the Manx legend with which it is most associated,
to provides travelers with a charm that will help them bounce back should they
encounter difficulties on their journey.

Ellan Vannin, or the Isle of Man, is well known for its mix of Viking and Celtic history.
Its chief insignia, the triskelion, has its origins in the mists of time—the earliest

## HOW TO CAST THE SPELL

### YOU WILL NEED

One pale blue candle, 6–8"/15–20 cm
in length

Matches or a lighter

One small single scallop shell, drilled

One fine paintbrush

One tube of vermilion oil paint

One 24"/60 cm length of fine black cord

**TIMING** Cast on a waxing moon and on a
Sunday, sacred to the sun.

### CASTING THE SPELL

1 Cast a circle in accordance with the
guidelines on pages 32–35.

2 Light the candle, saying:
*Mannanan of the waters*
*Mannanan the traveler*
*Look well upon [name]*
*That they are hale going out*
*And hale coming in.*

3 Paint on the inside of the scallop shell
the outline of a triskelion.

depictions of this sign are found in prehistoric rock carvings in Italy—but it is linked to a most intriguing legend. The magician Manannan guarded the island with magical mists. Sensing the coming of Christianity and the new age that was at hand, he turned his followers into triskelions and rolled them down Snaefell, the Isle of Man's highest mountain, and into the sea, to dwell in a kingdom beneath the waves. This tale of transformation and survival gave the Manx their motto: *Quocunque Jeceris Stabit*, which Manx folk prefer to translate as "However you throw us, we stand."

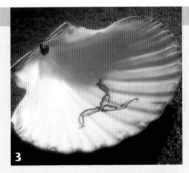

4 Sit in the center of the circle with the upturned shell in your upturned right palm, which should be placed over your upturned left palm. Close your eyes, and visualize the triskelion you have painted spinning clockwise, faster and faster until it is a blur.

5 When you are ready, blow onto the shell with your breath to bless it with the power of air. When the paint dries, thread it with the cord, and dip it into natural saltwater at the earliest opportunity.

6 The triskelion pendant should be worn around the neck of those who would call on its protective powers.

# WITCHWOOD SPELL
## TO DISPEL EVIL INTENT

**PURPOSE**   To drive evil away.

**BACKGROUND**   Mountain ash (rowan) is considered by magicians to offer magical protection of the highest order. There are many old country sayings and saws relating to mountain ash, nearly all of them referring to the mountain ash's power to dispel evil and protect bearers of the wood from harm. Apparently, mountain ash trees keep witches away, this belief coming from a time when the word *witch* was synonymous with evil. However, witches, who have never yet been "kept away" by mountain ash, tend to refer to it as *witchwood* precisely because of its reputation for goodness!

Mountain ash are wonderful trees that grow very quickly if planted in groves with other trees, making them good protection for saplings of slower-growing trees that are less hardy. They like lots of air and light and are often found growing in high places; they are common in the Scottish Highlands. They live up to two hundred years and are less prone to disease and breakage than many other trees. This hardiness makes them an appropriate symbol of endurance and protection.

## HOW TO CAST THE SPELL

### YOU WILL NEED

One charcoal disk in a fireproof dish

One red candle, 6–8"/15–20 cm in length

Matches or a lighter

One 2"/5 cm section of a small branch of mountain ash, drilled through ½"/1 cm from the top

One sharp whittling knife

One 36"/90 cm length of red wool thread

**TIMING** Cast this spell on a dark moon in the Fall to grow your protective shield. Cull a small branch and seal the raw edge.

### CASTING THE SPELL

1 Cast a circle in accordance with the guidelines on pages 32–35.

2 Light the charcoal, then the candle. Cut a 4"/10 cm strip of wool, and burn it over the flame, saying:

*As this flame dissolves this thread*
*Mountain ash wood shall deal all dread.*

3 Whittle away the bark, and place it on the charcoal to smolder. Cut away a strip of the wood to just below the drilled hole, making a flat surface.

4 Cut into this surface an upward-pointing equilateral triangle with a horizontal line through the center.

5 Hold the pendant over the smoking bark, saying:

*All good enter in*
*All evil to flee*
*Within my good hand*
*All evil withstand.*

6 Wind the thread three times around the top of the charm, and secure it; then thread it through the drilled hole, forming a pendant to be worn around the neck.

# DAEG RUNE SPELL
## TO COMBAT DECEIT

**PURPOSE** To help you see clearly through lies and deceit.

**BACKGROUND** *Daeg*, the rune on which this spell is based, is one of the eight symbols representing the last third of the ancient twenty-four character runic script. This group of runes is known as *Tyr's aett* and is the set most associated with human matters and characteristics. As Tyr is a god of justice and a great defender against wrongs, all of these runes have something of his nature in them. In the case of daeg, literally "day" or "daylight," the wrongs to be fought are related to deceit and the need to see things clearly.

As we go through life, there is a tendency to trust less after we have experienced deceit. Sometimes this is what is needed, for as the saying goes: "If a man deceive me once, shame on him. If he deceive me twice, shame on me." However, sometimes we need a little help in training our instincts, and this is where the Daeg Rune Spell comes in.

Daeg represents clear seeing and our ability to turn our understanding around 180° where necessary. This rune is also associated with necessary change. All of this makes daeg the ideal rune to call on when you wish to guard yourself from the deceits of others.

## HOW TO CAST THE SPELL

**3**

### YOU WILL NEED

One gold orange candle, 6–8"/15–20 cm in length

Matches or a lighter

One stub of white chalk

One coaster-size (minimum) piece of slate or stone

One container of salt with a flow hole

**TIMING** Cast on a waxing moon, on a Sunday, day of the all-seeing sun.

### CASTING THE SPELL

1 Cast a circle in accordance with the guidelines on pages 32–35.

2 Light the candle, and whisper the name of the person you think may be deceiving you, close enough to the flame to make it flicker.

3 Take the chalk, and draw the rune daeg onto the piece of slate or stone. Pour the salt in an unbroken line, tracing it over the chalk marks you have made.

4 Hold this up before the candle, saying:
*Let it be uncovered*
*That which was hidden*
*And [name of potential deceiver] tell*
*    the truth*
*As [she/he] is bidden.*

5 Blow away the salt, and show the chalked rune to the candle flame.

6 Place the chalked rune outside until the rain washes it away. You should discover the truth of the matter within three moon cycles.

**319**

# HERB POPPET SPELL
## TO PROTECT AGAINST HARDSHIP

PURPOSE   Cast this spell to guard against privation.

BACKGROUND   This spell uses a poppet (sometimes referred to as a *fith-fath*), a very old magical technique that embodies a wish or a person. A poppet is a stuffed figure made from two sections of cloth that are cut to a roughly humanoid shape, then sewn together and stuffed. An old charm to ward off nasty people is to stuff a poppet with stinging nettles and thorns. This spell rests on a similar principle, although the object of the working is to fend off the unpleasantness of hardship rather than unpleasant people.

## HOW TO CAST THE SPELL

### YOU WILL NEED

One black candle, 6–8"/15–20 cm in length

Matches or a lighter

One charcoal disk in a fireproof dish

Two pieces of cloth cut identically into a humanoid shape approximately 6"/15 cm high

One sewing needle

One 36"/90 cm length of black cotton thread

One large bundle of dried dandelions

One large bundle of dried thyme

Three finely chopped thistle heads

**TIMING**  Work on a waning moon to dispel negativity and deflect hardship.

**CASTING THE SPELL**

1 Cast a circle in accordance with the guidelines on pages 32–36.

2 Light the charcoal, then the candle. Place a little of each herb onto the charcoal.

3 Sew the two pieces of cloth together around the edges, leaving the head edges open, chanting the following:

*Guard my wealth and guard my weal*
*None to envy, none to steal.*

The herbs used here are known for their properties to attract good fortune and fend off bad. Dandelions are particularly lucky and attract good friends for bad times. Thistles are highly protective, and thyme is renowned for its ability to repel negativity. All of these should be collected in the wild and dried naturally prior to the spell casting.

It doesn't matter where you keep this poppet, as long as it never leaves your home or is found by one who envies you. Should either event occur, cast the spell again as soon as possible, as all the good you have achieved will have been undone.

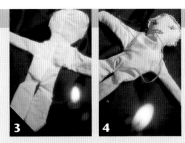

Stuff the legs with dandelion, saying:
*Walk in the way of fortune.*
Stuff the rest of the body with thyme, saying:
*Protect all I need.*

Now stuff the head with the thistle heads, saying:
*Guard against wrath*
*Avarice and greed.*

4 Sew up the head; then embroider eyes and a mouth.

5 Hold the poppet over the incense smoke, and show it to the candle flame, saying:
*Bend to no will but mine.*

6 Keep the poppet safely in your home, and guard it from envious eyes.

# HEARTH SPELL
## TO BLESS YOUR HOME

PURPOSE   Use this spell to bless your home and all who live in it.

BACKGROUND   It is such a natural thing to wish to bless your home with good fortune that we are spoiled with choices when selecting a spell to do the job—there are simply hundreds of them! This spell fits the bill, however, and has been included for its simplicity and beauty. But why a Hearth Spell? Because the hearth has been considered since ancient times the heart of the home. The Celtic fire goddess, Brigid, is called on here to bless your home, and the symbol constructed in the course of the spell work is sometimes referred to as Brigid's Cross.

## HOW TO CAST THE SPELL

### YOU WILL NEED

One charcoal disk in a fireproof dish

One red candle, 6–8"/15–20 cm in length

Matches or a lighter

One teaspoon of benzoin gum

Twelve straight twigs approximately 6"/15 cm in length

One spool of natural twine

One pinch of cinnamon

**TIMING** Cast on a waxing moon to draw blessings forth, with Sunday or Monday—sun and moon days—being particularly favorable.

### CASTING THE SPELL

1 Cast a circle in accordance with the guidelines on pages 32–35.

2 Light the charcoal and the candle, saying:
*Holy Brigid of the sacred flame,*
*Bless the charm I make in your name.*
Place a little benzoin on the charcoal.

3 Using the twigs and twine, divide the twigs into four groups of three. Fasten them together so that a 2"/5 cm square is formed at the center. This involves placing the end of one bunch of three at right angles to another bunch, 2"/5 cm from the end of the first bunch.

When all homes had open fires, the hearth formed the focal point for cooking, drying, warmth, light, and company. Nowadays, in older houses, gas or electric heaters may have replaced the open grate of a coal, peat, or wood fire; in this case, your hearth is probably where it always was. If your home was built with central heating and without open fire grates, you will have to decide where the focal point of your home is. Think about a spot where everyone gathers and that, intuitively, you feel is the heart of the home. This is the place where you should hang your charm.

4 Repeat this around the square so that a cross is formed with a square as its center. Bind the twine around the bottom of the twigs to secure them.

5 Place more benzoin and the cinnamon onto the charcoal, and cense the *Bridiog*, or Brigid's cross, in the smoke, saying:
*I call upon the four winds*
*To breathe lightly on this house,*
*I call upon Brigid's blessing.*

6 Hang the Brigid's Cross over the hearth.

# BAY CRADLE CHARM
## TO BLESS AND PROTECT A NEWBORN BABY

PURPOSE   To bring blessings to a new baby.

BACKGROUND   The leaves of the sweet bay, or *Laurus nobilis*, are well known for their culinary uses, but, magically, bay is used for its protective and positive properties. It is often used in vision-inducing incenses, carried as an amulet, or placed in sachets for healing and protection. Occasionally it is scattered on the floor in circles where negativity is being combated.

In this spell, it is used for protection, but mainly for its many blessings. Its virtues in dispelling evil thoughts and intents are legendary, and its wholesome nature makes it a particularly good herb to use to protect and bless a newborn. One of the properties of bay is that it invokes the energies of its planetary ruler—the sun—and all the associated blessings of health, success, prosperity, and joy. In magical terms, bay is synonymous with success, recognition, achievement, and realizing your potential for goodness. All deities associated with this plant represent growth and prosperity, reflecting bay's favorable aspects.

Ensure, for safety, that this sachet is properly secured under a crib mattress. It is not intended for an infant beyond six weeks old.

# HOW TO CAST THE SPELL

**TIMING** Work on a waxing moon to bring blessings, and on a Sunday, sacred to the sun gods and goddesses linked with bay.

### CASTING THE SPELL

1 Cast a circle in accordance with the guidelines on pages 32–35.

2 Sew three red Xs in a circular position at one end of the strip of cheesecloth.

3 Fold the cheesecloth in half with the Xs on the inside, and sew up two seams; then turn it right side outward.

4 Light the candle, saying:
*Lamp of the sun*
*Show your face*
*To this child*
*Warm [his/her] life*
*With your joy.*

5 Place the bay leaves one by one into the sachet, saying:
*One to shine upon your face*
*Two to keep you in good grace*
*Three to make your heart to sing*
*Four good fortune so to bring*
*Five for strength in any danger*
*Six for kindness from a stranger*
*Seven for good wisdom's crown*
*Eight for gathering high renown*
*Nine by which this spell is bound.*

### YOU WILL NEED

One 4" x 2"/10 cm x 5 cm strip of cheesecloth

One embroidery needle

One skein of red embroidery silk

One gold or orange candle, 6–8"/15–20 cm in length

Matches or a lighter

Nine bay leaves

6 Sew up the remaining side, and attach it to the baby's cradle.

# RING OF ROSES SPELL
## TO BLESS AND PROTECT A COUPLE AND THEIR RELATIONSHIP

PURPOSE  To bless and protect a couple and their relationship. You can perform this charm for yourself or to offer to newlyweds, or to a couple setting up home together.

BACKGROUND  It can be hard work keeping a relationship going once the early days of romance fade into everyday reality. This spell is for keeping a relationship strong and magically blessing it with endurance. It could be that you have friends who are truly inspirational in their devotion to each other, and you wish to mark your appreciation of what their warm and stable relationship means to those around them. In that case, this is a lovely gift, as it dries to an attractive appearance.

Roses are the archetypal symbol of love—especially red, pink, and white ones. Yellow roses, according to the lexicon of flowers and love, are for platonic friendship only and should not be offered to lovers, as they have the reputation of sending the wrong message! Red roses symbolize love and passion, while pink roses speak of loving affection and a true liking and admiration for a partner. White roses represent love in a pure form and show that your feelings are open, honest, and unselfish.

Needless to say, this spell favors red, pink, and white roses, with the last representing the kind of friendship that true love offers.

## HOW TO CAST THE SPELL

**TIMING** Cast this spell on a waxing moon to bring blessings, and on a Friday, sacred to Venus, the love planet.

### CASTING THE SPELL

1 Cast a circle in accordance with the guidelines on pages 32–35.

2 Light the red candle, saying:
*Bind it with passion.*

3 Light the pink candle, saying:
*Bind it with kindness*
Light the white candle, saying:
*Bind it with light.*

4 Using the florist wire and interspersing the colors, fasten the roses into a ring, securing each rose approximately 1"/2.5 cm below the flower head to 1"/2.5 cm below the flower of the rose before. Use the remaining lengths of stem to strengthen the ring, fastening them with the wire and covering them with tape.

5 When the ring is complete, wind twine clockwise around it between the rose heads, chanting:
*As I wind this circle round*
*Love and blessings shall be found.*

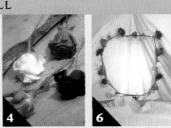

### YOU WILL NEED

One red, one pink, and one white candle, all 6-8"/15–20 cm in length

Matches or a lighter

Six each of red, pink, and white roses

One reel of green florist wire

One reel of green florist tape

One spool of natural twine

6 The ring should be hung in the couple's bedroom.

# WAYFARER SPELL
## A BLESSING SPELL FOR TRAVELERS

PURPOSE   To bring blessings to those about to set out on their travels.

BACKGROUND   One famous Irish blessing begins: "May the road rise up to meet you." This is a poetic way of wishing the traveler a pleasant journey free of the usual hardships to be met on the road. This spell has a similar intention, as it is designed to attract all of the blessings that make traveling a worthwhile, safe, and interesting experience. The needs of even the most weathered traveler include the basics that most people require in their own homes: shelter, warmth, food, health, good company, and a little luck. This spell is directed toward ensuring that these are granted.

This spell calls on the powers of three goddesses associated with the open road and invokes their abilities to steer travelers in the right direction. Annis, a goddess beloved of the traveling peoples of Britain and Europe, is a good friend of travelers who wander from well-trodden paths. Helen, a Welsh deity, is a goddess of crossroads and for those who have directions to choose from, while Cardea, a Roman goddess of gateways, opens the way to learning experiences and wisdom.

## HOW TO CAST THE SPELL

### YOU WILL NEED

One tea-light in a jar

Matches or a lighter

One pouch containing a mixture of the following:

One tablespoon of ash from a home fire or bonfire at your home

One tablespoon of dried hyssop

Three teaspoons each of dried mint, sugar, and breadcrumbs

Three leaves of fresh basil

**TIMING** Cast this spell outside on a waxing moon, on the evening before you travel.

### CASTING THE SPELL

1 Visualize a white circle of light surrounding you to a distance of approximately 12 feet/3.6 meters.

2 Light the tea-light, saying:
> Goddess of travelers, hear me
> Lady of the crossroads, hear me
> Bright one at the gateway, hear me.

3 Turn to the east, and cast some mixture in that direction, saying:
> Spirits of air, grant me easy passage.

Repeat in the south, saying:
> Spirits of fire, grant me fireside
>   companions.

Face west, and repeat, saying:
> Spirits of water, grant me the good
>   opinion of
> Those I meet.

Cast the remainder to the north, saying:
> Spirits of the earth, grant me food,
>   shelter, and protection.

4 Standing in the center and facing the direction in which your journey will take you, call out:
> Annis, Cardea, Helen of the ways
> Hold me safe leaving and returning
> Shower your blessings upon me
> As the rain refreshes the earth I
>   walk upon.

# SHIELD SPELL
## FOR PROTECTION IN STRESSFUL SITUATIONS

PURPOSE   To ward off stress.

BACKGROUND   It is now generally recognized that an overload of stress is very bad for our physical and mental health. One effect of being placed in stressful situations too often is that our physical and psychological responses make us less able to cope with problems with which we are presented. Adrenaline helps us flee from danger, but it undermines our thought processes when our habitual response, when faced with pressure or the unexpected, is to panic. This spell wields protection from excess stress both generally and in given situations.

## HOW TO CAST THE SPELL

**YOU WILL NEED**

One black candle, 6–8"/15–20 cm in length

Matches or a lighter

One 12"/30 cm length of string

One small, lockable box

**TIMING** Work on a waning moon to turn anxiety aside, and on Tuesday, day of defensive Mars.

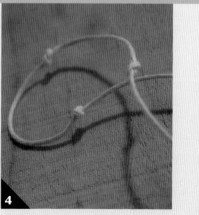

Once you have cast this spell, it is easy to summon up its power at exactly the right moment. This does demand concentration and an ability to shut out invasive thoughts, but this in itself is quite good practice for focusing, and for keeping stress at bay.

The image deployed here is that of a wall of shields, an infantry maneuver known as the *testudo* or "tortoise," used by the Roman army to protect forward-moving troops. This spell will protect you as you progress through workaday worries and enable you to continue to move forward positively even when faced with difficulties.

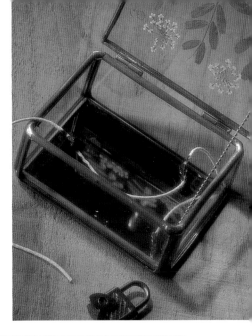

### CASTING THE SPELL

1 Cast a circle in accordance with the guidelines on pages 32–35.

2 Light the candle, saying:
*Banish my fears.*

3 Sit on the floor in the center of the circle, facing north. Close your eyes and slow your breathing, then clear your mind. When you are ready, visualize an oblong shield protecting you from chin to knee. Tie a knot in the string.

4 Now visualize more shields overlapping to cover your sides, back, and head, and tie another knot for each. Relax within your shield "shell," allowing yourself to feel secure and protected.

5 When you are ready, open your eyes, and drip wax from the candle onto each knot you have tied.

6 Lock the knotted string in the box, and keep it in a safe place. Whenever you feel the need to invoke your shield, summon up the image of the testudo covering and defending you.

# SALT AND WATER SPELL
## A SELF-BLESSING FOR TIMES OF TROUBLE

PURPOSE   To use in difficult times, when you need great inner strength.

BACKGROUND   When we find ourselves in difficult circumstances that are unlikely to find a simple solution, it may be difficult to remember how strong we really are. Sometimes the situation will require our attention for a long period of time, and it is when we face what seems to be an unending tunnel that we need to provide a little light for ourselves.

This self-blessing should be used only when in need, to preserve its potency. Many witches and magicians recognize that the spiritual value of this type of ritual is made stronger by using it very seldom. The symbolism is very simple: salt represents the shield and protection of earth; the candlelight brings hope and courage; the water brings spiritual transformation and cleansing; and the incense carries our prayer of blessing into the ether, to be relayed into the web of spirit.

Prior to using this blessing, think about a god or goddess with whom you have a strong natural affinity, and call on them by name in this spell to witness your self-blessing. It can be profoundly self-empowering and strengthening to keep a symbol or totem of that deity close to you in times of trouble.

## HOW TO CAST THE SPELL

### YOU WILL NEED

One charcoal disk in a fireproof dish

One white candle, 6–8"/15–20 cm
in length

Matches or a lighter

One teaspoon of frankincense

One container of salt with a flow hole

One wineglass filled with spring water

**TIMING** To be cast when in need, rather
than at any particular phase of the moon.

3

### CASTING THE SPELL

1 Cast a circle in accordance with the
guidelines on pages 32–35.

2 Light the charcoal, then the candle,
saying:
*I walk the path of courage*
*Where truth brings light.*

3 Sprinkle the frankincense onto the
charcoal, and inhale the scent, saying:
*May [God/Goddess name] hear me in*
*the darkest night.*

4 Pour some salt into your left palm,
and place your right palm over the water,
saying:
*Water, wash away all evil.*

Place your right hand over the salt,
and say:
*Salt, cast out impurity.*
Add the salt to the water, and anoint your
feet, knees, navel, breast, and forehead
with it.

5 Pour the salt all around you in a
clockwise circle, saying:
*[God/Goddess name], walk with me*
*in my footsteps.*
Treading on the salt, walk around it
clockwise in a complete circle; then return
to the center.

6 Close your eyes and silently ask to
be blessed with whatever qualities you
feel will carry you through your time
of trouble.

# DIVINATION SPELLS

# INTRODUCTION TO DIVINATION SPELLS

The annals of magic are replete with old country customs that lay claim to the ability to see into the future. Tales of unmarried women placing wedding cake beneath their pillows to dream of a future husband rub shoulders with rather more morbid theories for predicting who will die in the next year. Beneath the superstitions and the bloodcurdling stories can be found the skeletal frame of magical traditions. In this section you will find spells containing formulas that may seem faintly familiar, precisely because their genesis is in the origins of some well-known customs.

Divination, of course, is not just about foretelling the future. It is also about reading patterns that already exist in order to get a better picture of what is possible. The majority of tarot card readers, for example, are not "fortune-tellers" but experienced readers of the patterns of the present, symbolized within the various permutations of the card spreads. Similarly, palm readers may have predictive abilities, but much of their wisdom relies on reading your past and present in patterns set against a system of planetary symbolism. All of the magical recipes in this section are included within a broad interpretation of divination that goes beyond simply predicting what the future has in store.

The spells in this section are likewise diverse and are ranged around a number of different purposes. Here you will find the means by which to find solutions to problems and to discover who is false and who is true. For the romantic soul, there are traditional spells to discover the identity of your true love, to find out if your affections are returned, and to offer clues as to the nature of a future partner. There are, of course, spells for reading the patterns of what is likely to come.

You should remember, when using any of these spells, that the future is not set in stone—it hasn't happened yet! All that any of these spells can show— in common with any self-styled fortune-teller—are the likely configurations of what is coming. How you respond to that likelihood is what will make your future. Belief in "fate" can be stultifying—and, indeed, the opposite of magic, which is always about change and transformation. A warning: if you keep repeating the same spell in pursuit of the same problem, you will get distorted readings. If you approach these spells with respect and common sense, you will not be disappointed.

# BONES AND STONES SPELL
## TO CAST ONE'S FUTURE

PURPOSE  To give a reading on which to base future choices in your life.

BACKGROUND  A custom in South Africa, which appears to be based on very ancient ancestor worship, is the use of bones in divination. The use of a relative's finger bones is thought to invoke the knowledge of those who stand outside the world of the living in order to gain insights into the future. The person reading the bones has a personal set, each of which has different meanings well known to them. The method by which they are read is very simple: they are cast into a marked-out circle, and the pattern in which they fall, and their relationship to each other, offer a message for the soothsayer to divine.

In this spell, you will be combining this old method with that of lithomancy—the practice of reading stones. The stones in question can be obtained from most crystal or rock stores as well as from your surroundings. The "bones" are yarrow stems trimmed to various lengths, as specified on the opposite page.

You will need to use your imagination and your creative and intuitive abilities to read the stones and bones in the combination in which they fall, as each reading is unique. What you divine in your first reading, in a magical circle, is bound to be powerful and meaningful, so if at first you do not understand, try to match the pattern to what is happening in your life at the moment.

## HOW TO CAST THE SPELL

**TIMING** Cast your stones on a dark moon, in accordance with the ancient customs from which this spell originates.

### CASTING THE SPELL

Cast a circle in accordance with the guidelines on pages 32–35.

1 Light the black candle to your left and the white candle to your right.

2 With your finger, mark a large circle in the sand with a horizontal line through the center.

3 Shake up the "stones and bones" in your hands, and cast them onto the sand circle.

4 Divine their meaning as follows:

| | |
|---|---|
| TOP OF THE CIRCLE: | *public life* |
| BOTTOM OF THE CIRCLE: | *private life* |
| TO THE LEFT: | *challenges* |
| TO THE RIGHT: | *the material world* |
| THE 1"/2.5 CM STEM: | *soon* |
| THE 2"/5 CM STEM: | *the near future* |
| THE 3"/7.5 CM STEM: | *the long term* |
| SHORELINE PEBBLE: | *where problems lie* |
| CLEAR QUARTZ: | *friends* |
| ROSE QUARTZ: | *the heart* |
| AMETHYST: | *skills and career* |
| CITRINE: | *knowledge* |
| FLINT: | *beginnings.* |

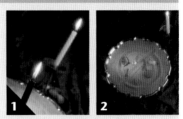

### YOU WILL NEED

One white candle, 6–8"/15–20 cm in length

One black candle, 6–8"/15–20 cm in length

Matches or a lighter

One tea tray filled with sand

Three yarrow stems, respectively 1"/2.5 cm, 2"/5 cm, and 3"/7.5 cm in length

One pebble from a shoreline

One tumbled clear quartz

One tumbled rose quartz

One tumbled amethyst

One tumbled citrine

One small sharp flint

# MAJOR ARCANA SPELL
## TO FIND THE ANSWER TO A QUESTION

PURPOSE  To find the answer to a question that is troubling you.

BACKGROUND  Tarot cards are consulted for guidance rather than for "yes" or "no" answers, generally speaking, and given the many permutations possible with readings involving seventy-eight cards, advice can indeed be very subtle. Most seasoned tarot readers agree, however, that there are ways in which to work out the timing of events predicted and even means of using the guidance of the cards to offer likely solutions to problems. Some of these methods are generally agreed, whereas others differ between readers. Those who work closely with the

## HOW TO CAST THE SPELL

### YOU WILL NEED

One purple candle, 6–8"/15–20 cm in length

Matches or a lighter

Twenty-two major arcana tarot cards

**TIMING** Lay your cards out on a waxing half-moon (sometimes known as the first quarter) to divine all possibilities offered in the spread.

### CASTING THE SPELL

Cast a circle in accordance with the guidelines on pages 32–35.

1 Light the purple candle, saying:
   *Fortuna, goddess of the wheel*
   *Look kindly on my quest for truth.*

2 Shuffle the cards, and lay all of them face down in the center of the circle.

3 With your question in mind, pass your writing hand over them, and pick up three that you are drawn to.

4 Lay them face up before you, from left to right, in the order in which you chose them.

tarot often note that when particular cards appear, they always carry a particular message to them, even if this is outside of the usual meaning ascribed to that card in the deck.

This spell rests on principles that are based upon generally agreed tarot wisdom. You should be prepared to do some hard thinking if the answer offered by the cards appears to be more subtle than you had hoped, but be assured that the guidance offered will be genuine if your need is sincere. Accept the first casting and read your answer on the basis of the guidance offered below.

5 The card on the left represents the basis of your problem; the one in the center represents its present effects; and the card on the right represents the outcome.

6 Refer to the following guidelines to features that appear on any of the cards in order to read your answer accurately:

| | |
|---|---|
| EVEN NUMBER: | truth |
| ODD NUMBER: | falsehood |
| MAN: | immediately |
| WOMAN: | within a year |
| MAN AND WOMAN: | leave it be |
| A CUP: | yes |
| A SWORD: | no |
| SUN, MOON, OR STAR: | your own judgment is correct |
| ANIMAL: | justice will be attained |
| WATER: | movement, travel, change. |

# PENDULUM SPELL
## TO DETECT A LOST OR DESIRED ITEM

PURPOSE   To locate a lost item or to locate something you have been looking for.

BACKGROUND   Pendulums are ancient divination tools, favored for their simplicity as well as their amazing powers. A more recent use to which they have been put involves maps, where a pendulum is suspended over a two-dimensional representation of an area being searched.

Traditionally, this technique uses one of two methods, the first being that of reaction and the second that of confirmation and negation. The former is based on any reaction at all from the pendulum: if it moves, the location is confirmed. It may also react very strongly over the correct point. The latter, based on a "yes" or "no" response, relies on the direction in which the pendulum rotates. Rotation clockwise denotes "yes," and counterclockwise means "no."

Before casting this circle, you will need to test your pendulum to see how it reacts when you use it. Test it by asking questions to which the answers are obvious, for example— "Is today Monday?"—and see what sort of response you get. This will guide you when it comes to divining the location of your lost or sought-after object.

## HOW TO CAST THE SPELL

### YOU WILL NEED

One white candle, 6–8"/15–20 cm in length

Matches or a lighter

One black ink pen

One sheet of office paper
*or*
One map of the search area

One sewing needle

One 24"/60 cm length of black cotton thread

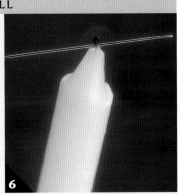

**TIMING** Test your divination abilities on the dark of the moon.

### CASTING THE SPELL

1 Cast a circle in accordance with the guidelines on pages 32–35.

2 Light the candle, saying:
*Spirit that aids the traveler and*
*Guides the birds in their flight*
*Empower this spell to find [name object]*
*Guide and help me in my quest*
*North to south and east to west.*

3 Draw a simple map of your home if the object you are seeking lies there, or use the map, as appropriate.

4 Thread the needle, then double the thread over, and fasten it. Suspend the needle over the map, pinching the knot at the end of the thread between the thumb and forefinger of your writing hand.

5 Allow your mind to go blank as you move to different locations on the map to test the response of the pendulum. Be patient, and take as long as you need to judge the response of the pendulum.

6 When you are satisfied with your answer, blow out the candle, and pierce the wick through the molten wax at the top with the needle of the pendulum.

# NEEDLE AND CANDLE SPELL
## TO UNCOVER A LIAR

PURPOSE   To discover deceit in another.

BACKGROUND   This magical equivalent of a polygraph test has an interesting pedigree. For hundreds of years, a test for a thief was to place needles in the side of a candle and seat all the suspects around it. As the candle burned down, the needles would fall, and the first to fall would be denounced as a thief. This spell is more of a lie detector than a thief catcher, but the principle is very much the same. Before putting this spell to the test, however, you should ask yourself some hard questions. First of all,

## HOW TO CAST THE SPELL

### YOU WILL NEED

One white candle, 6–8"/15–20 cm in length

Matches or a lighter

One sheet of office paper

One pen with green ink

One beeswax candle, 6–8"/15–20 cm in length

Seven sewing needles

**TIMING** Cast this spell at the full moon.

### CASTING THE SPELL

1 Cast a circle in accordance with the guidelines on pages 32–35.

2 Light the white candle, saying:
   *Shadows take flight*
   *In the moon's light.*

3 Turn the paper so that its longest side is horizontal, and draw a vertical line straight through the middle of it. On one half of the paper, draw the outline of seven swords, pointing inward. On the other half, draw a circle with a dot in the center. Place the beeswax candle in a secure holder on the center of the paper.

ask yourself whether you are right to suspect deceit or simply being paranoid or unreasonable. If you are being foolish, you will simply get a skewed answer from this test. Secondly, ask whether by casting this spell you are simply opting out of a much-needed confrontation. If you are, the person who is deceiving you will continue to believe that you are soft enough to fall for the same tricks again.

If you can answer the above questions to your own satisfaction, press on with the spell, which should help you to judge who is lying and who is telling the truth.

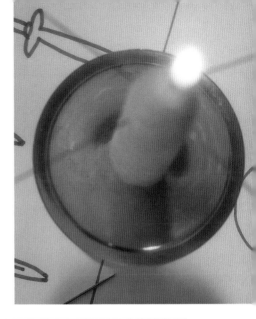

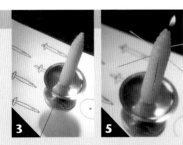

4 Heat the points of the needles and place them at equal distances and at the same level into the beeswax, about 1"/2.5 cm below the wick, so that they stick out from it horizontally.

5 Light the candle, saying:
*The seven swords*
*Shall judge thy words.*
While you are waiting for the candle to burn down to the needles, chant the following words:
*Will know you*
*When you fall.*

6 If the first needle to fall comes down on the side of the swords, you are being deceived; if it comes down on the side of the circle and dot, you are deceiving yourself.

# DAISY SPELL
## TO DISCOVER YOUR LIFE'S TASK

PURPOSE  To help you to find your purpose in life.

BACKGROUND  One of the most important questions
we ever ask ourselves is why we are here and what our task is
in this life. This goes beyond searching for a career path, a partner, or
surroundings in which we feel settled—it goes right to the heart of finding
purpose in our existence. Whatever your religious or spiritual beliefs, it is
possible to ask this question in order to seek self-knowledge and to search
for your place and purpose in the world. The final answer will come with
experience and revelation, but setting off on this path of discovery
without any idea of direction can be daunting. This spell will help you to
find your way.

You will need to cast this spell when daisies are in season, as they are its
main ingredient. Daisies have long been used for divination purposes. Children
are often seen tearing the petals off one by one, chanting, "She loves me, she
loves me not." Sometimes they are used in very much the same way as
cherry stones, to find out what your future status in life is likely to be.
Here they are used to offer you clues as to the gift that you bring to
others in your lifetime.

## HOW TO CAST THE SPELL

### YOU WILL NEED

One stick of sandalwood incense in a holder

One white candle, 6–8"/15–20 cm in length

Matches or a lighter

One sewing needle

Seven daisies, freshly picked

**TIMING** This spell is best cast on the night of the full moon.

### CASTING THE SPELL

1 Cast a circle in accordance with the guidelines on pages 32–35.

2 Light the incense, then the candle.

3 Using the needle, make a daisy chain by piercing a hole near the end of six of them and threading them together in a ring.

4 Holding the remaining daisy in your left hand, remove the petals one by one, chanting the following lines in order of their removal:

MAKER

SHAKER

CARER

SHARER

HEALER

5 The word on which the last petal is shed indicates which gifts you have to offer others:

MAKER: you have the gift of creating things of great practical use or beauty.

SHAKER: you have the ability to get things changed by word and action.

CARER: your strength lies in supporting others.

SHARER: you are a negotiator, a peacemaker, and one who achieves justice and fairness.

HEALER: you have the gift of healing.

6 Place the daisy chain under your pillow, as dreams over the next seven nights will offer further clues to your life's task.

# FETCH SPELL
## TO DISCOVER IF THE PERSON YOU DESIRE RETURNS YOUR FEELINGS

PURPOSE  To find out whether the object of your affections has feelings for you.

BACKGROUND  The tradition of the fetch has a number of different stories attached to it. In the Irish tradition, a *fetch* is a likeness of a person seen before their death, while Nordic traditions see a fetch as something akin to a totem, or personal power animal. English customs understand fetch to mean a likeness that is sent by a living person to take a message to a specified individual.

In this spell, you will send your fetch to put the person you desire in mind of you and to establish whether or not they return your interest. In terms of sending a likeness of yourself to visit someone, this spell is similar to the Magic Mirror Spell on pages 56–57, which is designed to help you send a comfort or reminder to a lover. This spell, however, is intended to draw out a reaction from the person to whom you are sending your fetch, and the methodology is somewhat different.

There is a magical "health warning" attached to this spell: if your intended is not interested, do not continue to send your fetch, as you will find yourself drained of energy. This is not because the magic employed involves a dangerous amount of effort but because obsession itself can exact a toll all its own, and magic will simply amplify this process.

## HOW TO CAST THE SPELL

**TIMING** The best time to send out your fetch is on a full moon.

### CASTING THE SPELL

1 Cast a circle in accordance with the guidelines on pages 32–35.

2 Light the charcoal, then the candle, saying:

*I call upon she who is queen of*
*All witcheries*
*To lend me her power*
*Hail, triple Hecate.*

3 Mix the orris root, bay leaves, and mugwort in the mortar with the pestle until it is thoroughly mixed, and sprinkle it onto the charcoal.

**YOU WILL NEED**

One charcoal disk in a fireproof dish

One silver or gray candle, 6–8"/15–20 cm in length

Matches or a lighter

One pinch of powdered orris root

One teaspoon of dried bay leaves

One pinch of mugwort

Mortar and pestle

4 Sitting in the center of the circle and facing north, close your eyes, and slow your breathing. Imagine stepping out of your body, getting up from the floor, and turning to face yourself. Keeping the image of the standing figure, return to your perspective in the seated position.

5 Allow the figure before you to turn and face you, and when it does, tell it where it should go and to whom it should appear. Add that it has only one month's life and that after that it will dissolve.

6 If the desired one returns your interest, they will approach you within forty days.

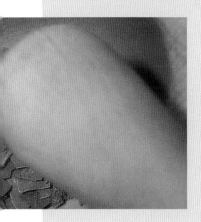

# TEA LEAF SPELL
## TO READ FORTUNES

PURPOSE  To help identify where your fortune lies.

BACKGROUND  The art of tea leaf reading, or tasseography, is thought to be thousands of years old and possibly originated in China. It is a psychic art, with guidelines rather than hard-and-fast rules. Individual tea leaf readers build a vocabulary of meanings that match the patterns formed during a reading; their methods are refined through experience rather than through rote learning of the shapes and correspondences. Happily for beginners, however, there are a few simple guidelines to help you get started.

This spell is undertaken to find out and identify where your fortune will be taking you in the next year, so you should not perform this spell for yourself again until at least another thirteen moon cycles have passed. If, following this spell, you wish to develop your skills in reading the tea leaves, you should practice this outside of the circle and try it on willing friends.

If you wish to ask specific questions for yourself within a year of casting this spell, they should be very focussed and not a general fortune reading, as you will get distorted readings and break faith with your own developing skills.

## HOW TO CAST THE SPELL

### YOU WILL NEED

One purple candle, 6–8"/15–20 cm in length

Matches or a lighter

One teapot containing a teaspoon of loose tea leaves and a cupful of boiling water

One teacup and saucer

**TIMING** This spell, to seek your fortune in the coming year, is best cast on a waxing or full moon. Readings outside of the circle can take place on any phase of the moon.

### CASTING THE SPELL

1 Cast a circle in accordance with the guidelines on pages 32–35.

2 Light the candle, saying:
*Spirit of fortune*
*Guide me and show*
*The line of my fortune*
*And all I must know.*

3 Pour unstrained tea into the cup.

4 Sip it until one teaspoon of tea remains in the bottom.

5 Swirl the leaves around thirteen times; then turn the cup over onto the saucer.

6 Read the residue of leaves as follows, from these very general guidelines:

| | |
|---|---|
| *LEAVES NEAR THE RIM OF THE CUP:* | *events coming soon* |
| *LEAVES AROUND THE SIDE:* | *events in the near future* |
| *LEAVES IN THE BOTTOM OF THE CUP:* | *in the long term* |
| *HORSESHOE:* | *good fortune, travel, a wedding* |
| *BALL:* | *there will be ups and downs* |
| *CIRCLE:* | *life has surprises in store* |
| *ARROW:* | *news coming soon* |
| *DISKS:* | *money coming in* |
| *BASKET OR BAG:* | *a baby* |
| *NEAR THE HANDLE:* | *traps and deceit* |
| *ELSEWHERE:* | *money coming in* |
| *ANIMALS:* | *be on your guard* |
| *LINES:* | *worries* |
| *SQUARES:* | *security.* |

# CONFETTI SPELL
## TO DISCOVER THE IDENTITY OF YOUR FUTURE PARTNER

PURPOSE  To help singles to discover the identity of a future partner.

BACKGROUND  There must be thousands of customs and traditions that claim to reveal the identity of your future life partner. This in itself indicates how important we consider committed relationships in our lives. If you are single, looking for a serious romance, and ready to find the right person long term, then this spell is for you.

In sympathetic magic, "like represents like," as they say. But like also begets like, which is why so many superstitions referring to finding a partner are linked to weddings. This spell requires you to collect the main ingredient for it—confetti—from a wedding that has just taken place. This means some detective work and a little skulking around, and it may also depend on the inefficiency of cleaning services at the local church, registry office, or town hall!

It is best to take a bag with you, so that you can scoop up a good quantity of the confetti deposited by a wedding party as the bride and groom leave the ceremony.

## HOW TO CAST THE SPELL

### YOU WILL NEED

One white candle, 6–8"/15–20 cm in length

Matches or a lighter

One large bag of confetti, collected after a wedding ceremony

**TIMING** Work when the first visible crescent after the dark moon can actually be seen in the sky.

### CASTING THE SPELL

1 Cast a circle in accordance with the guidelines on pages 32–35.

2 Light the white candle in the east of the circle, saying:

*Bright morning star rising*
*And shining above*
*Shine down on this circle*
*Reveal my true love.*

3 Stand in the middle of the circle, and bow to the north. Then face east, closing your eyes, and shower all of the confetti onto your head.

4 Keep your eyes closed and count to thirteen, then open them.

5 Examine the patterns of the confetti as it has fallen around you, and judge the likely identity of your future partner from these guidelines:

*AN EVEN CIRCLE AROUND YOU*
*It is someone you know.*

*SMALL PILES*
*It will be somebody who is good with money.*

*STRAIGHT LINES*
*Look out for an honest stranger.*

*ARCS AND SMALL CIRCLES*
*It will be someone gentle and kind.*

*ANGLES AND SQUARES*
*You will marry somebody tall and serious.*

*UNEVEN DISTRIBUTION*
*It will be somebody exciting and sensual.*

*NO DISCERNIBLE PATTERNS*
*You will meet in unusual circumstances.*

*MORE BEHIND THAN BEFORE YOU*
*It will be somebody older than you.*

*MORE BEFORE THAN BEHIND YOU*
*Your happiness will be long-lived.*

# GRAVEYARD DUST SPELL
## TO UNCOVER AN ENEMY

PURPOSE  To provide a way of discovering one who wishes you ill.

BACKGROUND  The origins of this spell are lost in the mists of time, but different versions of it emerge from time to time as ways of discovering evildoers or secret enemies. The main intent of this spell is to uncover one who is acting against your interests while playing the friend; it works best either if you already have your

suspicions about someone, or if the person upsetting you has been approaching your home. This may sound rather odd, but the behavior of people who set out to deceive very often *is* odd. Sometimes they might do upsetting things, such as post poison-pen letters by hand, or alert you by asking strange questions or being around at times you do not expect them to be. That said, if you do suspect someone is playing you false, set your trap for a time when you know they will be coming to your home. Otherwise, leave their coming to chance.

Needless to say, if you suspect dangerous or compulsive behavior, you should get help and advice immediately; but if you wish to uncover an enemy yourself, then this ancient spell may help stop them in their tracks—literally.

## HOW TO CAST THE SPELL

**TIMING** Carry out the first part of this spell on the night of the dark moon, and thereafter at dusk on the next day.

### CASTING THE SPELL

1 Cast a circle in accordance with the guidelines on pages 32–35.

2 Light the black candle, saying:
*By the skull of the moon*
*Mine enemy be shown.*

3 Pour the ash cinders into the bowl, and place both hands palm down upon it, saying:
*Betwixt these hands*
*All safe and sound*
*Below them the path of*
*Truth.*

4 Spread the ash on your front walk or driveway. At dusk the next evening, go out to see if the footprint of the suspected enemy is on the ground, or if an unknown foot has trodden near your home.

5 Using the knife, draw a circle in the ground around it. Drive a nail into the footprint, saying:
*Fare as fair as you would merit*
*Merit as fair as you would fare.*

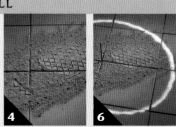

### YOU WILL NEED

One black candle, 6–8"/15–20 cm in length

Matches or a lighter

Ash from an ash (wood) fire, 1 lb/450 g

One bowl

One black-handled knife

One hammer and nail

One container of salt with a flow hole

6 Pour a circle of salt around the footprint. Within a moon, the enemy will betray themselves.

# ACORN SPELL
## TO PREDICT IF YOU WILL MARRY OR MEET YOUR LIFETIME PARTNER WITHIN A YEAR

PURPOSE  To help singles find out if they are likely to meet their lifetime partner within the next twelve months.

BACKGROUND  This is a delightful spell to share with friends, if they are willing. It is ideal for a bridal or groom shower—especially if there are a number of singles at the party—or even for a New Year's celebration. The idea of this spell is to predict whether you will marry or meet your lifetime partner in the course of the coming year. Although it is a fun

spell, it also has its serious side; if you call on magic to predict, then you should respect what it has to say and not cast this more than once in a twelve-month period.

This spell is based on a very old custom regarding trees. Many trees in ancient cultures were considered sacred. Oak trees are still held in great reverence in parts of England and Ireland and symbolize, among other things, truth and steadfastness. Acorns, the seeds of these mighty trees, sprout inside cups that at one time were thought to be the drinking vessels of fairies. In particular, the cups represent sacred potential, for they bear and carry a small seed that grows into a gigantic tree. To use acorn cups in a spell to divine future happiness is to use a potent and magical ingredient, for as the country folk say: "From little acorns there do grow mighty oaks!"

# HOW TO CAST THE SPELL

### YOU WILL NEED

One acorn cup for each person

One indelible soft-tip pen

One green candle, 6–8"/15–20 cm in length

Matches or a lighter

One large bowl

One long-handled wooden spoon

**TIMING** Cast this spell at any phase of the moon and on any day of the week—but cast it only once a year.

### CASTING THE SPELL

1 Get everyone involved to write their initials with the indelible ink pen on the inside of their acorn cup.

2 Light the green candle, and get everyone involved to repeat the following words when it is lit:

*Mighty oak*
*Greenwood tree*
*When is*
*Happiness to be?*

3 Take the wooden spoon, and stir the waters three times clockwise, three times counterclockwise, and then once clockwise, in quick succession.

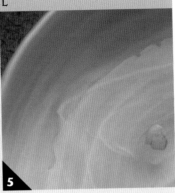

4 Get the first candidate to drop in their acorn cup, and count to seven.

5 If the acorn cup touches the side of the bowl within that time, they will marry or meet their lifetime partner in the course of the next year.

357

# ANCIENT KNOT SPELL
## TO FIND A SOLUTION TO A PROBLEM

PURPOSE   To bring inspiration to those seeking to find the answer to
a tricky problem.

BACKGROUND   To those facing a predicament and struggling to find the best
way to deal with it, the notion that a spell can help may seem ridiculous. However,
when a decision requiring both imagination and common sense is required—and
soon—it is often the case that what is lacking is inspiration. Much of the time we
subconsciously know the solution to problems in our lives, even if we are consciously
avoiding it. Unlocking that knowledge is the object of this spell, which is based on
a very old charm.

### HOW TO CAST THE SPELL

**YOU WILL NEED**

One charcoal disk in a fireproof dish

One pale blue candle, 6–8"/15–20 cm
in length

Matches or a lighter

One teaspoon of wormwood (*Artemisia
absinthium*)

One 9"/22.5 cm length of string

**TIMING** This spell should be cast at any
phase after the full moon until the day
after the dark moon.

**CASTING THE SPELL**

1 Cast a circle in accordance with the
guidelines on pages 32–35.

2 Light the incense, then the candle,
saying:

*You who know the secret*
*Of the unhewn stone*
*Whose light shines*
*In darkness*
*Light my way.*

3 Sprinkle the wormwood onto
the charcoal.

In the West, we often use the language of struggle and capture when we speak of dilemmas. We speak of "wrestling" with a problem, being "in" a quandary, or "tied up" in difficulties. Complex issues are spoken of as "knotty"—in line with the notion that we are constrained, held back, or even held captive when beset by them. This spell uses the age-old magical device of tying knots in order to help unravel a tangle. Keep a dream diary for seven days following the casting of this spell to find clues to the answer, looking out for puns and symbols, and trust your wise self to show the way forward.

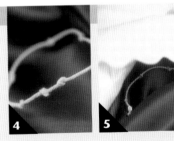

*Three for the moon who sails the sky*
*Four for the clouds that pass her by*
*Five for the babe that's in the moon*
*Six for the question on my tongue*
*Seven for secrets yet unknown*
*Within a se'night all undone.*

4 Tie seven knots into the string, reciting a line of the following for each one, in the order indicated:

*One for the sun who brings the light*
*Two for the stars that shine at night*

5 Place the knotted string under your pillow for the next seven nights, undoing one knot each night before you go to sleep.

6 The answer to your problem will come to you in your dreams.

# APPLE SPELL
## TO DREAM OF YOUR TRUE LOVE

**PURPOSE**  To reveal the identity of your true love in a dream.

**BACKGROUND**  Apples and love go together like a hand in a glove. As well as being the fruit of the Celtic otherworld, apples are closely linked with the element of water, the magical domain of feelings, emotions—and dreams. They are often mentioned in world myths, usually epitomizing that which we most desire. Here, the apple represents news of your future love, and both peel and flesh are featured in the spell.

One of the first spells I ever learned as a child was an old English charm that used apple peel as a way of finding out the name of your future husband. It was specifically

## HOW TO CAST THE SPELL

### YOU WILL NEED

One charcoal disk in a fireproof dish

One red candle, 6–8"/15–20 cm in length

Matches or a lighter

One teaspoon equal parts orris root and dill

One fresh rosy apple

One sharp black-handled knife

One portable mirror at least 6"/15 cm square

One 3"/7.5 cm square drawstring cheesecloth pouch

**TIMING** Cast this spell on the night of the full moon.

### CASTING THE SPELL

1 Cast a circle in accordance with the guidelines on pages 32–35.

2 Light the charcoal, then the candle, saying:

> Goddess of love
> True may you prove
> Show me [his/her] face
> By your good grace.

Sprinkle the incense onto the charcoal.

for girls and women, and it involved peeling an apple, keeping the peel intact, and throwing it over your shoulder to reveal the first letter of your true love's name. A variation of this was to do it at midnight in front of a mirror, and not only would you know his initial, but you would see his face in the mirror. A friend and I tried this, but she went first and was so spooked by the experience that we abandoned the experiment and never did it again!

Although this spell does involve an unbroken apple peel, your true love is reflected in your dreams, rather than in a physical mirror.

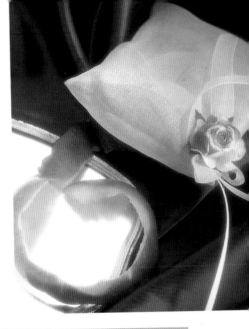

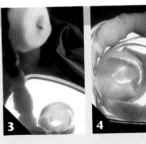

5 Eat the apple. Looking into the mirror, say:

*I have eaten knowledge*
*But not the skin*
*The skin is returned*
*When the secret is learned.*

6 Place the peel in the pouch, and hang it above your bed until you dream of your true love. The next day, bury the peel in the earth.

3 Peel the apple thinly over the mirror, without breaking the peel.

4 Allow the peel to fall on the mirror. Lifting the mirror, pass it three times in a clockwise circle through the incense smoke.

# BANISHING AND
# BINDING SPELLS

# INTRODUCTION TO BANISHING AND BINDING SPELLS

When magicians are approached for help when someone is behaving badly, there is an expectation, and sometimes a fear, that stopping the person necessarily means inflicting harm. These concerns are directly related to the belief that spells that prevent this behavior are hexes or curses intended to harm or damage. Nothing could be farther from the truth; spells that stop bullies, oppressors, and tormentors are designed to prevent harm—not inflict it! The terms *banishing* and *binding* bear this out. To *banish* may mean either to move someone on to another place or to banish an aspect of their behavior that is proving a problem to their peers, neighbors, or co-workers. *To bind someone* is to inhibit their ability to cause damage to others.

Banishing spells work on several levels; they can serve to shift a person away from the context in which they are doing harm, as in the Seat of Thorns Spell in this section, or they can work toward diminishing their power, as in the Cord

and Candle Spell. There is another sense in which banishment is used in magic, and that is to diminish the worst of the damage left in the wake of destructive behavior, as seen in the Ink Wash Spell. This is extended to include emotional detritus left following sad or traumatic events; here the Severing Spell is designed to help break with the past. Banishing spells can help banish your own bad habits if, with a little imagination, you adapt some of those in the following section. As you can see, there is a lot of scope for addressing harm in the range of banishing spells offered here—and not a curse in sight!

Binding spells are particularly persuasive when used to force someone to acknowledge the consequences of their actions. The Circle of Salt Spell in this section imprisons an evildoer by their own behavior, which will continue to bounce back to them until they decide to behave decently. The Bird's Nest Spell continues this theme, this time providing a more in-your-face, confrontational method, which means that the culprit will find the outcomes of their actions returning to their own doorstep. This type of confrontation offers the chance to the perpetrator to "make good." If they choose not to, then the consequences of their conduct will continue to bedevil them until they cease. Sometimes bindings depend on making visible to others the deceitful deeds of a wrongdoer—and here the powerful Water Elemental Spell provides the means by which to do this.

# CIRCLE OF SALT SPELL
## TO BIND A WRONGDOER BY THEIR OWN ACTIONS

PURPOSE  To prevent a malefactor from continuing to work harm to others.

BACKGROUND  When somebody's bad behavior impacts detrimentally on others, and understanding, persuasion, and even confrontation have not worked, it is time for magic to step in. This spell is a classical binding spell and works on the basis of psychic confinement. To place a representation of the troublemaker within a binding circle of salt is to surround them with a barrier that protects others, while confining the effects of any behavior to the immediate vicinity of its originator. In short, the "harm" created

## HOW TO CAST THE SPELL

### YOU WILL NEED

One black candle, 6–8"/15–20 cm in length

Matches or a lighter

Strands of hair from the wrongdoer

One 4"/10 cm length of black woolen thread

One circular mirror at least 4"/10 cm in diameter

One container of salt with a flow hole

An open fire in a grate, a brazier, or a bonfire outside

**TIMING** This spell can be cast at any time, according to need, but it is most powerful if cast on a dark moon, the best time to construct psychic barriers.

**CASTING THE SPELL**

1 Cast a circle in accordance with the guidelines on pages 32–35.

2 Light the candle, saying:
   *Dark of moon*
   *All powers surround*
   *Bless this space as sacred ground*
   *Ill confine and harm confound*
   *As I walk this circle round.*

will not get out to damage others but land right back at the feet of its creator. This can be enormously useful not only to those who have hitherto suffered from the wrongdoer's behavior, but to the perpetrator themselves; confronted by their behavior, they have a chance to change it.

In magic, salt is a purifying substance and is often mixed with water and sprinkled around a ritual space to psychically clear it before a ritual. Salt also represents the wholesome and defensive nature of this element and here provides a shield against harm.

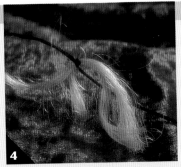

**3** Walk the circle in a counterclockwise direction, carrying the candle with you. Return to the center, and set the candle down.

**4** Tie the strands of hair in a tight knot using the black wool, saying:
> *[Name of wrongdoer], by my actions yours are bound.*

**5** Place the hair in the center of the mirror, and pour a circle of salt around it, saying:
> *As I make this circle round.*

**6** Breathe onto the mirror, and throw the hair and salt into the fire, saying:
> *Evil's death*
> *By my breath.*

# CORD AND CANDLE SPELL
## TO DIMINISH THE POWER
## OF A DECEITFUL PERSON

**PURPOSE**  To take away the power of another to deceive.

**BACKGROUND**  When the burden of proof is not in your favor, but you know that another person is being deceitful to friends, colleagues, or to yourself, this spell is absolutely ideal. Like many other magical workings in this book, the built-in philosophy is to reflect the deeds of the person on whom the spell is focused. If you are wrong or have got the wrong person, then there is nothing to fear in using this on an innocent one. If they are blameless, their honesty will shine through. If not, however, their ability

to deceive will be diminished, and their plans will begin to backfire.

It is important that you place the candleholder securely in a dish, as once the candle burns down, the flame will consume the cord and paper tied around it. Needless to say, all candles allowed to burn down should be properly supervised at all times, but this spell requires a little more care as the cord and paper may fall burning from the candle once it ignites. The paper, which should bear the signature or photocopy of the signature of the person you believe is being dishonest, should be cut down to the minimum size possible without compromising the signature itself.

## HOW TO CAST THE SPELL

**TIMING** This spell can be used at any time, if your need is urgent, but the most favorable time is the day after the new moon.

### CASTING THE SPELL

1 Cast a circle in accordance with the guidelines on pages 32–35.

2 Light the tea-light, and heat the point of the nail in its flame.

3 Use the hot tip of the nail to inscribe into the side of the white candle, about 1"/2.5 cm from the wick, the outline of an eye.

4 Roll the paper bearing the signature into a tight scroll, and tie it to the center of the black cotton thread. Tie the scroll and thread around the candle, passing the thread over the center of the eye. Fasten it tightly.

5 Light the candle, saying:
*[Name of suspect], if thou a liar be*
*Thou shalt find discovery*
*And all thy deeds be marked to thee*
*As I will it, so mote it be!*

### YOU WILL NEED

One tea-light in a holder

Matches or a lighter

One sharp iron nail

One white candle, 6–8"/15–20 cm in length

One slim piece of paper bearing the signature of the deceiver

One 6"/15 cm length of black cotton embroidery thread

Witness the candle burning down to consume the inscribed eye, the cotton thread, and the paper scroll.

6 Extinguish it, and bury it in earth where it will not be disturbed.

# MIRROR IMAGE SPELL
## TO CONFUSE AN ENEMY

PURPOSE   This spell is designed to frustrate the plans of one who is doing you harm.

BACKGROUND   Mirrors turn up in many spells all over the world, and they certainly have a reputation for mystery and magic. They symbolize the fine line between truth and illusion, because what they show is not always as simple as it seems. Perhaps this has something to do with the fact that a mirror can offer the illusion of space and entry to a three-dimensional world, when in fact it simply reflects what is in front of it as a two-dimensional object. Often a mirror can conceal as much

## HOW TO CAST THE SPELL

### YOU WILL NEED

One charcoal disk in a fireproof dish

One blue candle, 6–8"/15–20 cm in length

Matches or a lighter

One teaspoon of mugwort

Two identical circular mirrors approximately 4"/10 cm in diameter

One teaspoon of poppy seeds

One tube of strong glue

One spool of pliable wire

**TIMING** Weave this spell on the night of the full moon, mistress of both truth and illusion.

**CASTING THE SPELL**

1 Cast a circle in accordance with the guidelines on pages 32–35.

2 Light the charcoal, then the candle, saying:

*Child of the moon*
*Element of water*
*Reflect, distract*
*Direction alter*
*Shine upon [Name of wrongdoer]*
*Make their steps falter.*

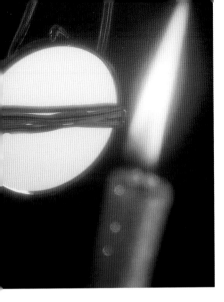

as it reveals, and in this spell it is this potential for confusion that is exploited in order to derail a troublemaker.

The tradition of placing a mirror in the window to deflect the evil eye relates to its ability to reflect, or bounce back, bad energy to its sender. Here, the mirrors are used to confuse and confound and also to radiate outward a shield against the bad intentions of the wrongdoer. The spell will create a double-sided mirror, which should be suspended over your front door outside the house. Ensure that all attachments are secure.

3 Sprinkle the mugwort onto the charcoal, take a mirror in each hand, then cense their reflective surfaces in the incense smoke, saying:

*I hereby empower you*
*To show the truth.*

4 Sprinkle on the poppy seeds, and repeat, saying:

*I hereby empower you*
*To delude and confuse.*

5 Firmly glue the backs of the mirrors together, and fasten the wire around and across the double-sided result, leaving a loop from which it can be suspended.

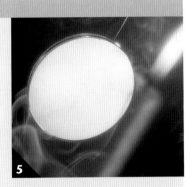

6 Hold this in front of the candle, saying:

*Confusion to the enemy*
*As I have spoken*
*Let it be.*

# SEAT OF THORNS SPELL
## TO RID YOURSELF OF A BULLY

PURPOSE   To remove a bully from power.

BACKGROUND   Bullying behavior comes in many forms and should always and without exception be challenged. It is not always easy for a person or a group of people who are being browbeaten to confront the bully who has already intimidated them, and this is why it is important to take practical steps in seeking outside help. If you are being intimidated by a housemate or a colleague at work, you need to seek help from the person leasing to you or from your union or personnel department, respectively. If you are being harassed and threatened in your own home by a partner, consult

## HOW TO CAST THE SPELL

### YOU WILL NEED

One black candle, 6–8"/15–20 cm in length

Matches or a lighter

One charcoal disk in a fireproof dish

Six large dried bramble thorns

Six dressmaker's pins

One small glass jar with a screw cap

**TIMING** Cast this spell at any time, but if you have a choice, plump for the waning moon, as this phase is best for carrying unwanted things away on the outgoing tide.

### CASTING THE SPELL

1 Cast a circle in accordance with the guidelines on pages 32–35.

2 Light the candle, saying:
   *I cast you out*
   *I sent you hence*
   *Let none protect*
   *And none defend*
   *Your rule of force*
   *Is hereby ended.*

3 Light the charcoal burner. Place five of the thorns on the charcoal, and allow them to burn to ash.

a support group or agency, and get legal advice. It might seem strange to you that a book on spells should advise you to take these measures, but magic is built on resourcefulness, and this includes using common sense.

This said, magic has its part to play and has long been the resort of those who are feeling powerless in the face of adversity. This is why there are so many spells for protection and defense in the tradition! This spell should be used in tandem with the practical steps you should be taking to end the rule of the bully in question.

4 Place the pins in the jar, with the ashes from the burned thorns, saying:

*I hold the means of your dismay*
*Until your cruelty goes away*
*As you are cruel*
*These thorns shall be*
*When you are kind*
*You'll kindness find.*

5 Screw the lid to the jar tightly, and keep it in a safe place until the bully departs.

6 Place the remaining thorn within or beneath the seat—wherever it is less likely to be detected—of the chair that the bully sits on.

# BIRD'S NEST SPELL
## TO SEND BACK TO AN EVILDOER THE RESULTS OF THEIR ACTIONS

PURPOSE  To ensure that a wrongdoer is faced with the consequences of their behavior.

BACKGROUND  There is an old English saying that opines, "It's a poor bird that fouls its own nest." This sentiment refers to the stupidity of behaving badly too close to home, where you will suffer the consequences of your actions because of your proximity to the fallout from them. This magician holds no brief for behaving badly away from home either, but there is something in this that does hold true. If the results of deeds are presented back to the person responsible, they will have to suffer what others have had to suffer from them. As well as ensuring that the wrongdoer is left in no doubt as to how unpleasant it is to be on the receiving end of bad behavior, it will also make obvious to all around them just who is responsible for any trouble being caused. This offers an obvious choice to the miscreant: desist or make amends, and your troubles will cease!

For this spell you will need the remnants of an old nest. If you keep a nest box, you will probably already be familiar with the practice of clearing out last year's nests to make room for a new clutch of eggs in the spring. If not, you may have to beg this from a more experienced neighbor or make friends with the wardens at a local nature reserve. Try to keep the nest as intact as possible.

## HOW TO CAST THE SPELL

### YOU WILL NEED

One charcoal disk in a fireproof dish

One black candle, 6–8"/15–20 cm in length

One white candle, 6–8"/15–20 cm in length

Matches or a lighter

One teaspoon of dried juniper berries

One intact disused bird's nest

**TIMING** Cast on the dark moon, at the turning of the moon's tide, to ensure that the troublemaker in question receives what they have given.

### CASTING THE SPELL

1 Cast a circle in accordance with the guidelines on pages 32–35.

2 Light the charcoal, then the black candle to your left, saying:
*The time of sending is gone.*

3 Light the white candle, saying:
*The time of return is near.*

4 Sprinkle on the juniper berries.

5 Take the bird's nest in both hands and hold it in the incense smoke, chanting the following words:
*After the flow comes the ebb*
*Everything we give we get*
*After the ebb comes the flow*
*Everything we get we know.*

6 Place the bird's nest on your enemy's doorstep secretly the same night.

# WATER ELEMENTAL SPELL
## TO MAKE VISIBLE TO OTHERS THE ACTIONS OF AN EVILDOER

**PURPOSE** To unmask a wrongdoer and reveal their misdemeanors.

**BACKGROUND** Sometimes the worst punishment and best lesson for a troublemaker is exposure of their deeds. This will mean the loss of the good opinion of those they have been deceiving and will confront them with the inappropriateness or just plain unpleasantness of what they have been doing. Revealing the truth can also release those most affected by mischief from the frustration of being unable to prove what they know to be the case. This spell is also very useful in cases of mistaken

## HOW TO CAST THE SPELL

**YOU WILL NEED**

One tea-light in a jar

Matches or a lighter

One stick of sandalwood incense

One drum

**TIMING** Cast on the night of the full moon at the side of a lake, sea, or river.

**CASTING THE SPELL**

1 Cast a circle in accordance with the guidelines on pages 32–35.

2 Light the tea-light in the jar. Stick the incense in the ground, and light it.

3 Using your hands, tap out a regular 3/4 rhythm, and allow your mind to follow the rhythm. When you feel ready, mentally reach out to the spirits of the water, and call them forth.

4 When you sense that the energies around you are changing significantly, speak over the drumming, repeating the following lines three times in succession:

*Flowing mirror of the moon*
*Show [his/her] face in full*
*Show [him/her] as [his/her] true self*
*Show [him/her] in true form.*

identity; if you are blaming the wrong person, all that is revealed is their innocence.

This spell requires you to work outdoors, near an expanse of water. You will be using a quite advanced magical technique—evocation—so it is wise to get some other magical experience before attempting this. You will need a drum for this spell, and some practice prior to casting it is essential. Beat a rhythm in 3/4 time, as this is usually effective with water elementals. When you go, leave a gift such as a flower, shell, or leaf cast at the water's edge.

5 Continue drumming for as long as you feel the water spirits around you. As the energies diminish, try to visualize the water flowing to the door of the person whose infamy you wish to reveal.

6 Leave a small gift at the waterside to honor the spirits of water.

# INK WASH SPELL
## TO CANCEL OUT HARM CAUSED BY ANOTHER

PURPOSE  To be performed by the person who has been adversely affected by the dishonesty or poor behavior of another, as it has therapeutic as well as magical value.

BACKGROUND  The impact of a troublemaker's conduct can be felt long after the original deed has taken place. This is part of the ongoing damage that irresponsible and dishonest people can cause, and it is as true for unwitting bystanders and dupes as it is for those who have been directly targeted. A person being unfaithful to their partner, for example, may leave behind not only an injured and angry ex-partner, but also a string of disappointed and very hurt friends and relatives who may have been enlisted, unwittingly, in their efforts to deceive. Similarly, friends, relatives, and partners of people who have been attacked also sustain damage by proxy—and have to deal with feelings of guilt, powerlessness, and anger.

In cases such as these, and in addition to very practical steps that can be taken to support the direct victims of violence or other unacceptable acts, this spell can help to diminish the residual effects of harm in a very therapeutic way. Many psychologists acknowledge the value of expressing pain through ritual. This spell may have originated many ages before psychology or the life of the mind was recognized professionally, but its methods nonetheless are recognizably therapeutic.

## HOW TO CAST THE SPELL

One black candle, 6–8"/15–20 cm in length

Matches or a lighter

One bottle of purple water-based ink

One fountain pen

One sheet of office paper

One bowl of water

One small glass tumbler

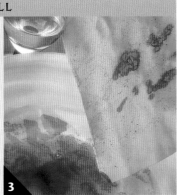

**TIMING** Cast on a waning moon, any time after the dark moon.

### CASTING THE SPELL

1 Cast a circle in accordance with the guidelines on pages 32–35.

2 Light the candle, saying:
*All that is valuable, I keep*
*All that is harmful, I discard.*

3 Dip the nib of the pen into the water-based ink, and write on one side of the paper, in three words, the harm that has been done to you. Holding this over the bowl of water, and using the tumbler as a scoop, wash the ink from the page.

4 Dry the paper over the candle flame, taking care not to set it alight.

5 Write on the paper three words that represent positive and healing things to replace the harm you have washed away.

6 Dry the ink over the candle flame, then roll up the paper, and keep it for a year and a day. After this, burn it and scatter the ashes in your garden.

**379**

# SEVERING SPELL
## TO BREAK WITH THE PAST

PURPOSE  To destroy the power that memories of past events have over you.

BACKGROUND  This is another very therapeutic spell, best performed by the person who wishes to break with the past. If memories of past events still wield an unhealthy amount of power over us, then it is not healthy to allow this to continue. To release the past with a spell is not to trivialize pain or suffering that may have come from past events, but to ensure that the best outcome can be achieved. In any case, letting the past run riot in the present gives it undue space in our lives, and the more

## HOW TO CAST THE SPELL

### YOU WILL NEED

One charcoal disk in a fireproof dish

One black candle, 6–8"/15–20 cm in length

Matches or a lighter

One teaspoon of myrrh

One 9"/22.5 cm length of black cord

One fireproof dish

One pinch of saffron

**TIMING** Cast on the dark moon, a powerful time for endings and new beginnings.

### CASTING THE SPELL

1 Cast a circle in accordance with the guidelines on pages 32–35.

2 Light the charcoal disc, then the candle, saying:

*By this token I am freed and come toward the light.*

3 Sprinkle the myrrh onto the charcoal.

4 Tie a knot toward one end of the cord: this represents the memories you wish to leave behind. Tie another knot toward the other end of the cord: this represents a future free from the feelings that are keeping you in the past.

attention we offer sadness, the more it will grow to block out our capacity for joy.

If you find that memories of a broken relationship, a bereavement, or traumatic events are still haunting you in a way that is not in keeping with the natural grieving process, then you should talk things through with a friend or counselor. If you wish to break with these feelings from the past, then this spell is absolutely ideal. At a psychic level, it severs your emotional links with the past to the extent that you will be able to live your life without those painful feelings.

5 Holding the "past" knot in your left hand and the "future" knot in your right, place the cord over the flame, and allow it to burn through. Burn the "past" knot entirely, placing it in the fireproof dish.

6 Place the saffron on the charcoal, and cense the knot that represents your future. Keep this in a safe place.

# FIRE STAIN SPELL
## TO FRUSTRATE ONE WHO IS DOING HARM TO OTHERS

PURPOSE   To foil the plans of a wrongdoer.

BACKGROUND   This spell is thought to originate from Scotland, but variations of it may be found in a number of European countries. It is based on an old form of ill-wishing reputedly used in circumstances such as illegal evictions, where families were removed from their homes by unscrupulous owners in order to sell property or land or to replace them with higher-paying tenants. It was the custom of the departing family, or at least those with some of the ancient knowledge, to leave stones in the fire grate in place of the usual coals, in order to wish the owner ill in return for their bad treatment. The wish is implicit: "May there be cold stones instead of hot coals at your hearth."

Leaving behind *stains,* as the Scots called them, was effectively a form of binding spell, to ensure that the wrongdoer's deeds would be returned to them. In this spell, you will be doing something very similar in order to frustrate the plans of one who intends to do harm to others. In this case, you will not need access to their fireplace, but you will reenact the fire stains tradition by building a cairn of special stones and leaving them in a pile on their wall or by their gate.

## HOW TO CAST THE SPELL

**TIMING** Cast this spell the night before the dark moon, so that the stains are in place by the next morning.

### CASTING THE SPELL

1 Cast a circle in accordance with the guidelines on pages 32–35.

2 Light the charcoal, then the candle. Place both palms against the sides of the candle, saying:

*All that burns between these hands is all the warmth you will receive [Name of wrongdoer].*

3 Sprinkle the rosemary onto the charcoal.

4 Sprinkle salt over all the pebbles, saying to each one:

*Nothing shall grow of thee.*

Pour water over all the pebbles, saying to each one:

*Nothing shall be nourished of thee.*

5 Now cense each pebble in the incense smoke, saying to each one:

*No grace shall be received of thee.*

Drip one drop of black wax onto each pebble from the candle.

6 Before morning, take the pebbles to the front gate or wall of the wrongdoer, and place them in a pile.

### YOU WILL NEED

One charcoal disk in a fireproof dish

One black candle, 6–8"/15–20 cm in length

Matches or a lighter

One tablespoon of dried rosemary

One container of salt with a flow hole

Five palm-size pebbles, naturally smoothed by water

One wineglass of spring water

# GLOSSARY

**AMULET** Strictly speaking, an item worn or displayed to attract certain energies such as luck, prosperity, health, love, and so on, but generally used as a term for a charm, often interchangeably with the term *talisman*.

**ATHAME** Witches' knife, used to direct magical energy.

**BALEFIRE** A fire used for magical purposes.

**BELTAINE** One of the eight Pagan festivals, celebrated traditionally from sundown on April 30 to sundown on May 1, or when the May tree is in bloom.

**CHARGE** To fill with magical energy or to entrust with a magical task.

**CLADDAGH** A traditional Irish village near a seashore where the claddagh design for a ring was used for centuries. It shows an Irish symbol of clasped hands, denoting true friendship, love, or amity.

**CLOUTIES** Rags or ribbons tied usually to a tree above a holy well, as an act of respect to a local deity or to symbolize a wish or hope.

**CORN DOLLIES** Items woven from ripe corn (wheat), charged with spiritual or magical meaning.

**CUNNING MAN** A traditional term for a man knowledgeable in magical and natural lore, and renowned for healing, dowsing, divination, or spell-casting powers.

**DARK MOON** The "new" moon phase, when the moon is completely overshadowed and invisible.

**DEOSIL** "Sun-wise"—meaning in a clockwise direction.

**ELEMENT CANDLES** Appropriately colored candles representing the five sacred elements.

**EOSTRE** One of the eight Pagan festivals, celebrated at the Vernal or Spring Equinox, usually March 21 or 22. The word derives from the Teutonic fertility goddess Oestra or Ostar.

**FETCH** A magical likeness of yourself, created magically and sent over a distance to appear to others.

**FITH-FATH** Another name for a "poppet" or symbolic representation of a person. It is usually, though not always, in the form of a simple doll.

**FIVE SACRED ELEMENTS** The symbolic and physical aspects of all existence, divided into earth, air, fire, water, and spirit.

**GOD-MAKING** The formation of an item used as a protective charm, usually wooden and taking the energies of the tree from which it is sourced.

**IMBOLC** One of the eight Pagan festivals, sacred to the Celtic goddess Brigid, and traditionally celebrated on or around February 1, or at the emergence of the first snowdrops.

**KNOTTING** A technique used in magic to secure energy in a cord, which is sometimes released when the knot is untied.

**LITHA** One of the eight Pagan festivals, celebrated on the day of the Summer Solstice, or "longest day," which occurs on or around June 21.

**LUGHNASADH** One of the eight Pagan festivals, celebrated toward the end of July, around the time of the cereal harvest.

**MABON** One of the eight Pagan festivals, celebrated at the autumnal Equinox, on or around September 21, and sacred to the fruitful mother goddess who bears its name.

**MAGICIAN'S CORDS** Cords used in spells for magical purposes, or as part of a spell.

**MEASURE** Traditionally lengths of cords that are measured directly from life, rather than a tape-measure; around the head, the heart, and the length of the body from head to toe—in short, shroud measurements—and thought to have a sympathetic connection with the person whose measurements are taken.

**OUROBORUS** An ancient symbol of eternity, depicting a snake swallowing its own tail.

**PENTACLE** A five-pointed star depicted with interwoven cross points visible. The sacred symbol of magic and elements conjoined, denoting the element of Earth, if encircled, or the element of spirit, if in its simple, five-pointed form. Traditionally, a distinction has been made between pentacle and pentagram, respectively a five-pointed star in a circle, or a star un-encircled, but sometimes this definition is reversed, and nowadays the terms are used with fairly careless interchangeability.

**PHILTER** A magical liquid, usually to be drunk.

**POPPET** A doll-like sachet made in order to represent a person for the purposes of a spell.

**RUNE** A figure from an ancient alphabet, originating from Northern Europe, and used for meditation, divination, or spell work to invoke an energy or meaning derived from its ancient origins, or in some cases to represent a person or situation for the purposes of magical work.

**SACHET** A small pillow sewn from fabric and stuffed with herbs or other materials.

**SAMHAIN** One of the eight Pagan festivals, celebrated on or around October 31, or when the first frosts set in.

**SIDHE** An Irish name for the faeries, or hill-folk.

**SIGIL** A mark or figure of magical relevance, used in a similar way to runes in magic.

**SUN-RETURN** Another name for the Winter Solstice, or "shortest day," which occurs on or around December 21.

**SUN-WISE** Clockwise, or *deosil*.

**SYMPATHETIC MAGIC** Sometimes called *like with like*, this is a system of magic that uses symbols to represent someone or something outside of themselves, and which may have a physical connection (i.e. hair, nail, or signature of the person in question) or a metaphorical or created one (a poppet or fith-fath). A spell-caster may then enact upon that symbol what they wish to happen to the person or something in everyday life.

**TALISMAN** Strictly speaking, this is a magical item worn or displayed by a person to ward off particular energies—for example, bad intents, jealousy, the evil eye, or bad luck—but is often used interchangeably with the word *amulet*. It is sometimes used simply to mean "charm."

**TASSEOGRAPHY** The art of reading tea leaves for divinatory purposes.

**THOUGHT-FORM** A magical form generated by your own thoughts and will, usually manufactured with the aid of a mirror.

**TISANE** Another word for a herbal tea, brewed with boiling water.

**TRANSFERENCE** Conveying a situation from one place to another by magical means. For example, transference occurs when a wart on a person is magically rubbed onto a stone, the stone is buried or thrown into deep water, and the wart disappears.

**TRIPLICITIES** The tendency, in magic, and in Celtic culture in particular, for symbols and supernatural or sacred beings to have a threefold aspect.

**TRISKELE** A Celtic symbol, originating in Brittany, depicting a three-legged spiral.

**TRUE MIDNIGHT** The middle point of the hours between sunset and sunrise.

**TUMBLED** Smoothed by a process of "tumbling." This term describes smoothed crystals or semi-precious stones.

**WANING MOON** The phase of the moon that sees its lit portion diminishing after the full phase until the dark or new moon phase; in the Northern Hemisphere the lit disc retains the circular curve on the left side, and appears to diminish from the right. This phase includes the last quarter, or waning half-moon.

**WAXING MOON** The phase of the moon following the new or dark phase and prior to the full phase. This phase sees the lit portion growing; in the Northern Hemisphere the lit disc retains the circular curve on the right side, and appears to grow from right to left. This phase includes the first quarter, or waxing half-moon.

**WHEEL OF THE YEAR** The solar year on Earth experienced as a cycle of seasons and change, and including the phases of sun, moon, stars, and nature.

**WISEWOMAN** A traditional term for a woman knowledgeable in magical and natural lore, and renowned for healing, dowsing, divination, or spell-casting powers—a witch.

**YULE** One of the eight Pagan festivals, celebrating the "shortest day" and held on or around December 21. Also known as *Sun-return*.

**387**

# INDEX

## C

# I

# ACKNOWLEDGMENTS

The Bridgewater Book Company would like to thank the following for the permission to reproduce copyright material:
**Corbis** pp. 18 background (Otto Rogge), 42/43 (Greenhalf Photography), 48/49 (Matthew Allen), 70/71 (Larry Williams), 76/77 (Rick Rappapart), 80/81 (Jens Haas), 96/97 (Owaki-Kulla), 109 (Jim Richardson), 118/119 (Michael St. Maur Sheil), 142 (Randy Faris), 154/155 (Anthony Cooper), 166/167 (Hanan Isachar), 168 (David Papazian), 175 (Steve Prezant), 182/183 (Matthew Allan), 184/185 (Leland Bobbé), 198/199 (James P. Blair), 210 (Matthew Kitto), 274/275 (Charles Krebs), 298/299 (Jennifer Kennard), 310/311 (Benjamin Rondel), 315 (Charles O'Rear), 316/317 (Raymond Gehman), 324 (Tim Pannell), 356 (Ralph A. Clevenger).
**Marc Henri** p. 64.